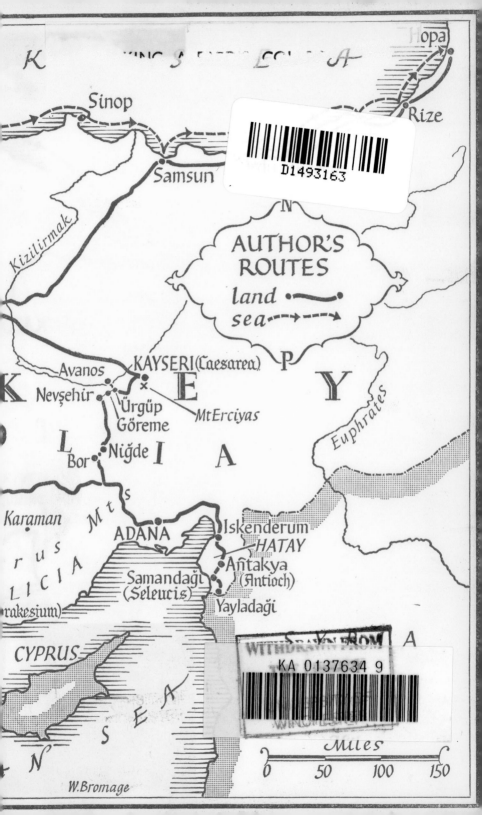

WELCOME THE WAYFARER

A Traveller in Modern Turkey

WELCOME
THE
WAYFARER

A Traveller in Modern Turkey

NANCY PHELAN

LONDON · MELBOURNE
MACMILLAN & CO LTD
NEW YORK
ST MARTIN'S PRESS
1965

MACMILLAN AND COMPANY LIMITED
St Martin's Street London WC 2
32-34 Flinders Street Melbourne C 1
also Bombay Calcutta Madras

THE MACMILLAN COMPANY OF CANADA
70 Bond Street Toronto 2

ST MARTIN'S PRESS INC
175 Fifth Avenue New York 10 NY

Library of Congress Catalogue Number 65-11366

PRINTED IN GREAT BRITAIN

TO BERIA
AND ALL MY
TURKISH FRIENDS

CONTENTS

ILLUSTRATIONS

Plates
following page 100

Maps

ACKNOWLEDGEMENTS

I AM very grateful to all the people who helped me in my travels in Turkey ... to the Turkish Press, Broadcasting and Tourist Department, who gave me a press card, and to Rüknettan *Bey* and Nimet Hanim, of that Department, who helped me with advice and information; and to the Turkish Consul-General in Sydney, who sponsored my credentials to the Turkish government.

I must specially thank Evelyn and Homer Kalças, of Istanbul, for their help and hospitality, and the late Gladys Moore, of the Australian Broadcasting Commission, Sydney, who gave me an introduction to the Kalçases. Through Evelyn and Homer, I met the Güneys, the Turkish family who did so much to help me see and understand Turkish life, and to whom I owe so much.

As to all the other Turkish friends who helped and entertained me all over the country, there is no way of thanking them except by trying to show my appreciation in these pages.

I took the photographs on a Rolleicord camera and I am most grateful to my husband, R. S. Phelan, for all his help in preparing the prints for this book.

To four generous writers I owe a tremendous debt for encouraging me to finish this book: Florence James, Kylie Tennant, L. G. Rodd and Lovat Dickson; and to the late Ida Leeson for compiling the bibliography.

Note: Although at times in this book the word policeman is used for *jandarma*, the *jandarmerie* are really military, serving in place of police in small country communities.

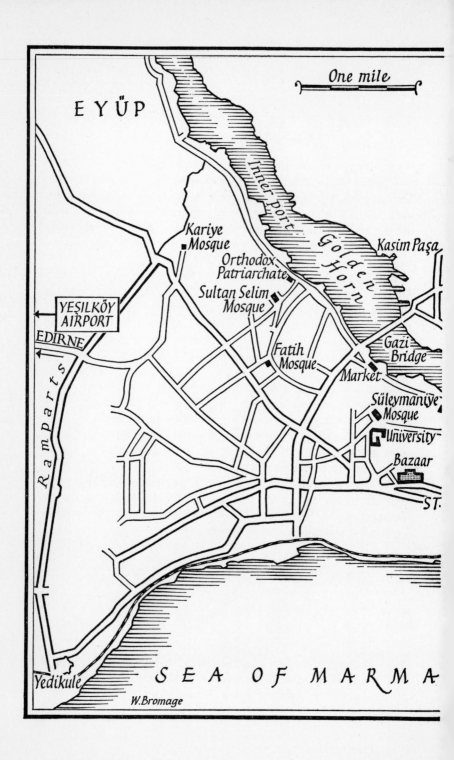

TURK, n. Ottoman, Osmanli; member of the race from which the Ottomans are derived; ferocious, wild or unmanageable person.

The Concise Oxford Dictionary.

CHAPTER ONE

WHAT DO WE KNOW OF THE TURKS?

It was from the island of Rhodes that I first saw Turkey.

Instructed by the taxi-driver I alighted at the edge of a cliff and stared obediently into the distance.

'Turkey!' the driver said, gesturing towards a low blue cloud. 'Turkish mainland. *Anatolie!*'

'Pow-pow-pow,' said my Greek companions disapprovingly.

I looked at Anatolia with apprehension and surprise; surprise at finding it so close, apprehension because quite soon I should be landing on its shores.

The Greeks waited a decent interval, then turned back to the car.

'Pow-pow-pow-pow-pow,' they said, fanning themselves, and we drove on with a slight feeling of having escaped contamination.

I looked back at the blue cloud. In love with Greece and the Greeks, identifying myself with them in the way of lovers, I had absorbed their views, their hatred of the Turks. On an earlier visit, staying in a Greek household, I had heard bitter stories from the older people of the burning of Smyrna, of massacres, of Greeks driven away from Asiatic Turkey (Anatolia) where they had lived for hundreds of years. Nothing good could be found in Turkey, they said. Better stay where life was civilized and people were *simpatico*; and because I had loved Greece at first sight, because I could not resist its beauty, the charm of its people, I had listened, hesitated and postponed.

This time I was on my way to see what the Turks were really like, for it is not only the Greeks who speak of them disparagingly. Every day airline passengers stream through the Istanbul Customs to the Hilton and Park Hotels, to Sancta Sophia and the Bazaar and the Bosphorus and back again to the airport, and many of them, really believing they have been in Turkey, bring home the strangest impressions. Tales of oriental sloth and cunning, of low-down thieving, undrinkable water and human packhorses are added to a background of tradition, of scratching Turks and finding Tartars, of Armenian Massacres, Bulgarian Atrocities, Sick Men of Europe, Unspeakable Turks and lascivious sultans with harems full of slaves, making an unappetizing picture.

It was not always so. In the days when people really travelled in Turkey, they knew better. In the nineteenth century Anatolia must have swarmed with travellers ... learned amateurs surveying the classical ruins, divines apostrophizing the sites of the Seven Churches of Asia, and English gentlewomen in search of drier climes, making water-colour sketches and writing in their journals, most of whom had a kind word for the Turks they encountered.

Then came the First World War; and after that, Atatürk and the Turkish War of Independence. The country was closed to foreign tourists while the Turks tried to put their house in order. Shocking reports were heard. The Greeks who had lived in Asia Minor for centuries were massacred and their remnants driven from the land; the Kurds were massacred; the Armenians were massacred; Atatürk was a bloodthirsty tyrant, a fiend, a monster. No tourist would want to visit such a country even if it were allowed, and very few did until after the Second World War.

Now, anyone can go there, but though there are plenty of Turkey books, few of them give much idea of the ordinary Turks. You can read how they came, led by a grey wolf, from the land of Touran, beyond the Caspian Sea; that they were brave and skilful fighters; that they were wandering shepherds, living in tents, wearing skins in winter and worshipping nature gods; that they strayed into Persia, seeking food for their flocks, and embraced Islam. You can read about Seljuk and Ottoman Turks and New Turks and modern education and agriculture and industry and politics but you can't find out much about Mehmet, Naci and Mustafa ... the Turkish equivalent of Tom, Dick and Harry ... unless you go there to see for yourself.

Though this seemed to me quite an adequate reason for going to Turkey, it was not good enough for friends and relations, most of whom looked pained and perplexed. People are so used to being organized, purposeful, constructive that they become disapproving, even suspicious when they catch someone doing things just for fun. As books must have a message, travellers must have a purpose . . . a survey, a report, a bridge to build, a community to develop, a mission to fulfil. To silence the questions, to appease the offended looks I said I was going to photograph the Turks.

At once everyone became helpful. I was wasting my time, they said. Turks, being Muslims, wouldn't allow their pictures taken; Turkey had no local colour any more; Turks looked just like anyone else, all in western clothes; I didn't speak Turkish; I would get typhoid from drinking the water; it was dangerous to eat Turkish food; I mustn't touch *yoghurt* or milk or any raw fruit; it wasn't safe for a woman to travel alone in Turkey, and finally, the government wouldn't let me.

I wrote to the Turkish government and told them all about it, and they wrote back saying they would give me a press card. This silenced the Anglo-Saxons, but not the Greeks. They looked cool, hurt, disapproving and reproachful. So vehement and convincing were their arguments and protests that when at last I tore myself from their country and set out for Anatolia it was with a bad grace and the belief that I should find nothing there to love as I loved Greece; no one so gay and friendly as the people I was leaving.

*   *   *

Although the Dodecanese are so close to Turkey, there is little communication between Greeks and Turks, but on Chios island I found a motor-boat that makes the crossing once a week. An hour after leaving Chios I was approaching the Turkish fishing village of Çesme, on the peninsular west of Izmir (Smyrna). Only my body travelled; my heart was still in Greece and I felt resentful when a Turkish flag appeared on the little boat's masthead, its brilliant scarlet overshadowing the faded blue-and-white stripes; yet to be honest there was nothing sinister or hostile in the sunlit scene ahead. Çesme, with its fishing-boats, its crumbling castle and its scattered houses seemed all innocence and domesticity.

The boat stopped and we floated, waiting. There was a dreamlike feeling of leisure over everything. Presently, a dinghy put out from the shore and slowly paddled towards us. Two slight, dark men in uniform climbed out and came aboard. The Greek deck-boy rolled his eyes at me in pantomime warning of tiresome formalities ahead, and the captain,

sighing, dug into a black plastic shopping-bag and brought out
an exercise-book which he laid on the cabin table. I produced
my passport.

The inspector did not take long.

'What's in here?' asked the first official, pointing to a flat
parcel.

'Discs . . . Greek songs,' I said.

He turned down the corners of his mouth.

'Oh, *Greek!*' he said, with the same inflexion the Greeks had
used when I declared my Turkish money at Chios.

I felt depressed and wished I were going back to Greece with
the boat, but things warmed up when the officials saw my
camera. Eagerly they offered to pose, and afterwards, saying
'Address . . . address . . .' they scrawled their names in my
little book. In an ambience of warmest friendship I was handed
into the dinghy and rowed ashore.

After the colours of the Greek islands Çesme was drab and
derelict, full of ruined buildings which, I was told, were relics
of the fighting between Greeks and Turks in the nineteen-
twenties. I wondered how I should occupy the three hours I
must wait for the Izmir bus.

I was led to the Customs house, into a small, stark room
containing a desk, bench and portrait of Mustafa Kemal
Atatürk, very handsome, dressed as though for a conjuring act
with white tie and gloves and top-hat. Here, beneath the Father
of Modern Turkey's cold pale eyes, I spent the three hours,
waiting for my two bags to be passed, benevolently tended by a
gentle, simple-minded gorilla in a shabby uniform. During this
time we managed to establish by pantomime and a jumble of
languages that I was from Australia ('*Ah! Avustralya! Gelibolu!
Anzac!*'); that I travelled alone; how much jewellery I wore
and how much money I had, apart from the black-market
currency concealed in the more inaccessible parts of my
person.

Remembering the warnings of the Greeks, I answered everything freely if not truthfully, smiled a great deal and did my
best to look harmless and non-political. When formalities were
over I was escorted by the gorilla, several policemen, some
soldiers and school-children to a fly-blown *gazino* (casino)
where a terrible meal was placed before me.

I ate everything they recommended, swallowed the drinks

they gave me, though I was sure the water was poisonous, and learnt to pronounce a few Turkish words. It was all very successful and at the end the *gazino* proprietor, the waiters and the cook, joined by the gorilla, the policemen and the school-children, rushed me to the crowded bus and stowed me in next to the driver.

This is the seat of honour in a Turkish bus, but as so often happens there was no back and little room for legs, while heat rising from the engine combined with the midday sun to scorch the face.

At the last moment the bus was halted by the gorilla, who was hovering about like an anxious mother, and a little police-man squeezed in, saying he would escort me to my destination; then with the air full of clamorous farewells from Customs staff, friends and onlookers we set off inland to where Izmir lies at the head of its gulf.

I had ascertained that the Turkish for 'beautiful' was *çok güzel*, since this is the best word to start with when arriving in a new country, and I now used it at every opportunity, to the gratification of the policeman and all the passengers. It was not hard to do so for the landscape was indeed beautiful and a continuous surprise as it unfolded. At first very arid, with sparse olive trees and glimpses of the sea, it soon changed to rolling hills and rivers lined with planes and oleanders. In the cornfields women in *şalvars* (baggy trousers) and yellow head-scarves worked beside men with wrapped-up heads and trousers shaped like jodhpurs. They were handsome people, many very fair with blue eyes and broad Saxon faces. They stood, unsmiling but not unfriendly, staring at the bus as though mesmerized.

My arrival was so quiet, everything was so disarmingly normal that I forgot about being in a strange land and one that was reputedly hostile. There was no sign of suspicion and I had no sense of being alien. Everyone was paying me little attentions. At a wayside *lokanta* (restaurant) the proprietor, having no flowers, picked a bunch of mint and pressed it into my hand; at a village a woman came to the bus window and offered me water from the *çeşme*, a piped spring, and my little policeman, who had an almost full set of gold teeth, jumped off at each little café to buy me tea, for which he refused payment, and addressing me as *Monsieur*, pointed out the sights in a strange language of his own.

B

'*Monsieur* . . . *monsieur* . . . *Chammels!*' he said with pleasure, waving at the camels on the road.

As far as I could see, the Turks, though perhaps slightly solemn, were very much like any other people, nor at first glance was there anything unfamiliar in the landscape; yet approaching Izmir I began to realize that there was a subtle difference in the scene. It was the churches that I missed, the little white buildings with pink or blue domes, the wayside shrines and crucifixes with their jam-jars of flowers and leaves, and the sound of distant bells, silvery and pure, or flat and slightly cracked. All these were left behind when I sailed from Chios; now, from the distant villages rose high pointed minarets with crescents shining out against the sky, and as we passed I heard the clear faint voice of the *muezzin* high above our heads.

CHAPTER TWO

A LAND OF SURPRISES

In travelling, several days should be allowed for hating the country just entered and comparing it unfavourably with the one just left. This may partly account for my dislike of Izmir, though I doubt if I should ever fully appreciate it. I should have seen it first from the railway, where the train slowly circles the hills, revealing an eastern-looking city unsuspected from other quarters; or from the water-front, which has all the life and colour lacking in the main streets. Here, ocean liners are tied up alongside brilliant *caïques*, and ferries move about among the fishing boats; and on fine days the harbour takes on the nacreous blue that is the essence of the Aegean; but arriving by bus from Çesme I saw none of these things. I saw only dusty streets, mud-coloured buildings and wide-open places where people rushed about dodging American cars. The city was full up, not with Greeks as in the old days, but with American soldiers, and American voices everywhere contended with the wailing of broadcast Turkish songs.

Hotels were crowded but by paying a high price I secured a room smelling of damp cement, opening upon a central shaft which acted as a sounding board for the voices of all whose rooms surrounded it. My neighbours were American soldiers whose uninhibited language, shouted from window to window, kept me awake most of the night.

Whatever I thought of Izmir, there is no doubt that it is an up-and-coming city. Factories smoke away round the bay and in the immense Kültür Park is the site of the Izmir International Fair, where exhibits are displayed each year by nations wishing to trade with Turkey. Ships, trains and planes come and go constantly, bringing goods and people to and from other parts of the world and giving an air of international bustle.

The town stretches back from the sea and up the slopes of Mount Pagus, where the houses, with their cypress trees, are arranged in terraces. There was an earlier Smyrna, built by

7

Greek colonists and named after an Amazon, which stood
slightly north-west of Izmir, but the site of the present city was
chosen by Alexander the Great after the liberation from the
Persians. It is said that as he lay on the slopes of Mount Pagus
the goddess Nemesis appeared in a dream and told him to
rebuild Smyrna on the place where he slept.

'Alexander the Big,' said the young man in the hotel office
who rather fancied his English. 'Alexander the Big decide the
place.'

For generations Smyrna was the chief Greek town in Anatolia.
The Turks called it *Giaour Smyrna* (Infidel Smyrna) but they
were not intolerant, and the Greeks thrived, building up a fine
trade in wheat and dried fruit. Kinglake, in 'Eothen', describes
the Greeks in the Ottoman Empire as better off than their
compatriots living in the newly constituted Greek kingdom;
but all this prosperity came to an end after the First World
War. Greek troops, with Allied naval support, occupied the
city, massacred Turks and invaded the interior. Guerilla war
broke out and fighting continued until 1922 when Atatürk's
forces defeated the Greeks. Smyrna was sacked, the Greek
citizens slaughtered or driven away and further hatred and
bitterness added to the long, long feud between Greeks and
Turks.

Away from the business and civic centres the town has more
character. The cobbled streets become narrow, full of life and
colour; there is a good deal of noise, radios play deafening
Turkish music and the general effect is like Singapore or any
eastern town where life goes on in the street. The gutters run
with slime, the smells are strong and flies and dust abound.
Between the little crowded shops, narrow doors and alleys lead
to dark and squalid courtyards where people, carts and animals
live together. Magnificent fruit and vegetables of every kind
are sold in open-fronted shops, and closed shops deal in hard-
ware, *yoğhurt*, goat cheese in hair-covered hides, bread, and cakes
and pastries swimming in sweet syrup. Barbers, shoe-makers
and photographs of Atatürk are everywhere.

Many of the streets are roofed with vines, and turning corners
you come suddenly upon covered fountains where chairs and
tables are set out, or queer-shaped mosques and buildings,
pink or white, with peeling walls, festooned with flowers and
creepers. The men in the cafés sip tea in little glasses or stare

blankly, fingering their prayer-beads. They have the air of sitting among ruins, for the broken pavements, running water, unmade roads and garbage in the gutters could be the aftermath of a cyclone or earthquake, and the crumbling old houses and unfinished new ones add to this impression. Uninhibited by the squalor of the quarter, the residents receive their visitors with simple dignity.

Above the city, on Mount Pagus, is the old citadel, and on the slopes are pine-woods and *gazinos* where the people go at weekends to drink samovar tea and smoke *narghilés* (hubble-bubble pipes) and enjoy the view. Buses and *dolmuşes* (shared taxis) struggle up the winding streets, disgorging families and sightseers and soldiers on leave, gentle shabby little creatures who look as though they are wearing each other's uniform by mistake and who walk hand-in-hand,[1] often carrying a bunch of flowers. Vendors of drinks, sweets, bread and pastries wander about or sell their wares from stalls, and donkeys carry the tanks of the water-sellers.

One blue day I lunched up there at the restaurant that looks across the city to the sea. From below it has a Riviera gaiety, with striped awnings and glittering lights, but though the view from the terrace is indeed marvellous a dry blasting wind soon blew us all into the dining-room, where we peered out through smeary windows, vaguely served by a little waiter in an off-white jacket several sizes too big. There was no Riviera gaiety. The décor was heavy Edwardian, the furniture pompous and on the walls a set of sepia ruins and an angry photograph of Atatürk; but the personnel were friendly. The waiter polished my plate with his own handkerchief and after lunch a soldier escorted me to the primitive lavatory and ushered me in, tut-tutting when he found no water in the carafe. When I reappeared, another waiter held my hat while I washed my hands at a vegetable sink in the kitchen and dried them on my slip.

* * *

How arrogant our ignorance can make us. I came to Turkey prejudiced against a landscape I had never seen, expecting only dust and heat, plateaux and steppes and cruel parching winds. I came, I thought, to see the modern Turks. I found

[1] In Turkey young men are often seen holding hands or walking arm-in-arm.

myself immediately involved with ancient Greeks and Byzantines, with Seljuk Turks and Ottomans, and everywhere confronted with a beauty so intense and varied that it threatened
to distract me from the people. I had forgotten that this Anatolian mainland was known as Asia Minor to the ancients because
it contained within its boundaries the diversities of climate,
physical formation and vegetation to be found in Asia itself.
All the more powerful for its unexpectedness, its beauty led me
on, down roads I never meant to take.

One of these roads took me, in strange company, to the ruined
Greek city of Pergamum, now called Bergama, north of Izmir.
Organized by the young man at the hotel desk, I shared a taxi
with a couple of Old Turkey Hands who had been in the country for two years, but spoke no Turkish and appeared to despise
everything but Greek ruins and antiquities. The taxi-driver,
wearing a cast-off American baseball cap and sun-glasses made
of greenish mirrors, quickly decided they were not for him,
and turned all his attentions to me, feeding me with sugar-
coated nuts out of a little paper twist, stopping the car at
frequent intervals and commanding me to take photographs,
to the disgust of our companions.

The highway runs for miles between the green hills and the
sea. Drifts of flowers are spread about the roadside and among
them storks meditate on one leg or prowl carefully in search of
food. Against this mellow landscape are Old Testament scenes,
men with short square beards driving primitive ploughs through
the dark earth and veiled women in baggy trousers advancing
in lines across the turned fields, sowing with immemorial
gestures . . . one arm embracing the bowl that holds the grain,
the other circling out and round as the seed is flung into the
furrows. In their yellow veils they gather at the wells and *çesmes*
with their pitchers, turning their faces from the passer-by or
shrinking down against the wall; but the men leading ox-carts
or strings of camels wave cheerfully, often exposing toothless
gums as they smile.

Bergama was in the midst of its annual Folklore Festival and
the streets were crowded with antique costumes, men in short
full bloomers, embroidered jackets and high boots, girls in
velvet waistcoats, coloured headkerchiefs and dangling earrings.
The older women, in black from head to foot, were like dark
bundles from which hands and feet protruded. People led

sheep and goats about, the bazaar was in full swing and in an open square before the mosque a dance was going on, a slow tottering Turkish dance in which the men reeled carefully round in a circle with arms held above their heads as though in surrender, to the music of drums and a melancholy pipe. The apparent clumsiness of the dancers' movements was studied and deceptive for at the moment you expected them to fall they would spring into the air, turn and come down lightly, holding their position with a combination of awkwardness and balance. Daggers were stuck into their striped sashes and on their heads were little fez-like turbans adorned with brightly-printed scarves.

A bust of Atatürk in the square looked sour, as well it might, surrounded on all sides by women whose faces were concealed in a way to make him turn in his grave.

From the acropolis of Pergamum, among the poppies and the brilliant little flowers of the Aegean, I looked down upon the roofs and minarets of Bergama, on the ruined basilica, the river curving into the distance, and beyond, the coloured squares of field and orchard, blue-tinged by the shadows of the passing clouds.

Rich, impregnable Pergamum on its hill-top was as famous for its learning as its commerce, adorned with fine buildings and proud of its museums and works of art. When it seemed that its library might rival that of Alexandria as the greatest in the world, the Egyptians prohibited the export of papyrus; but the scientists of Pergamum produced a substitute, from the tanned hides of sheep or goats, which they called *pergamem*, and we call parchment, and which long outlived the library of Alexandria.

Up on the hill, on the place where the altar of Zeus once stood, a family of Turks were picnicking with their shoes off. *Ekmek* (bread), *su* (water) and cucumbers were spread around where the sacrifices were made, and shoes and coats were strewn among the scattered marbles. The family called cheerfully, inviting me to join them. While the children ran about picking flowers for me, I sat with the parents, aunts and grandparents drinking water from a long-necked stone jar called a *testi*. I already knew the stories of undrinkable water were not true. The beautiful natural springs all over the country are a source of pride to the Turks and a blessing to travellers.

Picnics were going on everywhere. The fields separating Bergama from the ruins of the Aesculapium, the ancient sanctuary and health resort, were littered with holiday-makers, and painted carts trundled about carrying men in cloth caps and pyjama jackets, and the black forms that represent the women of the district. Tents and awnings were set up over the stalls of the food-vendors and a brisk trade was going on with cucumbers, bread and *köfte* or little fried meat balls.

Families were spread all over the classical ruins; fat ladies unpacked bags and distributed coats and sweaters as rain drizzled down and loving fathers in jade-green open-necked shirts and striped suits led their little children about by the hand, helping them up and down marble steps, taking them behind columns to unbutton their pants. The atmosphere was a family one and my impression of the Turks was of a homely people. This was the first time I had seen them out for enjoyment *en masse* and I was struck by the general seriousness of their demeanour. They were happy enough but expressed little of their pleasure on their faces.

On the way home I saw another aspect of these gentle people. In the town of Menemem is a memorial to Mustafa Fehmi Kubilay, killed in 1930 while trying to disperse a religious demonstration. Shot by the ringleader, Mehmet the Dervish, but still alive, his head was hacked off, while the crowd stood by and watched, after which they ran amok through the streets with it, until quelled by the military.

*　　　*　　　*

Having successfully despatched me to Pergamum, the young man at the hotel desk, who had become very chummy, now ordered me off to Ephesus in a bus full of Austrian tourists, assuring me, when I protested, that I need not stay with them.

I went, unwillingly, and fell in love with Ephesus. Compared with Pergamum it seems all grace and lightness, its marble streets, lined with fragmentary statues, brilliant against the blue Aegean sky. Heat shines off the worn and polished surfaces of surviving sculpture, and poppies grow among the cracks and joins of masonry or pavements where green lizards bask.

It is delicious to walk from the blazing sun and blinding marble into dim tunnels and archways, to crawl into dark unfinished openings in half-buried buildings. Much of the city still stretches under the earth. Scraps of walls emerge all round, like hands thrust up for deliverance, and in the great theatre the tiered seats have become a grassy slope strewn with flowers.

I quickly got away from the Austrians, who were talking knowledgeably about the city's Christian associations, about St Paul and Diana of the Ephesians, and the Cave of the Seven Sleepers, and the grave of John the Baptist. They also talked a great deal about whether or not the Virgin Mary came here to live after the Ascension, as legend says she did. *Panaya Kapulu*, the House of the Virgin, has been converted into a chapel and by the altar are hundreds of handkerchiefs, scraps of material, fragments of dresses strung up together, left by those who believe that the Virgin will answer their prayers if they leave a personal possession.

The site of *Panaya Kapulu*, unknown until the early nineteenth century, was revealed in a vision to Catharine Emmerich, the German mystic. Though she had never been to Ephesus her descriptions of the city and the house were so precise that investigators found it immediately.

Close to the marble streets and ruins of Ephesus is the Turkish town of Seljuk, built round the base and up the slopes of a high hill which rises suddenly from the plain, like a medieval fortress in the Drôme region of France. On the hill is a Byzantine castle with walls so well preserved that in the distance they appear complete, and below are minarets and domes where mosques and houses and old Seljuk tombs are mixed together, for the inhabitants have just added a few rooms here and there to ruined buildings and moved in. All round are the orchards, vineyards and cornfields of the Little Meander Valley, brilliant, virile, strong.

As the road climbs towards *Panaya Kapulu* there is a view back on this scene, on the hill and the great brown fortress with its square towers and scarlet flag. The past might still be living; there is a feeling that horsemen might gallop along the road at any minute and storm the castle, yet at the same time it basks in the benign peace which is only found in places now sleeping after a stormy life.

This little town was my first encounter with the Seljuks, the branch of the Turk family which overran Persia, Syria and Asia Minor, penetrating into the Holy Roman Empire until they reached the Bosphorus, opposite Constantinople; but it was not an exciting introduction, despite its ruins and its castle. The streets were full of the Austrians, who were letting no grass grow under their feet. It was clear that tourists were no novelty in the town and I was taken for one of the Austrians by a little girl and boy who hoped to sell me old coins.

With these two at my heels, chanting 'Bye-bye' and 'Spik English', I prowled wrathfully about the ruins. The inhabitants had turned out to see the visitors, the men sitting in the cafés, the women and babies crouching on the footpath or clustered together in corners, for rural cafés are a male preserve. There was no chance of getting portraits of Turks for it was impossible to approach them quietly or ask their permission. Those in favour of tourism were anxious to be photographed and were trying to attract my attention; the rest, the more interesting members, were hiding their faces or giving uninviting stares. One threw a stone ... a handsome woman with the broad cheek-bones, slanting eyes and small mouth seen in Seljuk portraits. Carrying a baby with an Eskimo face, she wore orange trousers, blue and scarlet tunic and a yellow veil.

Cheated of my portraits, dogged by the numismatists, I climbed the hill to the castle where I came upon the Austrians photographing each other on St John's grave. This done they strode off purposefully after their *Führer*, stopping suddenly to take a photograph, then hastening on, for time was limited. There was something so infectious about their urgency that I was swept up and borne along with them, through the dust and over the summer fields to a swamp of bulrushes and stagnant water where we all stopped dead. This, said the *Führer*, was the site of the Artemisium, the great temple of Diana, and after a rapid resumé of its history he made some ponderous comments about grandeur fallen into the dust while the Austrians wondered among themselves if it was worth wasting a shot on such an uninteresting sight.

There is something terrible in this abandoned swamp. Not a trace remains of all the wealth and splendour, genius and brilliance associated with the temple, one of the Seven Wonders of the World. On the night that Alexander the Great was born it was burnt down by a lunatic who hoped in this way to perpetuate his name. The Ephesians were still rebuilding it when Alexander came after defeating the Persians. He offered to help with the cost of reconstruction if his name were inscribed on the temple. Both these attempts at immortality failed, for the Ephesians condemned to oblivion the name of the lunatic and Alexander's offer was refused. The Artemisium needed neither of them. Now there is nothing but a rough field populated by a few Turkish peasants. Hundreds of years, thousands of people have been wiped out as though they never existed.

Even the landscape has changed. When Pliny wrote his Natural History the sea washed up to the temple steps; when St Paul preached against Diana, Ephesus was a port. Now the harbour has been silted up by the Little Meander River, and city and swamp lie inland.

As we stood gazing blankly a stork flew over, flopping and clattering, and one of the Austrians turned to me.

'Tis der stork vot goes, *ja*?' He twinkled roguishly and said daringly. 'Tis der stork vot brings der babies, *nein*?'

Shattered by his brilliance, the others went off into gales of hearty laughter, glad to be distracted from the gloomy spectacle of Diana's downfall.

Afterwards, I walked back down the empty Street of Marble, past the derelict shops like cool caverns smelling of earth, to the top of a mound where a little breeze came from the distant sea, and here I found a personal touch that suddenly made Ephesus a living place again. Clambering slowly among the fallen marble blocks, tracing with my finger the sculptured fragments and the smooth acanthus leaves I came on work that had never been finished, swirling patterns still picked out in little holes as though by a pin upon the stone, abandoned, never to be carved and smoothed and polished. That was the sad thing about Ephesus; not the lost grandeur, the vanished Artemisium, the broken statues or the buried houses but the touch of mortality, the message from unknown hands overtaken by night when they least expected it.

CHAPTER THREE

FROM AEGEAN TO MARMORA

I FELT like a tourist in Izmir, with the young man at the desk organizing my life. It was time to get on with my plans for meeting the Turks. I was making my way across country to Istanbul, where my press card was to be issued and where I had an introduction to an Australian woman married to an Istanbul Greek, and I found I had quite a choice of transport for this journey. I could go by ship, seeing nothing but the coastline; by air, seeing nothing much at all; by train, in a roundabout fashion or by bus in extreme discomfort. The last was the worst, I was told, the roads were terrible and the buses primitive and overcrowded, but since they pass through the villages and are patronized by the locals I decided to use them, breaking the journey at Bursa, then continuing on to Yalova, on the Sea of Marmora, where I could take a boat to Istanbul.

I made my reservation in plenty of time, for rural transport in Turkey is so crowded that you have to book well ahead, but when I arrived at the depot I found the ticket was made out for the wrong day. There was no room at all on my bus and no other for two days. All pleas and queries met the same answer ... 'Yok!' ... a word that was growing increasingly familiar and one which I finally came to hate, associating it with disaster, confusion, lost trains, non-existent buses, absence of meals or places to sleep. Yok, which is Turkish for 'There isn't any,' is usually accompanied by a lifted chin and raised eyebrows, and though I could accept the word itself as a negative, for no sound was ever more negative, the look of interrogation always suggests that perhaps there is hope after all.

This time, finding it entirely negative, I became desperate. I stamped my foot and demanded to be given a seat, refusing to listen to reason or persuasion. Without a word of common language we all understood each other perfectly, the bus officials, the conductor and driver, the food-vendors, the assembled passengers, the hangers-on who had gathered to watch the performance. At the end I was ashamed and ready to apologize but it seemed that my rage had roused only respect and desire to help. Murmuring soothingly, reassuringly, the Turks clustered round, trying to find a solution, and finally, when no other passenger would consent to be off-loaded, a canvas stool was fixed up in the aisle.

As I boarded the bus, I was congratulated by a soldier who spoke a few words of English.

'Turkish woman not get on bus,' he said admiringly. 'Turkish woman never argue ... Turkish woman obey, get pushed aside. Foreign woman not pushed aside.'

My improvised seat was hardly suitable for a journey of eleven hours on a rough road, and before long I was sore in every bone and muscle. The other passengers watched me kindly and sympathetically, offering food and drink at frequent intervals, and when at last someone alighted they demanded that the vacant seat be given to me instead of the incoming passenger who had reserved it.

They were as much concerned for my instruction as for my comfort, nudging my arm, tut-tutting with approval as they pointed out dry riverbeds flooded with pink oleanders, storks standing in fields of narcissi, opium poppies[1] flowering in the corn. For the most part their attitude was one of quiet pride but when from time to time we passed groups of wild, dark people in bright-coloured clothes they look disapproving and turned aside muttering '*Koorts*' (Kurds) as though in condemnation.

As the day advanced, the landscapes changed in character, deepening in colour, the pastel tones of olive groves and vineyards giving way to rich black soil and parklands of profound and penetrating green. Occasionally, we passed adobe villages where children in dark pinafores moved sedately in the streets, yet in the open country were no farms or cottages, only the tents and hovels of the nomads. Turkish peasants go each morning to the fields in waggons or on donkeys, returning to their villages at night.

Life in the bus was rather trying, for it was hot, and searing clouds of dust poured in through the empty window-frames. Everyone was well wrapped up, the men in woollen scarves

[1] Turkey produces a great deal of opium and fields of poppies are seen everywhere.

and waistcoats, the women in veils and *çarsafs*. *Çarsafs* are
straight lengths of material kept on with tapes round head and
waist, and though they vary slightly in different districts they
are all designed to conceal the wearer's form. It is strange to see
buses full of nun-like figures with husbands and children, and
the bizarre effect is quite startling when they carry young
babies in their arms, often breast-feeding them in quiet corners.

All day the wearers of these wintry garments groaned and
sweated grimly, but they cheered up as we approached Bursa,
for a cold wind rose suddenly and grey clouds clotted the sky.
Driving round the foot of Mount Olympus we came into a
drizzling rain which turned to a downpour as we made the
long zig-zag up the hill into the ancient capital of the Ottomans.

*   *   *

Pitchforked from the bus, which I had come to regard as my
home and refuge from life, I stood shivering. My raincoat was
in my luggage, my dress was thin and sleeveless, my legs were
bare. I was covered with dust, stiff in all joints and very tired.
I spoke no Turkish, knew no one and had no idea where I was
going to stay. Dusk was falling and I felt helpless and forlorn.
I hated Bursa.

A swarm of taxi-men gathered round me, shouting the names
of hotels, but I waved them back while I looked in my little
book from the Turkish Press, Broadcasting and Tourist
Department. With a weary kind of obstinacy I announced I
would go to the *X Palas* Hotel. If it was a palace it must have a
bath, I thought vaguely, and that was all I cared about.

X Palas was very hard to find but eventually the taxi turned
into a large garden and stopped at a rambling building with
a splendid view. I was too tired to question anything and after
an impossible discussion with a proprietor who spoke only
Turkish, a room was secured and the driver paid off.

The one thing I really understood in the proprietor's dis-
course was the word *banyo*, which he used frequently, but when
I set out to look for the bathroom I could not find it. The
Biblical females crouching on the hall floor had slunk away,
and I wandered about the house and gardens until rescued by
a plump French-speaking Turk who was sipping tea in the
rose-garden.

Side by side we pattered through the dark and echoing halls, for the bathroom was a long way from everywhere, and as we went I noticed there was something queer, almost macabre about the place and its inhabitants. All round, reflected in high tarnished mirrors were grotesque Hogarth figures, ancient, bent and lame, shuffling about or sitting listlessly at little tables, staring into space. They took no notice as we passed, our steps echoing round us hollowly, and I began to wonder how I should find this bathroom again. We descended a staircase, crossed a lower room and approached a second staircase made of stone. A curious smell was rising from below and for a second I wondered if it were a joke, even an ambush; then I realized what it was.

'*Banyo á la Turque?*' I asked. My companion nodded.

'*Oui madame. Banyo á la Turque. Beaucoup de vapeur.*'

He led me down the stairs, into the humid earthy smell and handed me over to a businesslike woman in a white overall, with wooden clogs on her feet and a towel round her head. Shutting the door, she demonstrated briskly that I was to remove my clothes. When this was done she handed me a pair of wooden pattens and directed me to a marble enclosure where water ran from silver taps into a marble bowl. Thrusting the soap into my hands she told me to wash myself, pointing to a little silver basin with which I was to bale the water from the marble bowl over my body.

It was a curious atmosphere, a combination of steam-laundry and catacomb. Steam was everywhere, and the damp, shut-in smell, slightly sour and repellent. We were under the ground where neither light nor fresh air ever entered. I was not sure that I really liked it but there was little I could do without my clothes, and the heavy door shut on me like a prison.

When the bathwoman returned she gave a cry of contempt at my slowness and snatched the soap from my hands. She set to work on me with a kind of dish-cloth, turning on all the taps till the water cascaded from the marble basin upon the floor, sloshing about to get a good lather, then applying it vigorously to my body as though to remove the outer skin. When all the lather had been washed off she led me, skating through the soapsuds in my pattens, to a chamber of tombs, where in long rows separated by a central aisle were marble sarcophagi, each without a lid, each with a curve cut from one end on which the neck might rest. Hot water from silver taps was running into the coffins, the surplus cascading into a marble gutter. Through the steamy air I was aware of a muted light and looking up at the domed ceiling I saw the daylight filtering in through small octagonal blisters of thick glass, those symmetrical bubbles like bottle-ends stuck in the roofs of Turkish baths.

I was led to a coffin and pushed down under the hot water until only my face emerged. An involuntary movement to escape from the sudden heat brought a shrill rebuke and I was thrust back with a firm hand. Emphasizing that I must not move, that I must stay boiling, the bathwoman tested the water with her hand, looked at a thermometer and clattered away to other victims.

Apart from the light and the heat it was not unlike being buried alive; there was the same restriction of movement and sense of suffocation that might be expected in such circumstances. I could hear a body being massaged in an adjoining room and someone had taken my place at the running tap in the ante-room, but I was alone as I lay in my coffin, sweating and stupified, listening to the ceaseless splash of the water running along the central aisle. When at last the bathwoman came to release me I feared to touch my scarlet skin lest it peel off.

It was right, of course, that my first introduction to Bursa should be a steam bath, for from the time of the Romans (who knew it as Brusa or Prusa) it has been famous for its baths, which come from natural hot and cold springs.

I dined that night in an open-air *gazino* adjoining the hotel, where the plane trees were strung with fairy-lights and roses grew by an artificial lake. Round me were family parties sitting in solemn silence, some eating, some sipping water, all looking blankly towards a large stage where chairs were set in rows. Presently several mournful musicians straggled in, and after shuffling about, began to play. The music, which was loud and Turkish, was all drums and pipes and twanging instruments and to my ears had a hard insistent rhythm, but the audience approved it.

A quintet of young women appeared and sat in the front row of chairs, bolt upright, ignoring the polite applause. They were all short and plump, with heavy hips and stomachs. Their dark hair was elaborately dressed and they wore taffeta and satin in the hardest of greens, purples and oranges. Tight round the hips and bottoms, the dresses burst out into ruffles, frills and flounces, berthas and ruches wherever possible, with artificial flowers pinned on here and there. One or two were draped in fringes and multi-coloured shawls and all were weighted down with rings and bangles. Stolidly they stared at the audience, who stolidly stared back at them. Occasionally one or other would get up and wander off the stage, then come back and compose herself again in her chair, and when, with eyelids drooping, I felt I could wait no longer, a girl stood up and walked to the microphone. Holding it with both hands, she delivered into it a wail so shrill, so piercing that my blood stopped circulating, following it with more and more fearful cries, uttered without feeling or variation. She was still at it when I tottered from the garden towards the hotel, leaving the audience spellbound with admiration.

*   *   *

It took me a couple of days to appreciate Bursa's charms, for mountain towns should be seen in summer or the heart of winter when they are deep in snow. Wet spring weather is depressing in such places. In the dismal grey light the streets were greasy and slippery, cold winds blew round the corners and the ancient buildings gave out a musty smell of long-stored damp. Yet it is a delightful town; a muddle of tottering buildings washed with yellow, pink and blue. Blue walls predominate and roofs of corrugated tiles surge up and fall away in greenish waves. Through this colour and confusion go the cobbled streets, dim, winding tunnels covered in with vines, leading to mosques and mossy steps and little shops dug into decaying walls. Bright streams rush down the hillside and from the gardens, terraces and cypress groves is a prospect upon the patterned plains below.

Above the streets, among princely gardens, lie the early Ottoman sultans and their families, in tombs of coloured tiles, and dominating all is Mount Olympus (*Ulu Dag*), in winter white with snow.

Despite the rain, I walked everywhere, for I found the buses very difficult to negotiate and feared that if I travelled in them I should spend my time whizzing past my destinations. Once in, the conductor would not open the door in any circumstances, however much you pleaded, and since I did not even know

c

where I should get off it was hard to reach any satisfactory conclusion. By the second day I had decided to find my way on foot and was standing in the street, cogitating, when a shabbily-dressed young man approached and offered his assistance in halting English. Still unfamiliar with Turkish ways, I took him for the kind of youth who gravitates towards foreign female travellers in Europe, but a second glance revealed that he was offering only kindness, friendliness and help.

This boy, Semsettin, took me in charge at once, guiding me through the streets, pointing out sights, coaching me in Turkish pronounciation, diving into bookshops to find me a phrase-book with what he called 'speak-sounds'. He had the heart of an artist. In the Green Mosque he led me to the walls to feel the carved niches, passing his hand lovingly over tiles and delicate wood-work; from a shelf he took a richly-gilded Koran, turning the pages with a book-lover's touch. He read me a verse or two, then broke off, shaking his head as though at the impossibility of commenting on such beauty, and shut the book reluctantly, as though he longed to keep it.

He made me ashamed. Bursa is acclaimed as a gem of Turkish architecture, the city where an indigenous art first flowered in a form no longer dominated by Persia, but I could not respond to its beauties. The endless wealth of detail, the constant repetition, the ubiquitous patterns baffled me. The plain octagonal tiles in their rich colours spoke irreverently of the bathroom, the stalactite *mihrabs* and doorways were like jelly-moulds, the light-wires criss-crossing the mosque interiors resembled overhead tramwires, and certain doorways and vistas recalled the elephant house at the Zoo or the Pavilion at Brighton. I wanted to understand and appreciate but I could not, and I was glad that Semsettin in his reverent trance was unaware of my real feelings as I repeated like a parrot, '*Çok güzel . . . çok güzel.*'

Outside the mosque I invited him to tea at the adjoining café, and afterwards, assured that I could find my way alone, he gracefully excused himself and left. When I asked for the bill I found he had forestalled me, leaving me still in his debt.

Next day the sun came out and Bursa was transformed. The little stage-property houses became infused with colour, the trees shone fresh and green. It was all pale domes, dark cypresses, mosques and gardens against a light blue sky, with tiers of richness cascading down to the tranquil plains.

I plunged into a street of coppersmiths where little men like stage dwarves hammer away in open-fronted shops. In another street are basket makers and coopers surrounded by their barrels. In the bazaars the famous Bursa silk is sold, spun by Bursa silkworms, woven by Bursa families. Foodshops are everywhere and, constantly on the move, boys with hanging brass trays bearing glasses of hot tea. It is a cheerful busy world inhabited by simple friendly people.

As I stood buying a casserole I heard a glad cry of recognition and Semsettin appeared before me, his handsome, kindly face smeared with black, his green eyes beaming with delight. At once a chair was brought and set for me, tea was ordered and I found myself the centre of a crowd of friendly coppersmiths who left their work to welcome me.

With the sun shining, the loveliest place in Bursa is the *Muradiye*, the burial gardens of the Ottoman Sultan Murad II. Here you may walk among magnolias and roses, bask in the sun or rest beneath majestic planes. There is a stillness and repose in the very air, evoked by the flowers and trees, the forms of the buildings and the dark shapes of the cypresses. It is a fitting resting-place for Murad, 'a just and valiant prince', whose virtues were acknowledged even by his Christian enemies. Twice this Sultan left his throne to live a holy life at Magnesia and twice, at the call of his people, returned to save them from disaster. He died before he could withdraw again to the life he loved.

Something of his humility remains in the *Muradiye*, in his tomb with the open dome. He did not wish to be buried like an Ottoman Sultan, shut away in gloomy magnificence; he chose to lie, like a poor man, in a grave exposed to the sun and rain of heaven.

*   *   *

On my last morning in Bursa I took a bus from the centre of the town, asking the conductor to set me down at *X Palas* Hotel, but when I rose to alight at the familiar gates he shook his head and signed that I was to wait. Nothing would induce him to open the door.

'*Yok!*' he said, pushing me back towards my seat. '*Yok!*'

I thought he had gone mad for he went on saying '*Yok*' to all my frenzied protests, supported by the other passengers who shouted at me kindly and helpfully while we rushed along the road to an area I did not know. Then the bus stopped, and ignoring my angry remarks, a woman took my arm.

'*X Palas Oteli*,' she said, pointing at a building I had never seen before. '*X Palas.*'

It was like a nightmare, for though everyone tried to explain I could not understand. When finally I reached my own hotel, late and harrassed, with fifteen minutes to change, pack, eat lunch and catch the Yalova bus, I made straight for the office where the proprietor sat.

'What is the name of this hotel?' I demanded. 'Is it not the *X Palas*?'

He handed me a card. On it I read a name I had never heard before and underneath a list of mineral baths and special services for invalids. It was a place for taking the cure ... Rheumatics ... arthritis ... No wonder the other inmates were so Hogarthian, so crippled, halt and lame.

*   *   *

After Bursa came the last lap of the road to Istanbul, over rich and lovely country to the Sea of Marmora, in another primitive bus full of peasants who fed me with nuts and lemonade all the way. Once more there were hills and mountains, winding roads and flowers, and in the distance the site of the ancient city of Nicea, where the Seljuks set up their first capital in Asia Minor. Then came Yalova, on the Marmora coast, and a hurry to catch the boat across to Thrace; and at last, in a grey misty dusk, the domes and minarets of Istanbul and the twinkling lights of the Golden Horn as we rounded Seraglio Point and drew into Galata Bridge.

CHAPTER FOUR

'NOT STRANGER, FAMILY NOW'

I COULD not have arrived in Istanbul at a more unpropitious moment or in a more unpropitious manner. Instead of landing at Yeşilköy airport or on the overseas quay or even at Sirkeci station, with all the dignity of an international traveller and access to the facilities provided for such, I stepped off the local boat from Yalova into the seething herd of workers on Galata Bridge at the peak of the rush hour.

Galata Bridge, which crosses the Golden Horn, is the terminus for the ferries that serve the Bosphorus and parts of the Marmora, and in the morning and evening is crowded with people fighting their way off or on the boats. As always in such places, officials love to slam gates in your face just as you think you have caught the ferry and this must have happened as we arrived at the wharf, for an angry crowd was gathered behind the iron grille, glaring in at us.

As we descended the gangway the gates opened and the crowd rushed forward. I was surrounded, completely losing sight of the kindly young Turk who had befriended me on the boat, bought me tea and carried my bags ashore. Wondering where I should get a taxi and how I should find a hotel I was relieved to be greeted by a tall, fair-haired woman who was standing near the exit, tensely scanning the faces of all who passed. It was Evelyn Kalças, the Australian married to an Istanbul Greek, to whom I had an introduction but had not yet met, and she had reason to look harrassed. The post office had omitted the time of arrival from my telegram, and she and her husband had spent the whole day at Galata Bridge, in shifts, meeting boats.

She explained this as she organized *hamels* (porters) to carry my luggage and fought a way through the crowd to the taxi rank. I followed her, overwhelmed by the noise, the dust, the reckless cars, the clattering trams, the surging herds of people. Was this really Istanbul . . . Byzantium . . . Constantinople . . .

the Scarlet Apple ... the Threshhold of Felicity, this grey, dirty, crowded city, like Liverpool or Leeds? Whatever I had expected, I was not prepared for this.

I had written asking Evelyn to book me into a hotel, but now she told me that when she mentioned my visit to her Turkish friend, Beria Güney, there was a typical Turkish reaction.

'She wants to see Turkish life? She will not see it in a hotel. She must come to our house. We have room.'

It was all arranged by the time I arrived and the taxi took us straight to the apartment where the Güney women received me warmly. Soft chairs, cool drinks and an elaborate meal were produced, and assured of my physical comfort, Beria interrogated Evelyn as to how she could help me in other ways, while her mother, silent, pale and serene, sat watching with folded hands, from time to time smiling at me with great sweetness.

Beria, small and pretty, with black hair and eyes and a magnolia skin, has the same beautiful facial bones as Princess Soraya – those indestructible good looks that are independent of youth and colouring. She seemed to be very intelligent, quick to understand and decisive in her reactions. I wondered how we were going to manage when Evelyn went back to her apartment at Beylerbeyi, on the Bosphorus, for Beria spoke only a few words of English, her mother none at all; but I was too sleepy to care very much. I gathered that plans were being made for me, that Beria, a schoolmistress on vacation, was proposing to accompany me on my travels in Anatolia to ensure that I saw everything of interest and importance; but that first I must wait in Istanbul for my press card, which would give me a chance to rest, to sort myself out, to see the city ...

Stunned with tiredness, unable to understand a word, I sat like a mute while my future was decided, agreeing gratefully when they suggested I might like to go to bed.

Next day, beaming with delight, Beria took me in charge.

'Today, *Basin Carte, Radio Evi*,' she announced, adding a few more Turkish words and a good many gestures. This meant that I must go to the Turkish Press, Broadcasting and Tourist Department, at Broadcasting House, for my press card, and that I must go alone, for she was occupied; but I was not alarmed. Already I was beginning to realize that though Turkey cannot yet always provide material comforts just when they are needed, she can and does give lavishly of human warmth and friendliness, even in the most unexpected places, and that in the main Turkish officials have remained human beings.

Behind the grand modern façade of *Radio Evi* is the same unpretentious kindness and desire to help found in Anatolian villages. The uniformed personage taking names at the entrance was fatherly, the attendant conducting me to my interview humble, and Nimet *Hanim*[1], the officer I was to interview, pretty, friendly and fluent in English and French. Nothing was too much trouble. Everyone was interested. Everyone wanted to know about broadcasting in Australia.

I was taken to see the building, to watch broadcasts, to meet personnel and artists, and when they found I was interested in music the librarian and his staff spent hours playing discs for me and writing down the names of those I liked.

Round the corner in the spanking new arcade by the Hilton Hotel is the travel section of this department. Here, in an elegant office, I found Rüknettan *Bey*[2], a slender, humorous Turk, speaking good English, whose job is to issue information, timetables and permits for tourists. Regarding me at first with slight bewilderment, he soon accepted my unorthodox ideas of tourism and set himself to help me. Whenever I came back to Istanbul from my travels I would call on him, and reclining in his best armchair, smoking his Turkish cigarettes, would regale him with tales of my hardships and adventures, at which he rocked with unsympathetic laughter.

I found it hard to orientate myself, to realize that though I was still in Turkey I was now in Europe again. The crossing from Yalova had brought me from Anatolia, in Asia, to Istanbul, in Thrace; and to make things worse Istanbul itself is a very confusing city. Seen on the map it resembles a cross-section in a gynaecological text-book, all promontories and inlets. The old city, Old Stamboul, Byzantium or Constantinople, lies on a triangular section bounded on one side by the Sea of Marmora and on the other by the inner harbour known as the Golden Horn. Behind the third side of the triangle, where the great land-walls of Constantinople still stand, are the rolling fields of Thrace. The Golden Horn separates the Old City from Galata and Pera, now called Beyoğlu, districts formerly inhabited by foreign

[1] and [2] *Bey* and *Hanim* (woman) are the old Turkish forms of address, now officially abandoned but still often encountered.

European residents, all known as Franks. Further up the hill is Taksim Square, the centre of the area – like Etoile in Paris, as a Turk explained to me – and beyond, past the Hilton Hotel, are the suburbs on the European bank of the Bosphorus.

Facing Istanbul, across the Bosphorus, is Üsküdar, or Scutari, the first of the suburbs on the Anatolian shore. Istanbul is in Europe; Üsküdar is in Asia. Without a map it is very easy to get direction mixed, with the three waterways – Marmora, Bosphorus and Golden Horn – going in different directions, for the Old City touches all three at Seraglio Point.

It is not a city to be loved easily or at first sight. Noisy, dirty, uncomfortable, hot in summer and cold in winter, covered with a grey pall of smoke and grime, it is a bitter disappointment to those who have been fed on colour photographs of the Bosphorus or fishing boats at Galata Bridge. Without the *camis* (mosques) it might be any unattractive European city. The bridge over the Golden Horn is dreary, dusty, crowded with people and thundering traffic, the Golden Horn itself at times as grey and uninviting as the Manchester Ship Canal. *Aya Sofia* (St Sophia), the wonder of the western world, at first sight seems a chill dark cavern smelling of mould, criss-crossed with overhead tramwires and gigantic chandeliers, its marble walls disfigured by great green discs like tea-trays, inscribed with Koran texts. The mosques are covered with dust and the streets often slimy with mud and grease, decaying food and refuse, the kind of dirt that is inescapable, being visible, tactile and oderiferous. Through the crowds go the porters, bent double, wearing saddles on their backs on which appalling loads are carried.

The whole city is in a chaotic state of demolition ... old buildings being pulled down everywhere to widen streets, create new squares and afford better views of famous monuments. This sort of thing not only causes noise, dust and confusion but clogs up transport. Many quarters might have been blitzed, and here the congestion is at its worst. Sometimes it is impossible to walk along the streets. Buildings crash round you on the footpath and when you step out on the road to avoid falling masonry you are hounded by trams and cars crowding hot on each other through the wreckage. Water gushes about underfoot and the periodical sound of collapsing buildings is augmented by the noise of dynamos, wrecking machines and pneumatic drills. The chaos is at its height at rush hours when everyone is dashing for their ferries, and it is only by looking across the Golden Horn to Eminönü Square that one can retain any sense of balance or faith in the future, for this large open *place* with its trams and stations for taxis and *dolmuşes*, and its wide view of Yeni Cami was once as crowded and chaotic as other parts are now.

Through it all the Istanbul trams groan and struggle their way, too few, too small, too antiquated; ugly, incredibly crowded. Very high, bucking and rocking, they have central aisles in which you become so inextricably jammed among human bodies that the thought of an approaching stop brings panic. Like people escaping from a fire, the passengers go mad, struggling and thrashing about with arms and feet in an effort to reach the exit before being whirled off again. Anyone wishing to fathom the secrets of the Turkish male body will find a brief ride in a tram completely illuminating, not because the Turks are importunate but because this propinquity makes it impossible to avoid the utmost intimacy. Locked together, the bodies strain, undulate and squirm, sighing, lip to lip, knee to knee, united not only physically but by the thought of escape.

The noise, the drabness, the chronic shortages, difficulties and delays of Istanbul life at first threatened to blind me, as they have blinded many visitors, to its real wonders. I hated it, I could not get any kind of *rapport* with it though I was anxious enough to try. It was like a rather nasty cake full of gorgeous fruit ... the Greek city; the Roman city; Byzantium; the Islamic city of the Caliphs; the city of the Ottoman Sultans; Pera, the city of Franks and Levantines; the poetic city of Pierre Loti and Gérard de Nerval, with its high walls and cemeteries ... all gummed up, embedded in the modern untidy city of today. If it had not been for Beria and the Kalçases and the fact that I had all the time I needed, I too might have left without ever getting to know or love it.

It takes time to see beyond the dirt and confusion, the crowds and ugliness; to see the Golden Horn as a long shining arm of water speckled with butterfly boats, with brilliant *caiques* clotted along its banks; to find old mosques and monuments, and cemeteries with cypress trees and strange turbanned headstones like little grey men. Alone or with Beria I explored the mosques and museums and strange hidden places to which she led me in triumph, saying 'Not touristik! Special. Turkish!'

and in time the wonders and delights obliterated all the trials and disillusionments. I fell in love with *Kahrije Cami*, with the Seraglio, the melancholy beauties of *Eyüp* and *Kasim Paşa*, with forgotten tombs, abandoned churches and lonely stretches by the broken walls of Constantinople. I read Kritovoulos'[1] eye-witness accounts of the fall of the city, of the streets running with blood, of women and children raped and slaughtered and tombs torn open and the dead flung out; how the Emperor Constantine died fighting by the walls and how Mehmed, entering the city at the end of the day, wept at the destruction his men had caused.

We went to weddings, funerals and circumcision parties, to *gazinos*, cinemas and cafés; we visited all sorts of households and met every kind of Turk. Beria had dedicated herself to showing me her city and her people, and though she loathed the heat, would come with me in the hottest weather to remote and inaccessible districts. Anatolia was all very well and it was right that I should travel there but Stamboul was a place apart and I must know that too. She made the difference clear. 'In Anatolia so-and-so is done,' she would say. 'But not in MY country; not in Stamboul.'

Her elder brother Naci was just as anxious to be helpful and often arranged little expeditions for my pleasure.

'Tomorrow Naci carry you Yediküle,' Beria would tell me; or, 'Tonight Naci carry us Çamlıça.'

One night, at full moon, Naci did carry us to Çamlıça, a high hill on the Anatolian shore. By day it is a popular park-like place where families come to drink the water and see the view, but on such nights it is transformed. The moonlight, turning all to silver, calls up an insubstantial shimmer over the distance. Behind are the hills leading to Ankara; below, the Marmora and the Princes' Islands. The Bosphorus, a wide white path studded with moving yellow lights, lies in the fore-ground, and beyond is the great city where a thousand diamonds flash and glitter.

I gradually came to love Istanbul as much as I hated it. Between my journeys to Anatolia or Thrace I would prowl alone in the old quarters or sit basking in the sun, in the gardens between the domes and minarets of *Aya Sofya* and *Sultan Ahmet*, the Blue Mosque, the glittering blue cave. I sought out the

[1] Kritovoulos: *History of Mehmed the Conqueror.*

scenes of Loti's novels, peered through iron grilles at tombs, and spent long happy hours with mosaics. For all my gratitude to Beria I liked to do these things alone, for sometimes her eagerness to show me the next marvel did not allow time to digest what I had seen; and though she was so conscientious about leading me to Christian relics, she naturally felt most attention should be given to Islamic monuments. So conscientious was she that one day she asked, with obvious effort, if I would like to go to the Greek Orthodox cathedral, and another day, led me, with an expression slightly resembling that of the Greeks as they looked across from Rhodes to Anatolia, to the house of the Greek Patriach.

To my surprise, the Topkapi Palace, the old Seraglio, became one of my favourite haunts. I was unprepared for its intimate character, its trees and rose-gardens. It is almost impossible, seeing it on a gentle spring day, to visualize bleeding heads piled by the gates or bodies strung up in the great plane trees outside the Janissaries' quarters. In the Sultan's private apartments there is an impression of domestic peace among the tulip beds and arcades, which banishes macabre thoughts ... of odalisques thrown in weighted sacks into the Bosphorus, of infant princes strangled by rival mothers, of heirs to the throne languishing for years in the terrible Princes' Cage, waiting to know if they were to become Sultan or be put out of the way. The sound of birds replaces the screams of young boys undergoing castration ... 'making all smooth as the back of the hand (whereof divers do dye in the cutting), who supply the uses of nature with a silver quill which they wear in their Turbants.'[1]

The only sinister note is in the *harem* building, despite the climbing roses on the yellow walls, the pretty rooms and courtyards. There is a darkness and a coldness in the passages, a shut-in feeling, almost a sense of death, which increased for me when one day I looked through a window in a forbidden area and saw a small room filled with cheap deal coffins.

You are not allowed into the *harem* without official guides, who are irritating, for they seem to feel they must make something spicy out of this melancholy building. 'Secret,' said one hopefully, pointing slyly to a hidden door in a wall. 'Secret ... Sultan go upstairs to lady.' Considering the publicity and protocol attending the distribution of the sultan's favours it is

[1] Sandys, George: *Sandys' Travels*, 1673.

possible the secret door was there for a far more sombre purpose.

My spirits sank each time I entered the *harem*; it is as though the walls emanate all the stored-up sighs of boredom, frustration and despair breathed by long-dead beauties, many of whom never reached the Sultan's bed at all, but who could neither escape, except in death. It was hard on the girls when the Sultan had abstemious habits, or preferred boys or one particular wife; on the other hand there were busy times, as in the reign of Murad III, whose diet consisted only of food with aphrodisiac effects. This Sultan had twenty sons, twenty-seven daughters and thirty other children who died young, and at one stage managed to have forty of his concubines pregnant at once.

The palace is now a museum, full of garments stiff with gold, jewels like hen's eggs, gem-studded thrones and corruscating swords and scimitars, carpets, textiles, porcelain. In the gallery are portraits of the sultans, showing every kind of human frailty – selfishness, greed, sensuality, cunning, weakness and debauchery. Among them are some thoughtful, noble, sensitive men but the majority are fascinating in their luxurious nastiness. With mosque-shaped bodies flowing to the ground in cascades of flesh and splendour, their dark heavy-lidded cynical eyes gaze out from under immense turbans, their beards merge into fur collars and their small, vicious, jewelled hands show white against the richness of their robes.

*   *   *

Beria only used the Istanbul apartment when she had to stay in town. Her real home was at Çengelköyü, on the Bosphorus, with her mother and younger brother Faruk. Only the gentle Naci occupied the flat but since he was at work all day and often out at night I did not see very much of him. Although he spoke no English we managed to communicate. At our first meal alone together we held a curious but triumphant conversation about Turkish food, all in pictures which we drew in turn on the morning newspaper, and from which I learnt that the jam was made of rose-petals and the cheese from sheep's milk, though Naci's animal drawing was rather confusing and appropriate noises were needed to amplify it.

When Beria gave me the keys of the apartment and of the house at Çengelköyü and told me to regard them as my own home I assumed we were to have a business arrangement of some sort, but when I brought up the subject she handled me kindly but firmly.

'Nothing ... nothing. You our guest.'

'Yes, but not for weeks on end ... not ...'

'Yes. All time. All time Stamboul.'

'No ... not all time.'

'Yes. All time Stamboul. No pay. Not Turkish.'

'I will go to a hotel,' I said one day, in desperation, but she looked at me with such hurt surprise that I quailed.

'Hotel? Not like our house?' That seemed to her the only possible reason for going. Any talk of imposing on their hospitality or causing inconvenience met with blank astonishment.

'But plenty room ... plenty room apartment ... Çengel-köyü ... plenty food. Good cooking my house. Not like?'

Of course I liked, but even if I hadn't I couldn't have said so. It wasn't Turkish to let strangers stay in hotels while you had a spare room, or lift a finger or pay a cent for anything. I protested over the habit of paying for taxis and meals in restaurants. She smiled.

'Ah! When we go in Anatolia maybe. Stamboul no. Stamboul our guest. NO pay. Not Turkish,' and when the conversation got out of hand she would give me a long steady stare and say slowly, 'I do not understand. I do not understand English!' Then seeing me look distressed she would press my hand and say consolingly, 'When I come in Australia, you pay ... I guest.'

So it went on. I was waited on hand and foot, fed, entertained and treated like a favoured child. Nothing was too much trouble, no unconsciously expressed wish allowed to pass. If I mentioned seeing a strange dish in a restaurant it would appear that night at the table; if I showed interest in some part of the city an expedition would be organized next day. They were forever thinking up things for me to do and see in Istanbul ... trips up the Bosphorus, to the Princes' Islands, drives along the European or Anatolian shores or expeditions to *gazinos* in the hills where people come to drink the special water of the district, sitting at tables, gravely sipping and appraising the quality, for Turks are connoisseurs of water. There seemed to be no end to the Güneys' generosity and kindness; but when I asked Beria if Turks were always so good to strangers she looked at me in surprise and said, 'NOT stranger ... family now.'

CHAPTER FIVE

IN LOVE WITH THE BOSPHORUS

BERIA was always happy at Çengelköyü. She loved the place and her life there in a way that communicated itself even in casual conversation; there was a note of satisfaction and pleasure in her voice whenever she spoke of it.

At night the house was scented with her roses and carnations, and she never passed a plant or flower without regarding it critically, with love and attention. Although she had her job as a schoolmistress, she was no career-woman in the western sense; her real life was at home and she was intensely domesticated; but there was nothing smug or dreary in her attitude to household activities, and it was clear that they were the things she really liked to do.

She was an excellent cook. Bringing food from the kitchen to the table was almost a ritual, and each dish was served with proper attention and respect. She and her mother loved to teach me how things were made, despite our language difficulties. Sometimes we would struggle on with dictionaries and pantomime; at others Beria would write the directions in her own English, as the recipe for cooking *semizotu*, (purslane):

> Onion, oil and meat. *Semizotu* wother.
> 15–20 minute cook
> after rice
> 5–10 minits cook

and the recipe for *Gül Receli* (Rose-Petal Jam):

> Rose cut petal 3–4 days
> On playter and limon sold
> after 250 gr. rose,[1] one kgr. sugar
> sugar and wother boil
> after rose put in.

[1] 250 grammes of rose petals is no problem in Turkey. Flowers of all kinds are abundant and magnificent.

When the men were not about we lapsed into a *harem* life of cooking and sewing and family visits. I learnt about Turkish embroidery; I developed a talent for sitting *á la Turque*, which means sitting, doing nothing. It was a tranquil, warmly affectionate world which though a little stifling at times had a curious charm.

Though my conversations with Beria's mother were limited to smiles and my few words of Turkish, we grew very fond of each other and I called her *Anne* (mother) as the family did. In this peaceful dignified woman with the magnolia skin and dark eyes I had a glimpse of an older Turkey, of a world foreign to me and even to Beria. *Anne* belonged to the days when women lived hidden from public life, concerned only with their families and households; when girls were married to men they had never seen, when houses were divided into two . . . the *haremlik* for women, and the *selâmlik* where husbands entertained male friends. She rarely went out by herself and when she did she wore a black veil over her head. Whenever I saw her among strangers – as on the Bosphorus ferry – she was sitting apart, with hands folded and her whole being withdrawn from her surroundings.

Both *Anne* and Beria were devout Moslems. Several times a day, while the wireless churned out strident Turkish music and people came and went all round, they would take their veils and mats to a quiet corner of the house to pray. Beria liked me to see the ritual of what she called 'Pryer Time'; it was part of my education in Turkish life – the washing of the face and hands, the spreading of the rug, the white veil, the movements, so serious and preoccupied. Although she had grown up at a time when there was no public religious instruction, she had learnt her devotions from *Anne*. She had also studied Arabic so that she could read the literature of Islam, for though the Koran has been translated into Turkish most of the sacred writings are still printed in Arabic characters which many young Turks do not understand.

I was lucky to have Beria as a companion, for though she is an independent modern Turk who has travelled in Europe and America she is deeply rooted in the old customs and traditions of her country.

Since Atatürk and the War of Independence, Turkish women have been encouraged to take part in public life. Some authorities claim that originally the Turks did not practise female seclusion; that it was adopted from the Arabs whose countries they overran, and that the Ottomans of Constantinople were further influenced by the Byzantine custom of concealing wives and daughters from the public eye. Whatever the truth, women are now free to train for any job they choose, from lawyer to Engineer-in-Charge at Broadcasting House; yet in a subtle way the old habits linger on and most of my female friends led rather restricted lives.

Their taboos came less from laws or men than from their own unwritten conventions, and might be described as things that were Not Done. Beria shared many of these views, feeling that certain activities were improper for a Turkish woman, sometimes even for a foreigner, such as my going to a cinema in a poor quarter of the Old City which she believed was quite unsafe. Nevertheless, even with these self-imposed restrictions, they have come a long way since the days of Lady Mary Wortley Montagu. In one of her letters from Constantinople she describes how the naked body of a murdered girl was found one morning in the streets of Pera, wrapped in a sack. It was so beautiful that men came from near and far to look at it, but no one could identify it because the face had never been seen before.

Much has been written about Turkish women in the past, and even today there are those who picture them as permanently dressed for the sultan's *harem*, lolling on divans or swaying in lascivious dances, when not driving tractors or flying aeroplanes in the Atatürk tradition. People are sometimes surprised and a little disappointed to hear that the average female Turk is neither exotic nor lascivious and that though they often have pretty faces their figures are pear-shaped, with small shoulders and large hips and stomachs. This curious shape is not a modern development. Miniatures of sixteenth-century ladies in the Topkapi Palace and little crude stone figures in the Hittite museum all have the same proportions.

On the whole, these pear-shaped ladies are homely rather than chic, comfortable rather than elegant and, to the casual observer, motherly rather than exotic. A nineteenth-century lady traveller, Miss Beaufort, thought them stupid and loud-voiced, sadly inane, immoral, vain, aimless and useless, and their conversation harsh birdlike chatter; but though they are rather preoccupied with gossip and their own and other

people's sex-lives, I found them kind, affectionate and demonstrative. They are much given to touching and stroking and
clinging to one's arm in public. They are good cooks and good
mothers and as they get older they are treated with increasing
respect by their families; and despite their outward submission
to husbands and sons they are the quiet rulers of the household,
the ones whose word usually counts.

*　　　*　　　*

I soon began to understand Beria's love for Çengelköyü – the
Village of the Hook, the Byzantine Sophiana. It is another world
to that of Istanbul, one of greenness, coolness and peace. In
the village all is bright and clean, the fruit and vegetables shine
as though polished, and splendid plane trees cast a pleasant
gloom. In an open space near the ferry wharf there are chairs
and tables by the water, and at night coloured lights hang in
the branches.

However tired, I always walked the distance from the ferry
to the house. I liked enduring heat and discomfort knowing
that a cool bath, soft chair and good meal lay ahead. Beyond
the village the asphalt road is lined with villas and apartments
where Turks, home early from work, relax in pyjama jackets,
or water their gardens, releasing into the evening air the scent
of flowers, of water on the dust; and drifting sweetnesses of hay
and summer meadows surrounded me as I walked, the road
still warm beneath my feet, my eyes upon the changing colours
of the Bosphorus.

At the end of my walk I came to an open square with noble
trees and lighted doorways from which the neighbours called
to me, wishing me good evening, asking where I had been; then
came the hill, with scents of roses and carnations drifting down,
and finally the steps up through the garden, the figs and loquats,
the flowers, the friendly voices. In the cool, tiled hall I would
remove my shoes and put on Turkish slippers and climb the
stairs to the sitting room where the family were gathered with
lokum (Turkish delight), cigarettes and *çay* (tea).

The old Turkish house was built of unpainted wood, set up
high with a view upon the Bosphorus. On summer evenings we
would sit in the window watching the ferries and *caiques* passing
up and down and the ships going to the Black Sea. The crowds
disembarking from the ferries, jumping off before the gang-

D

plank was down, might have been in Sydney, but for one difference. There are many times when the water of Sydney Harbour becomes like glass, with a dreaming quality and no winds or currents moving on the surface, but I never saw the Bosphorus like that. Always the strong, swift stream moved, hurrying from the wet grey *Kara Deniz* (Black Sea) to the warm blue Sea of Marmora.

I came to love the Bosphorus, not only as a place of relaxation but as a part of my life in Istanbul. After a hot day I would return to the apartment, snatch what I needed and run up the steps to *Tünel*, surely the world's shortest underground. Emerging at the other end, into the pandemonium of the street-works, I would pick my way over upheaved paving-blocks, round trucks or graders, through sleazy ponds of water to the sweet-shop on the corner; then with *lokum* or sugar-almonds for Çengelköyü, hurry on down the hill against the flood of *dolmuşes* and taxis.

What with the heat and noise and dust and the constant threat of hostile traffic I was always angry and fed-up by this time, hating Istanbul and comparing it savagely and to its detriment with other cities that I knew. As I approached Galata Bridge the first faint breeze would come from the Golden Horn and the ships tied up along Galata water-front stir gently in the golden light. Hunched against the sunset, *Süleyemaniye*, the mosque I loved best, would be gathering to itself its grey evening mists; but for the moment all was lost on me. Dashing across the Bridge with the crowds, dodging those coming in the opposite direction, trying to avoid *hamels* carrying grand pianos and wardrobes on their backs, I was just another Istanbuli rushing for the ferry home. There was no time to savour the fact that I was crossing the Golden Horn, that before me were *Aya Sofia* and the Seraglio, that the boat I caught would take me up the Bosphorus; but once on the ferry all this changed. After the heat and hurry, the infuriating business of gates slammed in your face, of waiting for the next ferry, of being caught up in the rush of maddened Turks fighting each other for a foothold on the gangway and then for a seat on the boat, I would find a place near the window and begin to relax.

This was the moment when all came into focus: the rich light of the sun setting across the Golden Horn, the grey mosques huddled round the water's edge like turbanned sultans in shawls; the ships lying in the harbour with their flags of different countries, the crescent-shaped *caïques* setting out for legendary seas – the Marmora, the Aegean, the *Kara Deniz*, the places of the Trojans and Ulysses and the Argonauts . . . yet of all these disturbing sights and sounds surely the most evocative is the hollow, haunting note of the ferries themselves, unlike any other sound I have ever heard; unforgettable, forever associated with Istanbul.

As soon as the passengers embark, they begin to eat and drink. Fruit, cakes and sweets are sold on the wharf, and nuts, bread and *simit*, (circular rolls with sesame seeds), are available on board. There are also sweet sticky biscuits and bottles of *gazöz* (sweetened aerated drink) and *limonata*. A popular delicacy is the *sondervidge*, which I always tried to avoid in Turkey, when pushed to it by starvation eating only the filling and throwing away the mountain of tough, indigestible bread in which it is embalmed. Even before the ferry leaves the wharf, trays of hot tea are circulating and vendors of safety-pins, hooks-and-eyes and other unlikely things wander about looking for custom.

With its melodious hoot the ferry moves off, weaving its way through the other boats coming and going from the neigh-bouring wharves. Galata Bridge draws away and becomes a crisscross silhouette against the sunset, where dark forms rush back and forth; the mosques give up their clear outlines and the minarets show paler against the deepening sky. In the Old City, beyond and below *Aya Sofia*, the trees in Seraglio Gardens are dark round the walls and domes of the *kiosks*, the tower of the *harem*. At the moment of passing Seraglio Point the breeze freshens, the heat of Istanbul falls behind and the boat is in the open neck of the channel where the Bosphorus flows past the Golden Horn, out into the Sea of Marmora. It is always cool passing Leander's Tower, and the air becomes softer and sweeter as the ferry moves on over to Üsküdar and up into the Bosphorus itself.

In this way, without fuss or formality, I crossed from Europe to Asia each evening without a passport, without even a ticket, since my *basin carte* (press card) gave me free transport all over Istanbul.

Only beyond Üsküdar does the real Bosphorus begin, with its gardens and palaces and *yalis* (summer villas). On the European shore Dolmabache stands out, all loops and columns, like a palace by Elinor Glyn, and further up, on the Anatolian shore, is Beylerbeyi, made of icing sugar, with bright windows reflecting the moving waters, the scene of a famous party given by Atatürk for Edward VIII and Mrs Simpson. Visitors sometimes laugh at these palaces, of which the Turks are proud, yet from the outside they have a nostalgic charm, and at night, with coloured lights in the trees, they are enchanting.

All along the water's edge buildings overhang the stream. Among the mosques and *gazinos* pink oleanders, blue hydrangeas are splashed across green lawns, and some of the older houses are painted, perhaps white, perhaps green or blue and sometimes a rusty pink that shines between the colours of the gardens and the sea. Many of the old buildings are not painted at all. They are of faded silver-grey or cinnamon wood, covered with ornaments and decorations, houses made from cigar-boxes by an enthusiast with a fretsaw. They have a fearful ramshackle look, with overhanging rooms and many windows lurching across their own reflections, as though too many people are standing on one side of the floor. Some have boatsheds in the basement, others have steps from the front door to the water. No doubt there are trapdoors in the floors, as in Gérard de Nerval's story, when his friend, caught in the sultan's *harem*, escaped this way into the Bosphorus.

Inside these houses life goes on for all to see. Men in pyjamas sit reading or staring, fat ladies sew or stare in turn. On the terraces are families eating, drinking, staring. Children run and climb, people dive and swim and wave as the ferry passes, and from the whole scene comes a feeling of holiday, of cool breezes, watered gardens and dinner on the terrace. The ferry passengers, whether standing up to disembark or still with some way to go, seem mentally to become clothed for this soft and easy place of sandals, bare legs and cotton dresses, as in Sydney when the ferries bring the workers home from the heat of the city to a world of garden-hoses, shorts and evening swims.

On Sundays there are steamer trips up the Bosphorus to the Black Sea entrance. The ferries, crowded with families carrying musical instruments and food parcels, zig-zag up the stream, past the ruins of *Anadolu Hisar* (the Anatolian Castle) and the walls and towers of *Rumeli Hisar* (the European Castle) both built by Mehmet the Conqueror for his final attack on Constantinople, and on beyond Beykoz to the military area into which they cannot go.

Along the banks, among the *yalis* and castles, are waterside *gazinos* and *lokantas*, sometimes on balconies or terraces, sometimes under the grapevines, with the Bosphorus lapping at their feet. Most people, after eating solidly from Galata Bridge to the Black Sea, descend at one of these places where they tuck into *dolmas* (stuffed vegetables, usually vine leaves), *şiş kebab* and fish, supported by plentiful quantities of bread and water.

The charms of the Bosphorus increase with familiarity, by day or night. On summer mornings it is delicious to walk to the little wharf at Cengelköyü or Beylerbeyi and take the early ferry into town. In the cobbled square at Beylerbeyi vivid fruit and vegetables are set out on open-air stalls and the sun sparkles on the roof and minarets of the eighteenth-century mosque. Coloured boats tied near the duck-egg blue wharf move about excitedly in the wake of departing ferries and the distant outline of *Rumeli Hisar* and the green hills beyond, the *caïques* passing up and down, the palaces and mosques are fresh and brilliant in the clear light. Later, as the day mellows, there is samovar tea taken in gardens of rose and wisteria, where white mulberries fall among petals, and on the Anatolian shore the Sweet Waters of Asia wandering in with singing boatloads, to the realms of grass and trees and picnics and weekend repose.

Lovely as the Bosphorus is by day, it is most beautiful of all at night, when the lights of the ferries are added to those of the fishing boats, and yellow lamplight shines from the houses on both shores. In the trees of the *gazinos* are coloured lights and from the bows of the ferries powerful searchlights sweep the water ahead, raking into the hills among the trees and houses. On hot nights, lying in bed or sitting in a darkened room, one is suddenly surprised by this beam of white light, illuminating everything brilliantly, picking out details and hidden objects, then sending them back to obscurity as the boat moves on.

The Turks find it amusing and do not seem to mind being spot-lit, and from the boat it is fascinating to see people displayed as though on a theatre set – dining in waterside restaurants, drinking tea under the trees, sitting on their balconies, hands folded on stomachs. At close quarters the searchlights give a carnival feeling and from the distance have a quality of magic, their long silver-white shafts driving through the night like the rays of a ghostly sun.

Of all the world's water-ways, the Bosphorus, like the Hellespont, must be one of those most steeped in history and legend. Its hills echoed the shouts of Jason and his Argonauts, invading an unknown land to seek the Golden Fleece; the foul-smelling Harpies shrieked round the Thracian shore, and the Symplegades, between which no boat could pass, clashed and foamed at the Black Sea entrance. It saw Xenophon's tattered heroes limping home to Greece, the splendour and arrogance of Darius the Persian; it knew Byzantine emperors and rich Venetian merchants, and the Ottomans, the sultans and the pashas with their garlanded *caïques* and summer palaces, their kiosks, trees and roses.

All these I could picture, all lived again for me except the legendary Greeks. It is as though they had never been there, and this puzzled me, for they survive so strongly in the Mediterranean and Aegean. Passing at sunset between Ithaca and Cephalonia, in a Greek arrested twilight, it would seem quite natural to meet Ulysses and his sailors rowing home; or from the heights beyond Catania to see them passing on their way to the Aeolian Islands; but I never expected to meet the Argonauts coming up the Bosphorus. It may be that one pictures gods and heroes in the brilliant light of Greece, so different from these hills and blue-grey waters; it may be that the cool air has dispersed their shades. Whatever is the reason, they have gone.

CHAPTER SIX

'SPECIAL – TURKISH'

ONE result of travel in Anatolia is that buses, like meals and lavatories, take on an importance quite removed from the roles they play in a normal urban life, dominating the mind and existence of the traveller. Apart from the features common to travel in most undeveloped countries – the roughness of conditions, the crowds, the garrulous friendliness of the passengers, the feeling that time is not of much account once on the road – the Turks have peculiarities of their own: the immense supplies of food they carry; their sickness and dislike of heat; the fatalism that attends most mishaps; their habit of stopping for water and refreshment at wayside springs, of splashing themselves with cologne, and writing pious and protective names and mottoes on their vehicles. 'God Preserve Us', 'In God's Hands', 'If God Will', are popular, and sometimes, fatalistically, 'Kismet', which is disturbing when allied to a mountain road and an offhand driver.

Turkish rural transport runs, more or less, on willpower and good nature. One has to admire the way the brave exhausted buses keep going through the wilds of Anatolia, without spare parts, with tottering engines and disintegrating frames, on roads that few western motorists would use. The drivers, battling against heavy odds, are sometimes alarming, for though the older men go carefully, nursing their sick buses and attending to hairpin bends, the young ones seem to feel that time lost groaning up a steep hill should be made up on the down-grade, and that they have some divine right-of-way even on precipitous roads. Allah has also given them assurance that it is quite safe to drive with one arm leaning out of the window and one hand on the wheel, while carrying on a heated discussion with the passengers behind.

There is certainly little to fear from oncoming traffic, for in the interior of Anatolia there are very few cars, and this, rather than careful driving, may be the reason why there are not more accidents. I think I only saw one real accident in all my travels, though minor incidents and breakdowns are going on all the time. Broken-down buses are found by the roadside, sometimes surrounded by stranded passengers, sometimes all alone in a wide flat plain, as though everyone had washed their hands of it and gone off; but usually, any stationary vehicle seen on the road in Anatolia, whether motor or horse-drawn, has a human form stretched under it. If the stranded vehicle is an automobile the form will be doing repairs; if horsedrawn, it will be having a siesta.

Eating is an important part of bus travel. The passengers' stocks of food are supplemented by goods bought on the way, and no one would think of tucking into his own provisions without first offering them to everyone else on board. This can be embarrassing, when stodgy bread and cucumber are involved, for refusal to accept brings a slightly hurt bewilderment, though the stranger's offerings are always declined with a graceful lift of the head and a hand on the heart.

When not eating or preparing to eat, the passengers suffer the effects of what they have already eaten, heaving into paper bags or out the windows if they are fortunate enough to be near them. Others content themselves with the floor.

Whether the journey is to be long or short, departures are usually excited and confusing. Hounded into their places by threats of imminent departure, the passengers sit in their appointed seats, shouting and waving good-byes for anything up to half an hour, while food vendors crowd round the windows in an urgent mass. Then the driver climbs into his cabin (decorated with coloured cards of the Hilton Hotel or Fatih Mosque or autumn scenes in the woods or Japan in cherry-blossom time, or perhaps with paper flowers or a little Turkish flag with a silver fringe) the engine roars, the vehicle quivers and followed by cries of farewell (*Güle güle ... güle güle*)[1] it dashes out of the bus station into the road. Sometimes it does not get further than the first corner before it breaks down and everyone has to get out and push; sometimes the surrounding streets are so narrow that it is difficult to negotiate them without running people down. Passengers and bystanders all give

[1] When saying goodbye in Turkish, the one leaving says *Allaha ismarladik'*, and the one staying behind answers '*Güle, güle*', which sounds like Goo-*Leg*oo-lay.

contradictory instructions, some beckoning forward and yelling
'*Kaç*' meaning to hurry ahead and others calling '*Dur*'.
meaning stop, while a third party call '*Tamam*' (Right ...
okay), so that the driver can have little idea where he is.

At other times the driver, having sat down, stands up again
and turns round to the passengers as though to give a lecture.
This means that people are in the wrong seats, or that the seats
have been over-sold and someone is going to have to get off
the bus; but first there will be a fearful row, everyone will argue
and shout, and it will go on for hours and hours. Half the
passengers climb out with resigned expressions and wait on the
pavement for the seats to be reshuffled, while the others,
shouting and gesticulating, clamber back and forth over the
seats or push each other up and down the aisle, dragging with
them babies, string bags, parcels of food and thermos flasks.

Often the crush is so intense that the owner loses sight of the
goods he is carrying and even the hand that holds them; then
he panics and tries to reclaim his arm, shouting and jerking so
violently that he falls over backwards, or would if there were
room to fall. If there is a small child on the end of the arm it
comes flying through to fall on its face. It then screams and
everyone shouts in sympathy and outrage.

Life in the bus is always animated. The wireless blares and
crackles and conversations take place in loud voices, often
turning suddenly into fierce shouting arguments from one end
of the vehicle to the other.

The loudest and most impassioned talker is usually the driver,
and when he is not twisting round to emphasize his points he is
shouting up at the boy on the roof who looks after the luggage
and who always seems to be called Osss-*mann*. The legend of
the silent undemonstrative Turk must have been started by
people who never travelled in Anatolia, where long-distance
buses are a kind of debating society.

An emergency, such as a breakdown, is always good for
drama. Having given the bus a push to get it moving, the men
panic. They rush after it, shouting distractedly, their wives
stand up and shriek, their children wail. It is always like this,
yet no one ever gets left behind and I'm quite sure the Turks
know it.

Considering their solicitude for strangers and even for animals,
they show extraordinary callousness to their own kind on the

road. Many times I have nearly been wiped up against a tree
by a driver trying to avoid a dog or cow, but stranded cars or
buses, injured human-beings are passed without a blink, even
with a heartless grin. One day my taxi-driver refused to pick
up a nomad boy seriously hurt in a shooting accident, saying
his car was not an ambulance and he didn't want blood all
over his upholstery. When I insisted, he callously bundled the
boy and his distraught mother into the boot, where they were
jolted over the rough road to the hospital.

'Good enough for Kurds,' he said, when I protested.

Another day we came upon some people weeping and wring-
ing their hands round a woman on the road. One of the men
had raised her to a sitting position, another held her arms
forward, limp as a rag doll. Her head had fallen back, and
seeing her grey and solemn face I realized she was dead or
dying; but to my astonishment the driver ignored my cries to
stop. There were too many people there, he said. They would
all want to get into the car.

I raged in English, French and impotently in Turkish but he
drove on, adding that the woman was probably dead already.
Seeing my distress Beria smiled kindly and stroked my hand,
pointing out that in Anatolia peasants were fairly expendable;
and when I asked how she would feel if it were her own mother,
she thought a moment and then said, 'But my mother Stamboul
woman . . . NOT Anatolian peasant.'

*   *   *

In general the Turks seemed to be rather off-hand about funerals.
Often visiting mosques, we found coffins lying unattended and
as though forgotten, on the steps or in the courtyard. I saw the
same thing in Jugo-slavia, at the mosque in Sarajevo, where
life in certain quarters still has a Turkish air.

Across the road from our apartment was a kind of cut-price
undertaker's depot, equipped with a ramshackle hearse and
a jolly fat man and woman who, between calls, sat laughing
and gossiping on kitchen-chairs in the courtyard. When a
summons came the hearse would be backed out of its shed,
a cheap unvarnished coffin slapped into position and covered
over with a dark green pall (green is the Moslem's sacred
colour). The woman would fetch a battered fibre case, a
bucket, a pair of gum-boots, some bundles and brushes, and

stow them in the back of the hearse, in a drawer beneath the coffin; the man would pull on a shabby robe and turban, transforming himself into a sort of *Imam*[1], and away they would go, laughing and chattering together. Sometimes I met the hearse rattling along the street with the *Imam* at the wheel and I must say it didn't look at all bad. It was only the thought of the bucket and gum-boots bouncing about inside that spoilt the effect.

Beria wanted me to see every aspect of Turkish life, and funerals were not excepted. One day as we sat in the courtyard of *Eyüp Sultan* mosque an animated crowd appeared, led by an *Imam* who talked and gesticulated gaily to a man carrying a white florist's box wrapped, as I thought, in red cellophane. After a quick prayer at the sacred tomb of *Eyüp* we all set off up the hill to the cemetery and I saw that the florist's box was in fact a flimsy coffin, big enough for a new-born baby. It was wrapped, not in cellophane but in cheap red silk with a foam of cotton-wool protruding here and there.

After the funeral, folded flat, it was carried away under one arm, the bearer still laughing and talking with the *Imam* as they moved off.

'Perhaps he is a very poor man,' said Beria when I remarked on the strangeness. 'Perhaps he has many children he cannot feed and it is good that the baby died.'

*　　　*　　　*

If I did not see tears shed for that death I saw them soon after for another. At Edirne (Adrianople), where I had gone alone against all Beria's instructions and advice, I shared a bedroom with a strange young woman and her string-bags full of food and water-bottles. We came from Istanbul on the same bus and she was all smiles and friendly gestures. Before turning in she ate several cucumbers, spread her mat and said her prayers, and in the morning when I got up she was still asleep, her face turned to the wall.

I went out early to see the *Selimiye*, the golden mosque of the architect Sinan, and mounting the stairs on my return I heard a dirge-like singing. A group of women were clustered together on the landing. They did not respond to my smile but stared at me gravely, pointing at my camera and fiercely shaking

[1] *Imams* are prayer-leaders, not priests.

their heads. I explained as best I could that I was not trying to photograph them, that I was going to my room, but at this they shook their heads again and made forbidding gestures. To my astonishment I saw that they were weeping.

Baffled, I proceeded to my room, but here was even more confusion. Outside the open door a party of weeping women squatted on the floor, clinging together, and from within there came the sound of singing and a male voice mumbling in a monotone.

It was a strange gathering. On my bed sat a girl playing a stringed instrument and singing sadly, and in a corner an *Imam* stood with a *tesbih* or prayer-beads in his hand, intoning prayers. A woman on a prayer-mat knelt facing the window and in the bed behind the door was my room-mate at the point of death.

She died before I could withdraw; and when I came back later to collect my clothes and move into another room she was still there. What happened I shall never know; but clearly she had no intimation of approaching death when on the previous night she smiled at me and offered to share her cucumbers.

CHAPTER SEVEN

FROM HITTITES TO SELJUKS

BERIA was very pleased when Rüknettan *Bey* arranged for me to see over some of Istanbul's modern buildings and hotels for she had very definite ideas about what a visitor should or should not see. She was all in favour of an interest in *Osmanli* relics and she could understand the attraction of the really *çok eski* (very old), the Greek and Roman ruins, but she was distressed by my lack of discrimination among people. I think she would have liked visitors to take their Turkey neatly classified ... the modern; the picturesque; the classical; the clean colourful museum specimens; the happy smiling peasants. Why did I want to look at dirty old houses and shabby people, when fine modern buildings and Turks in smart European clothes were to be had all round? She was not entirely consoled that I knew these things were a legacy of a long history of neglect, poverty and ignorance, for which her people were not to blame and against which they were now struggling; and that they counted little against the human qualities to be found in her country.

It was fatally easy to let time drift past in Istanbul, and I had to make an effort to think about moving off into Anatolia again. When I did, Beria became very active, despatching letters and postcards, for she had relations in most parts of the country, all of whom, she said, were dying to put me up.

When I protested she gave me the same hurt, bewildered looks with which she had scotched my efforts to temper her own hospitality, and said, 'But my uncle expects us ... There is plenty of room, plenty of food ...' or, 'But I haven't seen my cousin for three years ...' and so on.

Hers was a wide interpretation of the word relation for it included friends, neighbours' families, dependents and pensioners of all kinds. Such spaced-out connections are the main reason why Turks travel in Turkey, for apart from business they rarely move about unless they are visiting relations or family graves. They just do not go to see places, and though familiar with the habits of foreign visitors they cannot share them.

In this case there was a difference, for Beria had dedicated herself to showing me her native land; even so, she felt it was also a good chance to see as many relations as possible.

Though she feared the trip would be a dreadful ordeal she was determined that I should not go alone, convinced that disaster would befall me. She pointed to the business of the wrong hotel at Bursa, and when I laughed, reminded me of my visit to Troy, when I had to sleep in the hotel hall, and the affair at Edirne. Such things would not have happened if I had not gone off by myself in that headstrong way. She was prepared for every kind of nastiness and danger and made me promise we would go only to *çok güzel* hotels and always share a bedroom, for there were many bad men in Anatolia and in the southern districts everyone was *Arab*.

To please her I agreed to everything, even to staying at Ankara, where her favourite cousin lived, though my own instinct was to spend as little time as possible in this dusty modern town; and so we set out, light in luggage but overweight in food parcels. It was hot. We wore nylon dresses and sandals and I had a straw hat bought in Dubrovnik for sixpence. In our overnight bags were nylon dresses, raincoats, underwear. These bags, labelled simply BERIA – and NANCY – ANKARA, went up on the bus roof among the bulging Lux cartons, battered fibre cases and bundles of *kilim* rugs – Turks are not smart travellers – but the food parcels went inside with us.

Our route, via Izmet (Nicomedia) and Bolu (famous for its cooks) took us through forests of beech and plane and mountains strewn with rhododendrons, from the olive groves and cypresses of the Marmora to the earth-roofed adobe houses of the bare Hittite plateau, where shining heraldic goats climb in the dust.

We left Stamboul in high spirits; we reached Ankara depressed. For all its importance as the capital and symbol of the New Turkey it is not an attractive city. It is a kind of miracle, for its scented gardens, trees and fountains were created out of a bare and arid plateau by the faith and courage of the people and their leader Atatürk; but we did not like the modern town, and the old Angora on its dry brown hill has too many tourists and its occupants are hostile and suspicious.

'Not Turkish,' said Beria, when some of them threw stones at my camera. 'Turkish people speak gentle and nice. These bad people. *Koorts*.'

The Turks talk proudly of their new capital and they like to refer to its site in the Hittite country, but they rarely mention those who came in between the Hittites and the New Turks . . . the Persians and Phrygians and Macedonians, Romans and Byzantines, Crusaders and Mongols and early Christians who were there. In the old citadel there are walls in which fragments of marble, slabs engraved in Greek and Latin, sculptured heads, sections of friezes appear among the stone blocks, but in the modern city it is easy to forget the past, despite clusters of antiquities here and there. In my own case there was the added, rather shameful fact that I tend to put historical people and events into compartments. I never associated Alexander the Great or St Paul with Ankara, yet it was in St Paul's Galatia, and Alexander came here after cutting the Gordian knot. To me, Ankara's past was the Battle of Angora, or Ancyra, where Tamerlane and his Mongols defeated the Ottoman Sultan Beyazet, which I remember mainly because of the insults exchanged by the two leaders before the battle. Tamerlane called the Sultan a pismire, and advised him to surrender before the Mongolian elephants trampled him to death, and Beyazet replied, may his wives be thrice divorced from his bed if he capitulated, and may Tamerlane have to receive his own wives after they had been thrice subjected to the embraces of strangers, if he feared to meet him in battle. Tamerlane was so outraged that he ordered Beyazet's wives to wait on the tables at his victory feast, *unveiled*, among the ordinary slaves.

Some stories say that he treated the Sultan generously; others that he put him into an iron cage and carried him about Asia, exhibiting him like a wild beast. Possibly both could be true, for he was capable of every extreme.

*   *   *

Beria's cousin, who also seemed to be her aunt ('My mother's little sister Sabahat marry with my cousin Nazmi') welcomed us with shrieks of joy. She was gay and plump and pretty, speaking French but no English, though her daughter Meril and her husband Nazmi, a handsome army officer, spoke it well. They were an attractive family, living in a modern apartment

in a new part of the city. They were New Turks in the best
sense of the word, for though they were intensely Turkish in
their feeling for their country and their concern for her place
in the world, they were enlightened and open-minded. They
were also friendly, generous and hospitable to the point of
embarrassment. Sabahat's cooking was superb but I could not
live up to her standards of appetite.

'You are not like Englishwomen, you eat nothing,' she said.
Pretty as a picture, her mouth full, she described the eating
habits of the English.

'Bacon and eggs,' she would cry, reaching for another cutlet,
more *dolmas* and rice. 'Steak . . . sausages . . . all for breakfast!
Liver! *Porridge*!' – eyes cast up – 'Marmalade and toast. And
what *coffee*! And so *sad*, madame, such a sad country. So grey!'
And to cheer herself up she would take another helping. She
loved Paris, where Nazmi had been stationed, and she liked
Italy, but England's charms were not for her.

Nazmi was a country boy, from Bor, but Sabahat was an
Istanbuli. She pined for Istanbul, for the Bosphorus, her friends
and family. She did not feel happy in Ankara and I could not
blame her. The atmosphere at this time was bleak and a cold
dry wind blew all the time, swirling clouds of brown dust
everywhere. When I returned on a later visit a hot dry wind
was blowing, swirling the same brown dust about. The wind
was inescapable, the dust omnipresent. The modern city, good
in parts, patchy in others, seemed to sprawl about confusingly.

I did not like it but I admired it for being there at all, and
one cannot admire Ankara without admiring Atatürk and his
achievements. As we travelled about the country I developed
an increasing interest in him as a leader and a person, and since
his portrait hangs in every town and village in Turkey I was
able to trace with morbid fascination his progress from a
handsome young soldier to a nervy, dissipated dictator. When
one day I remarked on this to Beria she said, 'Atatürk very
good man for our people;' then she looked all round as though
not wishing to be overheard and added in a disapproving voice,
'But he *drank too much*!'

'It is disgraceful for a civilized society to seek help from the
dead,' said Atatürk in one of his speeches.

I thought of these words as I stood in the courtyard of the
Haci Bayrami mosque, in the Gazi's own capital, and watched

two peasant women, dressed in bright colours, heavily veiled. Earnestly, desperately they were passing a sick child over and under a marble bench where coffins rest. They had come from an inland village, they told us. Their local wise man had prescribed the treatment. They must come twice more and repeat the ritual before the boy would be cured.

*   *   *

Travelling from Ankara to Kayseri in our ramshackle bus we spanned hundreds of years in a matter of hours and miles. As we left Galatia for Cappadocia, Hittites for Seljuk Turks, we moved from the dusty plateau, through rich cornfields to a pale astringent land, bare and eternal as the sky. The austere hills are marked by downward-trickling lines of erosion and deep grooves full of shadow, and in the distance, ethereal, with snow spread on blue slopes, rises *Erciyas Dag*, Mount Erciyas. At its feet is Trajan's Caesarea, the Seljuk city, now called Kayseri.

Kayseri is bigger than most Anatolian towns; yet though it is the headquarters of the administrative province (*vilayet*) and has some industrial development, its atmosphere is more villagey than citified. Little painted low-sided carts trundle through the streets, and women on wooden pattens clatter to the water troughs carrying metal urns. All wear baggy trousers, and shawls drawn across the face. When busy with their hands they hold the shawl in position with their teeth. Some even wear a sketchy kind of *yaşmak*. From the rear they look like people who have been woken by fire in the middle of the night and have rushed out in their pyjamas, flinging the bedcover over head and shoulders to shield the face from the flames.

The town has the blitzed appearance of so many Turkish cities, though here it seems that the destruction took place long ago. The survivors have built themselves into the ruins, some attaching their houses to the crumbling walls, others using parts of the debris to erect separate structures. It is this growing together of past and present that gives Kayseri its special character.

The people are pleasant and friendly, with gentle manners. Many of them work in little factories, making rugs or *pastirma*, highly-spiced dried beef which I found very good. There is a busy air in certain quarters but it is the mild bustle of country people rather than the rush of a city.

E

We liked it all immediately, despite the rain and mud that splashed up to our knees. We liked the open feeling of the streets, the leisurely life, the Seljuk monuments. No one has done anything to beautify these ruins and most of them stand solitary, among decayed houses and empty fields, but somehow this desolation, in the sombre light of wintry weather, enhances their quality.

Beria's doubts and fears about the dangers of sleeping in strange hotels were quickly calmed. Our *Oteli* was clean and adequate, with quantities of cold cement ... steps, walls, floors and ceilings, all giving out a rather damp smell, for heavy rain had been falling for some days and started again soon after we arrived. From our room we could look down on the life of the town and hear the *muezzin* calling at prayer-time. Five times a day I listened for the quavering cry, floating above the noise of the streets, snatched away by the wind, fading completely as the caller moved to the far side of the minaret, growing stronger as he returned. I knew now why Byron described it as more moving than all the bells in Christendom, even those flat cracked bells that clank so evocatively in Greece and southern Italy. The very frailness of the sound, of the little voice so dissipated by height and distance, are part of its power. Bells speak to man as a social animal, calling him to the family gathering, but the *muezzin's* cry goes straight to the solitary places in his heart, awakening the loneliness that underlies all human companionship.

Already some of this magic has gone. Loudspeakers are installed on many minarets, and the cry that they broadcast has the harshness and strength of mechanical reproductions.

Our hotel had a cement bathroom with a European bath tub, but it was kept locked and the maid with the key could never be found, and even when she could there was no hot water unless several hours' notice had been given, so for the most part we had to wash in a sort of public ante-room. There are various grades of bathrooms in Turkish country districts, starting at the top with the real steam bath, as at Bursa, and ending low down with a kind of communal trough. In between are varying degrees of cleanliness or horror, the better places having taps and sometimes even a shower that give hot and cold water, and marble floors that slope downwards to an efficient drain. Fresh towels are provided and wooden clogs called *takunya*, and usually there is a clean dressing-gown hanging behind the door and a broom of some kind with which you hurry the water down the drain. In theory, having filled the marble basin with water, undressed and put on the wooden clogs, you soap and wash yourself, finally sloshing down as much as you like with water; but in practice there is often no marble basin, nothing but a battered tin one, no hot and cold water and no efficient drain, nor is there anywhere to put or hang dry clothes, so that with the floor awash with water and often mud from previous occupants it is exceedingly difficult to manage. Sometimes in extreme cases there is no light, and nine times out of ten the drain is blocked so that any additional water on the floor brings a fearful attack of regurgitation from the strangled pipe. When you get down to the communal washing trough there is little water, if any, perhaps a bucket on the floor containing a stagnant mixture, and the troughs, which are usually encrusted with very old dirt, are set out in a fairly regular manner with the lavatory adjoining but beyond, so that to reach it you must pass through the ranks of washing Turks, or they have to pass through you if you are the one at the trough.

Though the ante-room at Kayseri was clean it was laid out in this curious manner so that washing was a fairly gregarious affair. I was intrigued to see that Beria, though she accepted it bravely, was more surprised than I by the publicity of its appointments.

Our life was simple. We ate lunch and dinner in small restaurants and after several unhappy experiments I found that the way to breakfast was to take my instant coffee to a neighbouring shop and order hot water and a bun. While waiting for them I would go outside and get a cup of hot milk from a man who stood on the freezing pavement, with a cauldron teetering on a primus. Though the hot water was cold and the bun as hard as nails, everyone was very kind to me in this café and one morning when the waiter had spilt the water, a man at the next table pulled from his pocket a blackened piece of rag and offered to dry my plate. He made the gesture with such simple trust that I could not have refused and was saved only because the waiter forestalled him, wiping the plate with a corner of his grimy apron.

Beria was saying her prayers faithfully, five times a day, in our hotel bedroom, but when possible she liked to go to the mosque. I went with her. We never saw any other women there and always took care not to meet the men entering or leaving. It was pleasant to walk through the courtyard, where worshippers were washing themselves at the fountain, and enter the building as the *muezzin* called from his gallery, like a warning bell.

Stepping among the beggars on the porch, often so muffled up that nothing appears but an open hand waiting for alms, and leaving our sandals at the door among the discarded shoes, we scurried silently up the stairs to the women's gallery where we could see without being seen. I sat in the shadows while Beria, in her white veil, prayed alone. She was graceful and dignified in her movements, devout and preoccupied, touching the ground with her head, folding her hands on her bosom, whispering to herself as she knelt, while the men below, led by the *Imam*, murmured together ... *Allaha* ... *Allaha* ... *Allaha* ... In long rows, facing the *mihrab* where the *Imam* sat in his robes and red turban, holding his prayer beads, they moved forward ... *Allaha* ... *Allaha* ... The *Imam* faced the wall; up; down; bending; kneeling; heads to the ground, behinds in the air; then the gesture of supplication, the hands held open, palm upward; the touching of shoulders and heart, the heads turned to the side, the fingertips on the ears, then *Amen*, the hands wiped slowly downwards over the face.

Unlike churches in Protestant countries, the mosques are usually full, mostly with shabby and poorly-dressed men. There is a great deal of informality and commonsense in Moslem worship. People come in late at a rush and squeeze into the rows of praying figures, their caps in their hands, their feet barely dry from the fountain. So long as foreign visitors show consideration and respect Turks do not object to them in the mosques any more than they mind praying in public ... in railway carriages, in the fields, or, which I once saw, in Istanbul Post Office.

Our favourite mosque was the *Ulu Cami* or Great Mosque, a huge twelfth-century barracks hidden among the ruins. It lies in a maze of narrow streets where doorways and arches give glimpses of smoking *banyos* and houses with stone carvings and wooden balconies. There was a strange excitement in descending the great staircase into the mosque, it was like entering a subterranean cave to worship secretly in a hostile city, for the outside world was shut away completely. While Beria prayed and I watched the people below and listened to the voices intoning, I could peacefully take in all the details of the building, its pale grey arches and coloured beams across the ceilings; and as time went on there dawned an affection for it all, and for the people who had made it and lived with it. It was through such quiet hours in the mosques that I began to develop a feeling for the Turkish arts, for familiarity brought some understanding and appreciation of things that formerly had passed me by.

*　　*　　*

On the morning we left Ankara for Kayseri, just as the bus was about to start, a fattish pleasant-looking man hurried in rather out of breath and began hunting for a seat. We were having the usual confusion over tickets, forty-one having been sold instead of thirty-one, and people were sitting all up the aisle on little stools. The plump young man was obliged to take one of these, and being large he overflowed almost into Beria's lap. He took this indignity with such good grace and such a charming giggle that we were both drawn to him and he and Beria were soon deep in a conversation which continued for the whole of the journey. By the time we reached Kayseri he had volunteered to be our guide and chauffeur there. His name was Mustafa.

After all her stories of Bad Men in Anatolia I was surprised at the ease with which Beria succumbed to this offer, but to do her justice no one in their right mind could think anything but good of our new friend. His pink skin gleamed with health and wholesomeness and even his little moustache could not destroy his engaging schoolboy appearance; yet it was a mature face, full of kindness, honesty and generosity.

In Anatolia it is quite a distinction to know anyone with a private car and whenever Mustafa turned up at our hotel in his green station-waggon he caused tremendous interest. Crowds gathered round it, gaping as though at Apollo's chariot, and when we moved off little boys would run beside us, cheering and waving as people do for royalty.

Day after day Mustafa drove us about through mud and slush, cheerfully leading us to Seljuk buildings, for which Beria and I had developed a passion. We loved the mosques with their plain columns and pointed arches, the curious cylindrical tombs crowned with high octagonal roofs. Whatever the Seljuks did, one feels, they did on a grand scale. There was nothing petty about the people who designed these monuments. Solid, they are far from ponderous; austere, yet in no sense grim, they have the quality of Norman architecture as seen in Tewkesbury Abbey, where the same strength and simplicity create a feeling of harmony and space.

Despite their origins as pastoral nomads, the Seljuks who ruled Asia Minor were not crude barbarians. At a time when most of Europe was plunged into darkness, their dominions showed up as centres of light and splendour, tolerance and wisdom. They were at once savage fighters, artists and thinkers, capable of terrible cruelty, great piety, generosity, ruthlessness, pride and humility. Stories told of the Seljuk King, Arp Aslan (Valiant Lion), say that he honoured the defeated Byzantine Emperor Romanus Diogenes, then put him in a cage and exhibited him, as Tamerlane did Beyazet; and that he ordered a conquered enemy to be fastened to four stakes and left to die, but when the desperate man attacked and mortally wounded him with a dagger, died reflecting upon the transience of human glory, and was buried beneath an epitaph expressing the same sentiment.

His son, Malek Shah, was described as the Greatest Prince of his age – noble, generous, pious and enlightened, a protector of learning and a patron of fine buildings. But the price for the transition from wild nomads to rich and cultivated city-dwellers was degeneracy, and eventually the Seljuks were overcome by new invaders. The Seljuk faces on the tiles and carving at Kayseri and Konya are no longer those of fierce, slit-eyed warriors, but of people softened by comfort, fattened by self-indulgence.

Though I loved the Seljuk mosques it was their tombs that impressed me most. On the outskirts of the town are several of these strange monuments, one of which is the *Döner Türbe*, said to be the burial place of a Seljuk princess. The name means Turning Tomb and the locals offered us a variety of explanations for it, several old men assuring us that the tomb turned round in the night, while the women at a nearby spring claimed that if you stood inside and shut your eyes you could feel it turning in the darkness.

One day we drove in soft rain across bleak hills and muddy

fields to a group of these austere shapes, outlined against the
monochrome landscape. With much difficulty we secured the
key of the biggest, which, enclosed in a high wall, lies apart
from the others. Within the walls, in a courtyard strewn with
fallen stone-work, was the massive tomb, with broken walls
but pointed roof intact. To left and right of the courtyard
entrance dark narrow steps led to a second story, shadowy,
smelling of decay, and from this closed, abandoned place came
something so compelling, so charged with doom that we all
reacted to it, falling into an uneasy silence, at once frightened
and attracted; yet there was nothing morbid in this emanation.
Behind it was a vitality that was heroic and defiant rather than
ghoulish or defeated, an iron, uncompromising quality which,
underlying the finality of death, banished any sense of sadness
or tragedy.

With varying intensity these silent echoes linger in all the
Seljuk ruins, as inescapable as the decay that consumes them all,
for apart from the Princess Mahperi's tomb all are crumbling
away.

Grim and shadowy, the tomb of the Princess is in the old
quarter of the town, in the grounds of a *medrese*, or theological
school, now a museum, adjoining a mosque and the ruins of a
Turkish bath. I could not be dragged away from these buildings
and went prowling alone in the mud, climbing the crumbling
roof of the bath, peering down through the vents into tiled halls
with derelict fountains, smelling the damp earth-vapours that
rose up, chilling my blood with glimpses into rooms where all
has fallen in, creating dark archways giving into nothing, eerie,
sinister. From this scene of desolation I would enter the mosque,
translated suddenly to a world of white-washed columns and
pointed Seljuk arches, where murmuring voices rose and fell in
the heavy silence and people prayed on a floor ablaze with
colour.

Behind the wide and quiet streets of Kayseri is a swarming
world of narrow lanes and curious forgotten buildings. A honey-
comb of backstreets circles the town and one can go from one
end to the other without emerging into the main thoroughfares.
There is no knowing what may be discovered there.

One day we were led by a group of cheerful ragged children
into a dungeon where suddenly a door opened to reveal a little
Seljuk mosque, whitewashed, secret, with a musty closed-in

smell. Beyond this dungeon, through a broken archway, was an unsuspected quarter, shut away from the rest of the town. As I stood marvelling, Beria and the children vanished. I heard their voices echoing away in the distance; then with a rush the children were back, laughing and shouting, dragging me to a door in a high pale wall. Within was a courtyard and a white-washed house with ornate balconies and stairs; beyond again, another door in a blue wall.

I opened the second door and saw trees in an enclosed garden, carved stone door- and window-frames; then the door shut behind me and there was silence, the voices of the children cut off as though extinguished for ever.

It was an extraordinary moment, as though time had stopped. Behind the iron bars of a window I saw Beria, in a white dress, sitting as a woman might have done in the *harem*; but she pressed her unveiled face to the bars and called me to come quickly, and I realized that the moment meant nothing to her.

Beyond the splendid doorway was a great room like a ruined mosque. There were the remnants of a *mihrab*, and above, a frescoed dome. Pewter kitchen pots hung on the carved and panelled walls, and as I entered an old lady spoke to me from behind her *yaşmak*. In an inner room an old man with a saintly face and round black cap sat cross-legged on a divan by the ashes of a charcoal fire. Behind him the barred window gave upon lemon trees and blue-washed courtyard walls, but it was my immediate surroundings that held my eyes. In the dim light from the small windows, the baroque panels and ceiling, the carved furniture, the brilliant rugs on divan and floor had an illusory quality. Once more, time stopped. I felt I had passed through the hedge of thorns and entered the spellbound palace.

A dark young man, handsome as a prince, offered us coffee on a silver tray. This was part of the fantasy, yet at the same time nothing could be surprising in such a place. Afraid to stay too long lest the spell were broken, I declined his invitation to dinner and hurried away in the raw cold evening, back to the mundane hotel, hugging to myself the memory of the secret room.

There were many such rooms; many carved stairways, many fine examples of stone and iron-work buried in mud and decay; but though most of the ruins were inhabited, some of the occu-pants lived in anything but grandeur. Exploring the little

Kuluk Cami, one of the oldest mosques in the city, we wandered into the ruined theological school adjoining it and found a collection of delightful old women, existing in conditions of misery and squalor. Their rooms were black cells, without light or air, opening off a dank and slippery passage; their beds were bundles of straw or ragged clothing; the ceilings were so low that one could not stand upright.

Terrible though their conditions were, destitute though they were themselves, their charm and hospitality were unaffected. They collected round us in the little courtyard, lavishing on us affectionate attentions. They wanted to give us tea, to entertain us. With shrieks of laughter they dressed us up in shawls, showing us how to arrange the folds, posing with us for photographs. They stroked and fondled us, beamed at us lovingly and brought out their treasures . . . an old *kilim*, an embroidered veil, a pile of ancient banknotes printed in strange characters, which, said the owner, she had brought when she fled her own country. We could not find out which country, but whatever it was, whatever suffering exile had brought, her spirit was gay and her strong old face full of courage and character.

When we left, the old women crowded round the door, waving, calling, begging us to return. We never saw them again, for we left Kayseri next day, but the indomitable face of that woman looks out at me still from the photograph I took that morning and its battered austerity reminds me of the old city. Both had impressed themselves on my imagination, the woman with her unbroken strength and the city with its secrets and contrasts . . . the grey lava block houses and brown adobe walls, with eyes above veils watching from the doorways; the cheerful clatter of voices at the water troughs, the rattle of clogs on the cobbles, and the silence of the narrow hidden streets; the interiors of white pointed arches and brilliant carpets, and outside, the fine brown mud, the sharp wind at evening blowing off the snow, and the derelict tombs against a grey sky.

CHAPTER EIGHT

THE DOUR, UNSMILING TURKS

MUSTAFA was a government engineer specializing in the sinking of artesian wells, and since his work required him to drive about the countryside he proposed that he should take us on the next lap of our journey, from Kayseri, through the Göreme Valley to Niğde and Bor, where we were to stay with Beria's uncle, the father of Nazmi.

We had come to regard Mustafa as a benevolent brother, and though he and I could not converse in words, except through Beria, I was already very attached to him. He was so remarkably good-natured, his shy giggle was so engaging and his plump fresh face and hazel eyes so reassuring. He was very polite and slightly sentimental, and when Beria discovered he was newly married and that he pined for his bride he blushed each time she teased him.

On the morning of our departure he arrived early at the hotel, packed us into the station-wagon and drove off at breakneck speed across the plains in the direction of Ürgüp. He drove mainly on the wrong side of the road, and when other vehicles approached would rush flat-out towards them, swerving sharply at the last minute with a furious blasting of the horn.

It was a strange stony landscape that we passed, and as we approached the Göreme Valley it became even stranger. The earth was startlingly pale against the freshness of the vegetation, and the whitewashed villages on the slopes of lemon-coloured cliffs unlike anything we had seen before. Above and among the houses were nesting-places for pigeons, waffle-patterns carved in the rocks. The people we met were friendly and cheerful, the young girls wearing white shawls and coloured trousers, sometimes with *yaşmaks*, and hair braided in dozens of thin plaits; but they were not so archaic as they looked.

'*Cok güzel*,' they said, fingering my dress. '*Nailon?*'

Ürgüp is the first of the Göreme Valley towns on the road from Kayseri. In a sunken plateau of volcanic tufa, said to have

come from Mount Erciyas, the pale rock has weathered into
extraordinary forms and colours. Where it is softest it has been
carved into hundreds of tiny valleys, while the harder rock has
formed into grotesque upright shapes – tents, needles, mush-
rooms, witches' hats, peaks and wigwams. Charles Texier, the
nineteenth-century French traveller, seeing it by moonlight,
described it as a world of white cathedrals, where pale spires
crowd the sky and dark shadows resemble the forms of monks
wandering in procession; and among the less imaginative the
delicate colours and pixilated shapes have produced a string of
clichés about Fairy Toodstools, Fairy Chimneys, Fairy this and
that. In daylight there is nothing fairylike about the place at
all. It is the home of hardheaded, hardworking peasants who
plant their gardens round the fairy toodstools and use the
hollowed-out fairy chimneys as store-rooms for their apples. In
the past it was inhabited by holy men, communities of early
Christians who, going there for solitude, found refuge from
persecution and from raiding Arabs.

Nothing one reads about Göreme can lessen the impact of its
landscape and its little towns. In Ürgüp the houses are jumbled
one above the other, some whitewashed, some of light gold
stone. Women on donkeys patter up the zig-zag road, poplar
trees and minarets are sharp against a pale pure sky; at the
post office a mulberry tree throws green shadows on white
walls; Saracen arches and iron bedheads used as window grilles
demand attention. From the top of the town, among the
pigeon-roosts, is a prospect across a miniature Grand Canyon,
painted in water-colours – red, blue and purple where the rocks
are weathered and eroded, green where gardens and vineyards
grow in the coral-white soil.

We lunched in a homely *lokanta* where a demented proprietor
was trying to appease a bus-load of imperious German tourists.
Since so much Turkish food is already soft or cut up small,
country restaurants often don't bother about knives, but the
Germans demanded them and there weren't enough, even
when we handed over those on our table. Everyone got so
excited that Mustafa drank two glasses of *raki*[1] and Beria was
afraid he would be unable to drive or would take us over a
cliff.

Beyond the town we left the high ridge road and plunged on

[1] Anise-flavoured drink known as *arak* in Arab countries, *ouzo* in Greece.

foot down hillsides, our feet sinking into the atoll sand, scrambling into emerald pockets of young corn and fruit trees where peasants work, and where, in the creamy cliffs, entrances to hermits' cells gape. Around us were the *igde* trees, like fragile olives, silver-grey, with long and narrow leaves and little yellow flowers giving out a sweet elusive scent, so lingering and persuasive that even when the fruit is dried and sold in the bazaars it is still aromatic. All over central Anatolia in summer the air is full of this dusty fragrance, more complex than the scent of other flowers, subdued in itself but strong in its power of evocation.

Inside the cells are sinister passages, impossible to explore in the pitch darkness. In the more simple retreats the Turkish peasants have piled their hay, planting their crops up to the entrance of the caves.

In the main part of the valley, where the rock dwellings are like rabbit warrens, the holy men have carved out churches high in the cliffs. The frescoes, preserved in the dry air, still retain their colour and detail – Christ and the Virgin and the saints; curious animals, like aboriginal bark paintings, in browns and reds and yellows, spread about among crosses and formalized designs. There are domes and arches and altars; one large cavern is a refectory, furnished in stone: smaller ones, like black cells, used for prayers or sleeping. In one or two churches the sun touches the entrance, but most are dark and dim.

From these cells and churches are enchanting views down into the valley. Each tufa rock has weathered exactly as it chooses, without reference to its neighbour, and the forms are all different. Some rise to a sharp point, others have large flat rocks balanced on the top like hats, and scattered among the green patches of vegetation they have an immaculate beauty. But it is a dead world. The cells are abandoned, the churches disused. No one but curious visitors climb up to the entrances; no birds fly out from the waffled patches in the cliff faces. All is silent and deserted in this part of the valley.

*   *   *

Neither Mustafa nor Beria seemed to think it necessary to explain where we were going. They both exuded the pleased, rather maddening air of parents who have a treat in store for the children but refuse to say what it is. I was a prisoner, kindly, even tenderly treated, sitting mute in the station-wagon while they chattered away in Turkish. From time to time characters from the Bible passed us, Isaac and Abraham driving their sheep and goats, Joseph and Mary fleeing from Herod. In the golden light, against a blue-washed sky, they padded past on foot or on their donkeys, wearing the clothes of two thousand years ago.

Suddenly we were out of the valley. We had crossed a bridge over a wide river and were in a town spread along its banks. It was Avanos, on the Kizil-Irmak, a town of square and graceful houses, each one with wrought-iron window-bars and balconies. In the main square Mustafa alighted and at once was surrounded by a group of young men calling affectionate greetings. Tea was sent for and we drank it perched on shaky chairs, while vehicles skimmed past our toes and clouds of dust rose round us. It was hot but peaceful in the square. Dark-eyed people wandered about in antique robes and women came and went from the well with amphoras on their heads or shoulders. From time to time little girls staggered past with huge skeins of undyed wool to be used for prayer-rugs.

A crowd gathered at once, standing at a polite distance, watching our every move, heads raising and lowering as we lifted our glasses to our lips and set them down again. Teetering on our chairs on the uneven pavement we sipped and smiled and sipped again.

Mustafa's friends were delightful. They overwhelmed us with eager questions about our trip, about our plans, about Australia. They all wanted to migrate, to try life in a new country. Two of them spoke English, one fluently. How could they get to Australia? they asked. They had written to the Australian representative in Ankara but had had no reply. Where could they find out about emigrating? They were trained . . . they were prepared to work . . . why didn't the authorities answer their letters? Didn't Australia want new citizens?

Mustafa, smiling fatly, decided to emigrate too with his new wife; and carried away by the general enthusiasm I promised to sponsor them all.

We were surrounded by clay pots. Beautiful urns and pitchers stood about and several carts loaded with terracotta waited in the square. One of Mustafa's friends, who owned a pottery, led us into a dark cellar where the air smelt of damp clay and where little men with feet wrapped in sacking were working on a primitive wheel; but there was no time to enjoy the clean smell of the clay, the rhythmic movements of the men, the faint constant sounds of the wheel, for Mustafa, after a brief mysterious conference with his friends, suddenly hustled us back into the car. The young men climbed into another car and set off out of the square at a great rate, and Mustafa, with the air of a conjuror, drove after them.

The road winding through the tranquil countryside followed the line of the broad river. Coloured shadows lay in the white-ribbed hills, staining them blue and purple, and the fields were darkening green. The deep pastoral peace of the landscape could be felt even in our mad exhilarating drive, and its beauty was haunting, like the road in Provence that runs from Avignon to Tavel through just such scenery.

Suddenly the first car turned into a rough track leading towards the river, and following it we found our friends alighting in a grove of splendid trees.

'Hurry, hurry,' the boys called, as they spilled out of their car; and laughing, mystified, we hastened after them into the orchard.

How do you share an experience that is entirely personal, or impart such an intangible thing as the quality of that evening? We are all locked up inside ourselves, unable to communicate except in the most obvious ways. I looked at the others and found no contact in this moment. They were enjoying it but gave no sign that they found it in any way special. There was probably nothing to show that I found it so, but as in the ruins of Kayseri, it was something apart; and because the whole essence of such moments is the desire to share them, there was the familiar sharpness of despair at inadequacy to communicate an experience at once sensual and spiritual.

The scent of the trees, of all greenness came towards us as we ran into the shade, an emanation of rural peace and coolness, of long summer days and tranquil nights when the round white moon stares down on the sleeping world, and sunburned limbs lie carelessly spread, relaxed and lost in peace. Through the leaves came the sound of voices, quiet, slow, the voices of people absorbed in what they are doing, working without fuss or hurry. There is no mistaking such voices, they have the quality of poetry as their words fall slowly upon the warm air, sink down and become a part of it. They belong to summer evenings, to a world of children in pinafores and long grass under the apple trees. They are memory; they bring peace and reassurance; they are the voices of the grown-ups in the lighted room across the hall.

Beyond the voices, forms moved through the trees. Walking carefully through the red earth where vegetables grew, brushing low green boughs from our faces, we came upon the people we had heard, veiled women in *şalvars* and old men in round caps, charming, gracious and shy. As we appeared they came forward to greet us.

'Come!' called one of Mustafa's friends. 'Hurry!' Already he and his companions were kneeling, squatting on the ground under the trees. 'Help yourselves!' they called to us. 'Take all you can!'

The ground was littered with red mulberries fallen from the boughs. We sat cross-legged among them, eating as fast as we could, scooping up handfuls, thrusting them into our mouths, smearing our lips and chins with purple stains. We spoke little, finding in this childish behaviour an extraordinary sense of joy and completion. From time to time someone would laugh for sheer happiness and the laugh would be echoed by all the others. Children came from among the trees, bringing hard green plums and apples. The heat and dust of the road were forgotten, the discomforts and fatigues of the day wiped out.

The shadows were long when we stood up and the sun had almost vanished, but the air was warm and still and filled with scents and the sound of bees. On a brown bank were rough clay cylinders, country bee-hives, where moving bodies circled slowly, lazily, as though coming home from the day's work.

The boys led us through green alleys to the river bank. Like the bees, the water moved slowly. Purplish, almost red in colour, stained by rich mud, it wandered by as though gorged with rain, the Kizil Irmak, the Red River.

A great home-made wheel turned slowly, splashing as it went, scooping up water for the orchard, and in the distance the hills sank into coloured shadows. The scent of the mud, of the fields and the river were round us and over all the sweetness of the *igde* tree, less a scent than a memory, a unifying thread that tied together all these lovely things.

How far away was the heat of the plateau, the snowy Taurus

peaks. This Anatolia was gentle and benign, its air informed with serenity, as drowsy as the greenest heart of England. How different were these animated boys from the dour unsmiling Turks of popular belief. Behind them, beaming benevolently, were the older people with their veils and baggy trousers, their gnarled hands and smooth brown skins, and like an invisible background, the thought of the farmhouse, the cool adobe walls, the white-washed interior and the coloured *kilims* on the floor – the richness, peace and fulfilment of fortunate country life.

*   *   *

The drive back to Avanos was swift. In the square we said good-bye to the boys, and, anxious to lose none of the daylight, Mustafa made off over the bridge, away from the purple river, back towards the valley.

We were driving into the Old Testament again, for the village people were coming home. They drove their sheep or goats into the setting sun, they straggled along carrying pitchers on their shoulders or copper buckets knocking against their legs, and the silhouettes of the women seated side-saddle on their fragile donkeys were those of antiquity.

Mustafa was anxious, said Beria, to show us something special before it was too dark, which meant that we must drive to Niğde by a roundabout route. He drove fast through the purpling wigwams, through a cluster of rocks and caves and a river bed with poplars and a white road winding ahead towards a distant hill. Among the evening shadows were the cones and obelisks, some with flat-roofed additions, others with doors and columns carved in the rock. It was like a village of sandhills set among vineyards, gardens and trees, but unlike Göreme it was alive, inhabited.

'Avcilar,' Mustafa said, jerking his head towards the receding houses, but when I begged him to slow down he shook his head, promising me something even better further on, smiling as at a wonderful surprise in store.

Suddenly I saw it. At the top of the hill was a cluster of pale houses, built tier upon tier. Dominating the town, outlined against the darkening sky was an enormous rock, a jagged peak transformed by doors and windows into the likeness of a castle. Below us the last of the evening light shone out on the rocks and

vineyards of the valley and the snowy mountains fading in the
distance.

Without knowing why, I felt an intense excitement. Quite
suddenly I knew this was a place I must not pass. It spoke to
me so powerfully that I called out.

'Mustafa,' I cried. 'Please stop. I must stop here.'

Obligingly he slowed down and stopped the car. It was a
black and white world. The snow-white channels leading up
the hill were full of black-and-white goats, and white sheep with
black ears and noses were driven by black-veiled or white-
veiled women with smiling eyes. Men crowded round the car to
greet us, craning in the window, questioning us, inviting us to
alight and take tea or wine with them. From the dusk a voice
spoke in French, then in English, and an old old man came
from the crowd to shake my hand and tell me he had been to
Australia in a sailing ship. It was all so unreal that it did not
seem strange. I had never seen the village before, I did not even
know its name, but I knew in my bones that I belonged there;
that it was imperative I stop there.

'I must stay here,' I said to Beria. 'I must get out and stay the
night.'

She smiled tolerantly, and so did Mustafa, childishly pleased
with the success of his surprise; but they had no idea what was
in my mind. We could not stop now, Beria explained, there was
no inn; besides if we didn't get to Niğde that night all our
arrangements would be upset. I had not even thought of things
like inns or arrangements; I only knew I must stay in the village; but no one listened to me. They could not understand my
English or my agitation and presently we drove on. It was a
sensation comparable only to nightmares when the limbs are
paralyzed while the mind is driven by a fearful compulsion. It
was as though the place had put a spell on me.

The air was cool, the dusky scenery beautiful and soothing.
The only sounds were those of the donkeys coming home from
the fields, the padding of their feet on the dusty road and
occasionally their distant cries, the terrible harsh breath forced
from anguished lungs. All round us was the scent I loved, the
scent of the *igde* tree; but I thought only of the village.

Nothing could put it from my mind, none of the things that
should have consoled me . . . Nevşehir, with its ancient mosque
and *han* (a primitive inn where man and beast sometimes sleep

F

together); the pallid hillside houses; the flocks of strange long-haired sheep, the men returning from their work with tools upon their shoulders. Beyond the village a cemetery was dark against the corn, and further off the hills merged into clouds as evening fell over the plain; but I saw it all with absent eyes.

Although the sun had gone, the sky still shone with pink, and all was graced and enriched by the dying light. The tired, slow farm-carts coming home across the fields were touched with majesty, the fields themselves became more green than green; and an air of calm benevolence evoked by the time of day lay on the villages, softening their crudeness, giving an illusion of tranquillity.

These were the villages of the plain, unlike those from which we had come, more spacious and open against the wide corn-fields, their outlines marked with poplar trees. When a child is born to a peasant, said Mustafa, a tree is planted so that when the child is grown the tree will provide him with wood. In the creeping darkness there were few people to be seen and in one little town it seemed there were more dead than living for three great cemeteries surrounded it.

As night fell, there came a sharpness in the air, a touch of mountain snows, the crisp fresh chill of wide flat places when the sun has gone. The stars were immensely bright and clear, and the lonely road stretched far ahead, lit by our headlights, which from the darkness called forth trees, high walls, a fox in the corn. From time to time we passed benighted men; we drove through shuttered villages and more lonely cemeteries. Far off, lights of infrequent cars shone out across the plain. We were in a warm boat crossing the sea of night.

Then a clear stationary light shone ahead of us and as we approached we saw a tent, a tall tower with lamps and a huddle of machinery. It was only the routine sinking of a well, but the blanketing darkness had informed it with a foreign quality of excitement, blotting out the surrounding landscape, giving the little settlement the air of being set in space and isolated from the world.

Mustafa got out to speak to his workmen and we followed him. I sniffed the air with excitement. It was full of green scents of earth and growing corn, young scents already hinting of maturity and harvest. In the quickening atmosphere each sound became intensified, the first, the sole vibration in a listening world. It was a night when footsteps on the tarmac ring out with a metallic note, when the blood circulates more quickly and all senses are keenly alive; and standing in the darkness I suddenly knew what I must do. I must go back to the village.

CHAPTER NINE

A MOMENT OUT OF TIME

ONCE the decision was made I felt quite different and ready to cope with all obstacles and objections that might be raised. We dined very late when we reached Niğde, and Mustafa and I drank *raki*, which gave me the energy and courage needed to break the news to Beria.

She did not believe me at first; then she humoured me as though I were mad; then she pointed out that it would upset everything and complicate all our arrangements ... that her uncle at Bor expected us next day; that Mustafa was going to drive us there; that we would get behind in our timetable (hers, not mine) that it was eighty kilometres to Üchisar and there was no transport and even if there were, even if I got there, how should I get back?

None of these things made any impression. I suggested she should wait for me at Bor and I would find a bus or taxi or get a lift in a truck back to Nevşehir and from there get a cart or a donkey. If all else failed I would walk the remaining kilometres to the village.

She was stunned, but seeing that I was quite determined, temporized by saying 'Maybe, maybe,' and went to bed looking troubled. I think she hoped I would change my mind or that the formidable difficulties of transport would bring me round; but while she was telephoning Mustafa next morning, in the hope that he might be able to make me see sense, he arrived at our hotel door with surprising news. He could not take us to Bor after all; a telephone call had just come from Ankara instructing him to return to Kayseri at once. When I told him what I wanted to do he agreed to take me back to Üchisar on the way. Beria would continue by bus to Bor, where she would wait for me.

We set out immediately after breakfast. Mustafa was accompanied by a friend who spoke English, a fair-haired, blue-eyed

boy named Cengiz, full of gaiety and good humour. He was a
geologist and his opening remarks were very promising.

'I have never met an Australian lady before,' he said. 'I did
not know they were so beautiful.'

He never stopped talking and he was full of curious little
phrases. When thanked for anything he would say, 'You're
very welcome,' and he reeled off strange formal compliments at
every opportunity. When I remarked on his vivacity he was
very pleased and offered to sing. He gave us, not a Turkish
song, but an American pop tune with a perfect American accent.
He had learnt many such songs from discs, he said, giving me a
selection. Mustafa was deeply impressed but could not be persuaded to perform. His favourite song, he said, was 'I Love
Paris', but he was ashamed of his English.

Under the liberating influence of Cengiz, Mustafa threw off
his shyness with me and revealed himself as a kindred spirit.
Conversing through Beria I saw him as friendly but slightly
restrained, but now it appeared that he liked nothing better
than to let his hair down. He may have thought me a rather
earnest character, interested only in Seljuk ruins, but discover-
ing now that this was not the case he became quite uninhibited
and our ride grew increasingly hilarious.

Worried lest he could not bring me back from Üchisar, he
began to spin one of those webs of kindness the Turks were
always weaving round me for my protection. All along the
route, he decided, messages must be left and arrangements
made so that I could find transport or a bed, if needed, on the
journey back to Niğde. At Nevşehir he worked out an elaborate
plan with the hotel-keeper, who had never met any of us before,
but who immediately wrote a letter to his cousin, the mayor of
Üchisar, commending me to his care, and requesting that if no
car, jeep or donkey could bring me back to Nevşehir I was to be
given a bed in the village; and if transport could be organized
I was to be brought to Nevşehir, to his hotel, where a bed would
be ready for me at any hour.

Having laid this trail of alternative arrangements and
assured himself that I was not going to starve or get stranded,
Mustafa drove on with an easier mind.

The journey back over the plains was disappointing, for in
daylight their nocturnal excitement was gone, but after we
turned off the main road, towards Üchisar, I began to feel a

curious tension. Suddenly, unexpectedly, the rock castle appeared ahead, brilliantly lit by the sun, lemon-cream, tapering to a peak like a grotesque Klu Klux Klan hood through which peered multiple eyes. My involuntary cry of excitement so infected Cengiz that he suddenly announced Mustafa must manage without him in Kayseri, for he was coming with me to the village.

Mustafa left us at the mayor's office on the edge of the village and drove off into the valley. We mounted the steps and entered. A strong smell of urinals greeted us and a décor of dark grey walls, burnished by the shoulders of all who had leant or brushed against them. A gendarme led us through a crowd of men to an inner chamber where we were greeted by the mayor, a sad dignified person in a hat, who had been hurriedly fetched from his house by another policeman.

The mayor welcomed us courteously and offered us the freedom of the village. Then, followed by several policemen and attendants, he led us out into the open, towards the great rock which we were to climb. It was an immense white needle, worn and weathered into weird shapes, and scrambling up the giddy heights I saw the Göreme Valley spreading out below us, first the village at our feet, then the wide landscape studded with tufa cones and patterned with the dark symmetrical lines of orchards and vineyards, and in the background the pale petrified mountains.

At the top we rested. I had removed my sandals and climbed in bare feet, but the men had kept on their shoes and the mayor his hat as well. Proudly he led me about, showing the sights. People hid here, he told me, some were buried here, and he hung over a precipitous ledge pointing out tombs and the remains of a church dug out of the rock. It was çok eski, I said, and cok güzel. He beamed with delight.

As we basked in the sun on this eagles' roost a strange sound floated up, a dull rhythmical vibration accompanied by wailing pipes. It was a wedding, said the mayor, and the celebrations would be going on for four days. This morning everyone was at the bridegroom's house, but later in the evening the bride would be receiving friends and relations at her mother's house, and as distinguished visitors we would be very welcome.

During our absence from his office the mayor's henchmen had been organizing our lunch and when we returned we were

invited to sit down, watched with wonder by the villagers who
thronged round the door in the outer office. Lunch was brought
in little newspaper bundles by men in cloth caps, who, deposit-
ing their offerings on the table, bowed sheepishly and retired.
Having seen no sign of a shop or café in the streets I suspected
that our meal was being provided by the villagers.

The mayor carefully spread one of the crumpled newspapers
on a table and laid out the feast . . . bread, black olives and
helva (a Middle-Eastern sweet) in little bits of paper. He sat
back and watched us with satisfaction as we ate, for we were
ravenous; then tea was brought in little hot glasses and Turkish
cigarettes offered. His air of generous graciousness turned this
rough and simple snack into a banquet.

There were great goings-on at the bridegroom's house. A row
of women with faces completely concealed by *yaşmaks* were
squatting in the dust outside the gate, and close by, in a cleared
space, the musicians were seated, churning out their strange
monotonous music. A man in a felt hat was beating a drum and
a wild-haired youth blowing into a long pipe. In the centre of
the space a young man was dancing, with hair on end and a
couple of aprons tied round his waist like a skirt. He had a rose
in his mouth and another behind his ear and kept time to the
music with four wooden spoons, which he held, a pair in each
hand, at the end of his outstretched arms, clapping them together like castanets as he slowly gyrated in the dust. A laughing crowd was gathered round the group and in the middle was
the bridegroom, sheepish and dressy in a new turquoise-
coloured suit and tie that did not match his dark complexion.

Cengiz and I were given a warm welcome and the dancer
presented me with his roses. I pinned them to my dress and the
scent moved Cengiz to ecstasy.

'Oh,' he said, as we walked away down the hill. 'Can't you
hear the flowers smelling? Oh, they are coming from your
breasts.'

We had accepted an invitation to go to the bride's house at
six o'clock to see her in her wedding clothes, or rather I should
see her for Cengiz would not be admitted; meanwhile we
explored the village, climbing the steep rough streets that at
times were no more than narrow passages. Each house was completely individual; some domed, some flat, some carved out of
the rock, some built of stone blocks. There were square windows

with iron bars, and windows and doors with beautiful ornate carvings; loggias with Italianate arches, classical columns trailing vines. The walls were white or yellow or faded salmon-pink, and some were of pale natural stone and others of earth-coloured adobe. They rose one above the other, up the steep hillside, each looking out over the roof of the house below to the valley, or down upon the gardens and vines and terracotta pots where flowers grew on loggia or roof; and among these houses were others which were no more than caverns carved in the rock, like the churches at Göreme, with doorways and windows high up, some of them inhabited, others used as store-rooms for apples from the valley orchards.

The people in the narrow streets were as strange as the houses. Each woman wore a *yaşmak* tied across her face and a long white veil over her head, floating down below her knees. With their flowered trousers some of them wore padded jackets, roughly quilted, in strong colours. No female face was visible, but all the eyes that regarded us so keenly were friendly and kind. I commented on this to Cengiz and he replied, 'They smile because they like you and they like you because you are beautiful. Turkish people will do anything for beautiful ladies, they love beauty more than anything else. Only beauty of face,' he went on, 'that is all they notice. They do not care about the figure . . . they do not mind how ugly that may be.'

Beyond the houses the road descends towards Avcilar, the village in the valley which I had glimpsed the night before. The sun was shining and it was warm as we scrambled down the pale petrified sandhills. On the slopes below, people were working in their gardens and vineyards where the trees and vines were like spaced-out green dots in the white soil. Round them were soft, grey-banded cliffs and in the far distance the mountains, purple, red and blue. The rock-faces were honeycombed with pigeon-roosts, and at our feet brilliant pockets of young corn were splashed with poppies, cornflowers, yellow and purple pea-flowers. Ravished by the colours, the beauty, the clearness and cleanness of everything I sat down on a rock and refused to move, while Cengiz prowled round picking field-flowers for me. A man working in a tiny vineyard half-way down the cliff called to us, telling us how to descend, and in the warm sunny air his voice came flat and remote, like a voice in a dream. Behind us, Üchisar rose up on its hillside and in the distance

were the vibrations of the wedding drums. Below in the valley
an owl hooted. I lay back in the sun and basked, happy,
relaxed, at peace.

*   *   *

Some months before, travelling from Marseilles to Paris, I had
suddenly turned from my contemplation of the Rhône to see
through the opposite window a ruined castle high on a crag.
There are several of these castles in the stretch between Valence
and Lyons but this particular one made such a strong impression that I stood craning out the window, watching as it disappeared. I could not forget it, and when I returned to Provence
I went to find it. Though it appeared easy enough to reach, it
eluded me and several times I took the wrong road and finally
had to walk through rough and overgrown country. I found it
almost completely ruined, with trees and grass growing wild in
the courtyard, but to my astonishment, as I entered the building I saw whitewashed walls and vaulted ceiling, bright colours
on the floor and a kind of shelf or divan built under the wide
windows, through which I could see the medieval village and
the plains below.

The illusion was remarkably clear, but by the time I had
blinked my eyes it was gone, and I found I was standing in an
empty shell with rough stone walls and a floor of earth and
broken red tiles. It is so easy to have such visual deceptions that
I did not pay much attention to this one, but the place clearly
had some great attraction for me, and there was such a strong
feeling of belonging there that I began thinking of ways to
rent the ruins and move into that wonderful derelict room. Life
in Anatolia had rather put these things from my mind and as I
walked up the hill from Avcilar with Cengiz my thoughts were
all of the Turks and the village we had just left.

Women were coming to the doors of their houses to look at
us, discussing us among themselves, examining my clothes and
camera, not with the long whole-hearted stare of the male Turk
but a little bashfully, averting their eyes when they caught
mine.

'They like you,' Cengiz said, and this time did not make it a
back-handed compliment. 'They are saying, "She has beautiful eyes. Her eyes smile".' He took it as a personal compliment.
Although I think he regarded himself as very sophisticated, he

was so engagingly naïve that even his most flowery and ambitious remarks had a childlike innocence about them.

'I told them you were Australian,' he added. 'Australian ladies are not like English ladies. Sometimes English ladies are very coldly but Australian ladies are very warmly.'

For all their shyness the women were pressing in their invitations to enter their houses for rest and refreshment, and high above on the terrace of a white house two female figures were waving and beckoning to us. Now, suddenly, there appeared a little boy called Osman, who earlier in the afternoon had guided us down the hill to Avcilar, and who had come, he said, to take us to his house for tea. It was nearly time to go to the bride's house and I was about to refuse when Cengiz said, 'We had better accept someone's invitation, just for a minute. Which one shall we go to?'

For no reason I said, 'Let's go to the one up there where the women are.' Cengiz said, 'Don't you think we ought to go to Osman's house?' but Osman said excitedly, 'But that is my house . . . and that's my mother and grandmother calling you to come up.'

He led us up the hill, up a narrow street and through a door in a wall. We stepped down, sinking to our knees in fresh-cut hay and mint, and the sweet scent rose round us as we waded through to a little courtyard where the white-veiled women waited. Osman's mother kissed my hand and put it to her forehead, but the older woman stood looking at me for a long minute; then, ignoring Cengiz, she folded me in her arms and kissed me fervently on both cheeks, hugging me as though she could not let me go.

'Why have you been so long?' she said. 'I've been waiting and waiting.'

Cengiz, who translated this, explained that we had walked up from Avcilar, but she took no notice and said again, 'I've been waiting so long. Why didn't you come before?'

With her arm still round my shoulders she led me towards the house and invited me to enter. I walked through the door and stopped dead.

It was unbelievable.

I was in the room I had seen in Provence, months before.

There was no mistaking it . . . the whitewashed walls and vaulted ceiling, the long Turkish divan built under the window and the brilliant *kilims* on the floor. The only difference was the view from the window . . . a Turkish village instead of a French village, and the Göreme Valley instead of the plains of the Rhône; but the room was the same, and this time it did not vanish.

I don't know what was expressed on my face as I stood staring but when I turned to the old woman she was nodding and smiling with delight. She led me to the divan and sat me among the rugs and cushions, throwing open the window upon the divine view of valley and coloured plains. I was dazed, for the sensation was not the familiar one of 'I have been here before', but rather 'This is where I belong', with a curious feeling of lightness and comprehension, almost as though something that had puzzled me was now explained.

There was no time to analyse my sensations. The old woman, whose name was Emïne, sank down on the floor beside me while Osman and his mother Fatma came and went with bowls and plates. Cold water and towels were brought and Emïne knelt, washing my feet and pouring water over my outstretched hands; then on a small table she arranged the dishes the others brought in . . . *yoğhurt* and *yufka*, paper-thin bread made from barley, dried figs and *lokum*, and *pekmez*, a kind of molasses made from grape skins. She was a poor woman and it was a poor household, but everything in it was as it should be. The food was in copper dishes, the wooden spoons were painted with traditional designs and all were spotless. The room itself was one of the most restful I have ever seen. There were arched alcoves in the white walls, one holding the Koran, another an earthenware amphora with water, and in a wider shallower recess above the windows was a rough primitive painting in vivid colours. Who did the painting? Where did it come from? How did it come here? I asked Cengiz to enquire, but he, lapping up figs and *pekmez*, was concentrating on Emïne. She was gazing at me with strangely luminous grey-green eyes and saying something with immense earnestness.

'She says you are to stay here,' said Cengiz presently. 'They are ready for you . . . your bed is all prepared.' Fatma pulled back a curtain, showing a mattress with coloured cushions and rugs. 'This is for you; this is where you are to stay.' Then he added, 'But I've told her you can't stay . . . that we're expected at the wedding and the bride is waiting for us.'

I had forgotten all about the wedding, though now I could hear the drum and pipes in the distance, and I had no wish to go. I wanted to stay where I was, for in this peasant's house was the same sense of belonging that I had felt in the ruined castle, the same feeling of happiness and serenity and of always having been there. Outside the window a silky white goat with a golden kid walked delicately about on the roof below, eating the grape vines; down in the village a cock was crowing; white pigeons flew from below the window and out over the valley and back to the window ledge. The light of the setting sun shone down into the walled gardens and on a scarlet flag with the crescent and star, and on the houses on the opposite hill, turning them yellow and pink, and catching their western windows flashed out suddenly, dazzling our eyes and striking into the white room. All the little sounds of village life came up to us from below. It was absurd to think of leaving such a place when I had only just arrived and when it was clear that I belonged there. Even Cengiz, who had the air of one who is not sure what is happening, sympathized when I said I could not go; nevertheless he hauled me off, reminding me of my promises to the mayor and the bride, to Mustafa and Beria, for left to myself I should have accepted Emïne's offer and stayed where I was.

The departure was even stranger than our meeting, for I found it was not so hard to leave as I might have expected. Though I went reluctantly, I went in peace, with a sense of completion quite unlike the night before when I felt so compelled to return; and Emïne, though she embraced me lovingly, begging me to stay, seemed to accept my going in the same way.

'When will you come back?' she asked, and it did not enter my head to say, as one normally might, 'Oh, I'll come back some day.' The situation was far too serious and real for such evasions. 'I don't know,' I said. 'I want to come back . . . but . . . I don't know.'

She nodded and said, 'Whenever you're ready.'

There were more loving embraces and wet kisses pressed through veils and we were out in the street in the fading light, hurrying towards the wedding. I hardly noticed where I was going or even saw the slow procession of women coming home from the fields, the swathed white figures riding on their donkeys, the men in their round caps driving their flocks of

black-and-white goats and sheep. I heard nothing of what
Cengiz was saying, though he talked incessantly.

What did it mean? What was it all about? Such happenings
are beyond a world that attributes inexplicable things to co-
incidence. There was in the whole affair something as clear-cut
and inevitable as a well-planned campaign, but it was a campaign in which the protagonist acts under hypnosis. I had been
moved about like a doll by forces I did not understand. It was
not until I saw the inside of Emïne's house that I began to
understand why the village spoke to me as it had the night
before. In the general bewilderment of this discovery, and
astonishment at Emïne's behaviour, there was no chance to
think at all, and it was only now that the scattered incidents
were beginning to come together, making it clear that all
previous happenings had been leading me towards this place.
Why had I seen that Turkish room months before in Provence?
And why had I had the compulsion to return to that castle in
the first place if not to see that room? I thought of the extraordinary way my return to Üchisar had been made possible;
the telephone message from Ankara, recalling Mustafa; Osman,
so casually attaching himself to us; Emine calling to us from
the terrace. But why? Why had all these things happened?
Why had Mustafa decided to take that road to Niğde instead of
the normal direct route? What was the connecting link that
would make sense of it all? Why for that matter had I come to
Turkey, in the face of so much discouragement?

Suddenly I realized Cengiz was speaking.

'Emïne's eyes are just the same as yours,' he said; then he
added, 'She wanted to talk to you. She wanted to tell you something. When she was sitting on the floor she kept saying to you,
"If only I could talk to you . . . if only I could talk to you".'

'What did she want to say?' I cried. 'What was it? Why
didn't you tell me before?' But he did not know and I realized
that my agitation was childish. Supposing he could have interpreted for her, which I doubt, how could he have explained?
How could Emïne herself have explained whatever it was she
wanted to say? It was not only ignorance of my language that
prevented her; it was possibly something she herself did not
understand, could not express even in her own tongue. But
what? What did she want to tell me? What did it mean?

There seems to be no answer, no explanation, and as time

goes on I remain as far as ever from real understanding. Is it possible perhaps that at the moment when I, in Provence, saw Emïne's room, she, in Üchisar, saw me; and that was the reason for her greeting, the extraordinary welcome she gave me? It was so much stronger than an ordinary case of *déjà vu*; it was more like a reunion, a mutual recognition from an earlier existence. Or, more disturbing, could it be a glimpse into the future? But why? What was the reason for it?

CHAPTER TEN

ŞARAP AND SAZ

THE bride's reception, though an anticlimax, was a good sequel to the mystery of Emïne's house, providing the complete contrast that was needed. Everything was on the most earthy level, the people, the noise, the general excitement. We found the house at the end of a long lane, enclosed behind high walls, with a narrow gate beyond which Cengiz was not allowed to penetrate. He sat himself down on the ground, joining the circle of men round the band, now playing rather wildly, and the young man who was still dancing, clattering his wooden spoons.

With much giggling and whispering I was ushered into a courtyard so full of people that there was literally no room for another body and several women had to leave to make space for me and my escorts. Not only was the courtyard full but the high walls surrounding it and the roof of the next-door house were crowded with women all squeezed together, clucking and dithering with excitement. Packed in among her friends was the bride, dressed in her best clothes. Long black plaits came down past her knees and round her neck, and from her ears dangled immense gold coins, wealth that her parents had saved for her. Her dress was a screaming-pink satin and the colour of the material was almost as bright as the flush on her cheeks, for she seemed on the verge of hysteria, with an exhausted, terrified expression in her eyes. I have seen all sorts of brides in different parts of the world but this was about the most harassed I ever saw. It was not really surprising, for she was only 15, and she was probably worn out with excitement and the celebrations. Her female relations surrounded her on every side, holding her arms as though to keep her upright, though if she had lost consciousness she could not have fallen, so closely did the crowd press round her. She took my hand, bent and kissed it and held it to her forehead, but when I kissed her on both cheeks she gave a kind of sob and flung her arms round me, embracing me fervently. All the women nearby stretched out their hands to pat my shoulders and stroke my head in an orgy of affection, and led by the bride, whose dubloons clanked each time she moved, I shuffled and wormed through the crowd to be presented to her mother, who was sitting bolt upright, veiled and *yaşmaked* on a kitchen chair. Except for the children present, the bride was the only one whose face and head were uncovered, and she had a strange bare look beside the ranks of swathed heads.

The object of this gathering, I was told, was for the bride to meet officially her new family. All the bridegroom's female relations were there as well as her own, and from the time she became his wife they would be her close concern. Such a thought was enough to harass any teenage girl, but the look of desperation upon her face might also have been caused by the fact that she did not want to be married, or to be married to that particular bridegroom. Such things must often happen in Turkey, where marriages are still so commonly arranged by parents. I photographed her with her attendants, rigid, staring into the camera, and then the women besieged me, begging me to take their pictures. When everyone had stroked and patted me and fingered my dress and had a good look at my red nails and camera I felt it was time to go, and kissing the bride I tentatively put some notes into her hand. She looked thunderstruck and for a terrible second I was afraid I had done the wrong thing, but her astonishment quickly turned to rapture and once more she embraced me, sobbing openly, pressing wet kisses on both my cheeks and calling on Allah to bless me. The other women clamoured frantically to see the present and on being shown flung themselves upon me like teenagers on a film star. I have never been such a success anywhere. It was terrifying. Smiling fixedly, waving feverishly, I battled my way to the gate, and with a last shriek of farewell escaped out to the open air while the women surged after me, screaming with excitement.

'Whoever said the Turks were not excitable?' I asked Cengiz as I sank down on the ground beside him, deafened by the musicians, mazed by the gyrating dancer who was now performing with a crowd of children in his train.

Cengiz shook his head.

'Turks,' he said. 'Feel things just like any other people. Why should they be any different?'

We were tired when we reached the mayor's office and glad to sit quietly, waiting for Mustafa. If he had not come by nine o'clock, he said, we were to sleep in the village, unless the mayor could find us transport to Nevşehir, where his cousin awaited us at the hotel. Much as I loved Mustafa I hoped he would not come. I wanted to stay in the village, to go back to Emïne's house and sleep in that vaulted room. I knew how it would be in the morning, facing east, with the sun rising over the valley and shining in the long windows, and the colours from the *kilims* on the floor thrown up on the white walls and ceiling, and all the village waking below. But though I wanted to go back there I was peaceful now, as though I had done what I had come to do.

As the sun went down and night came on, the hillside grew colder. There was a sharp chill in the air and almost a suggestion of autumn, and the feeling of being in a mountain place. Outside in the darkness the bridal procession, now greatly depleted, was still staggering through the village behind the band. Mainly composed of over-excited children, it tottered from house to house with the female impersonator dancing and capering ahead. In the office the mayor sat with us, gentle and kind, while a gendarme pumped up a pressure lamp for our illumination. When it was lit, hissing and roaring, I was astonished to see there was no glass and the naked flame was quite exposed to the outer air. The policeman, balancing on a rickety chair, hung it above our heads, where it swung in the draught, its hard white light throwing black shadows that rose and fell on the dark grey walls.

It was quiet in the office, but as we sat waiting, men crept to the door, standing shyly in the darkness, gazing in at us. Each one, invited by the mayor, entered sheepishly, bowed to me and acknowledged my smile with a hand on the heart. Soon there was a whole circle of them seated on wooden chairs against the wall, gazing at us solemnly. Cengiz was delighted to have an audience. Acting as a sort of stage-manager he embarked on a detailed account of my life, my travels, my accomplishments and my views on Turkey. As these last were favourable, the atmosphere soon warmed up and the men began to whisper among themselves. Cengiz knew that Beria was teaching me Turkish cooking, and he was describing my gifts as a cook and my interest in wines, when the mayor suddenly leant forward and interrupted. Üchisar was a wine-growing village. ... Would Madame not like to taste some of the local wine? At

G

once a policeman was despatched into the night, returning with seven bottles which were laid before me. All different, the mayor explained, one of each kind, so I could try them all.

I was only too happy, and as Cengiz struggled with the corks, the mayor told me how he himself had made *şarap* (wine) and even *raki* in the old days and how good it had been; but now, he said, all that was finished and the wine of Uchisar went into the *Ko-operative* in Nevşehir. The office had suddenly become very matey and policemen were running in and out bringing cups and glasses, and when at last the bottles were open and the tasting could begin I realized I was in the mood for it.

Presently, hot food was brought in, and though I suspected someone's house had been robbed of its evening meal there was no question of demurring. The dish was put on a chair and Cengiz, the mayor and I dipped into it in turn, watched by the sixteen pairs of eyes around us. Only Cengiz and I drank the *şarap*, which was excellent, for the mayor refused, his hand on his heart.

'He does not take wine because he has heartbreak,' Cengiz explained, and added 'I, too, but only for pretty ladies.' As the wine flowed and Cengiz warmed up, his stories of my exploits became more and more colourful, ending with the rash statement that I spoke fluent Turkish. I recited all the Turkish words I knew, which caused shouts of laughter. Noticing a gleam in the eyes of our audience I asked Cengiz why he did not offer the wine all round. He replied in a loud whisper that the policemen could not drink in the mayor's presence; then with the cunning of the slightly foxed he called one of them over to him.

'Here,' he said in a cross voice. 'This glass is not clean. Take it out and wash it for me.' He held out a glass three-quarters full of *şarap*, with his hand ostentatiously concealing the contents from the mayor. The policeman took it humbly and left the room, returning after a few minutes, flushed and happy, with wet lips and an empty glass. Pleased with his own subtlety, Cengiz now tried to do the same for the other policeman, but the ruse was so obvious that it was greeted with a burst of laughter and the mayor suggested that those who cared to take *şarap* might go ahead. Although only a few accepted, the atmosphere of the stark room was becoming animated and more and more men were creeping in at the door to be presented. From

time to time a little *jandarma* clambered up on the rickety chair
and brought down the failing lamp which he pumped up and
returned to the ceiling.

Cengiz, now full of wine and very gay, asked if there was anything I would like, and when I suggested music burst at once
into song. He sang well, in Turkish, with much expression, and
the performance was received with applause. Then Mustafa
arrived, cold and hungry, and was swept up into the party.
More wine was brought and the remains of the food spread
before him. In a very short time he had caught up with us and
was quaffing the Üchisar vintages as though they were water.

At first the men were shy and would not sing, but after a
whispered discussion someone produced a *saz*, a stringed instrument like a mandolin with a thin elongated keyboard. The
coming of the music brought a transformation, for the two
smallest and saddest little men in the room turned out to be the
best performers. One of them, in a green cord coat several sizes
too big, who had come to the office on business and had been
agitating piteously about a little piece of paper and a sum of
money which he claimed he should not have to pay, now
became a different being. Seizing the *saz* he began to sing, first
explaining shyly that it was to be a serenade to Madame, a long
strange wandering air which took his voice up into the regions
of falsetto, but powerfully sweet and moving, ('Very good,'
Cengiz whispered to me with the air of an expert) with a terrible
sadness in it; and afterwards came another song from a bashful
little man with a shorn head, who giggled as he took the instrument but sang with a longing note in his voice, most sweetly, his
eyes fixed sadly upon me all the time. ('He sings of the beautiful
black eyebrows of his sweetheart,' said Cengiz.) The notes of
the *saz* were haunting, the songs strange and melodious, and the
two little men sang in a manner to bring tears.

The other spectators clapped wholeheartedly and the instrument was passed from hand to hand, for it seemed that everyone
could play, some in a simple way, others with remarkable skill
and feeling. Two of the policemen performed a rather meaning-
less dance, a simple shuffling movement round and round in a
circle, and then Cengiz, suddenly inspired, leapt into the middle
of the floor and announced that he was going to show us an
Izmir dance. It was a tottering drunken dance such as I had
seen at Bergama, in which he leapt up light as a feather and

came down with marvellous grace, while all the men applauded. He was prepared to go on all night but nothing could persuade Mustafa to perform. Wreathed in smiles, the picture of bene-volence, he sat tucking into the *şarap*, watching the dancing and at the same time holding a theological discussion with four or five men round him.

The rest of the audience watched us intently, their faces lit by the harsh moving light of the swinging lamp. They were wonderful faces, not handsome, not brilliant or gay, but good, with a goodness common to them all. Warmed by the *şarap* I had drunk, by my wonderful day in the village, by the atmos-phere of *cameraderie*, I had one of those moments of universal brotherhood that we all believe in but so seldom experience in the true sense of the word; and although or perhaps because I was slightly drunk, fleetingly I felt at one with these Anatolian peasants. Their lives of hard work and poverty were written on their hands and faces, on their crude and clumsy outward forms, but down in the depths of these rough men was a feeling for beauty that found expression in their music. Their songs and singing revealed a sadness and a wistfulness for something different; the wandering spirit which lies, however deeply buried, in us all.

*   *   *

It was nearly morning when Mustafa left me at my hotel door. When the singing and dancing were finished and everyone had crowded round to say farewell and escort us to the car, he rose above himself. Waving good-bye to our friends he dashed off into the sandhills with tremendous bravado but in the wrong direction, singing with all his strength that he loved Paris, veer-ing about on the narrow track which became smaller and smaller until at last it disappeared altogether and we were in the middle of a queer white landscape which sparkled like snow under our headlights. Then the lights flickered and faded and both Cengiz and Mustafa had to get out and tinker with wires in the darkness, from time to time accidently sounding the horn which rang round the dark countryside eerily. Long after-wards, it seemed, for I was now asleep in the car, the lights were fixed and we returned to the village, which was in complete darkness, and finding the right road, set out on the long drive to Niğde.

CHAPTER ELEVEN

'YOU ARE OUR SISTER'

I T was not far to Bor, where Beria awaited me at her uncle's
house. Although we set out early, the dusty brown road already
glared with the heat that was settling over the flat landscape.

Guided by fleets of little boys, we drove slowly through the
narrow streets between earth-coloured houses, which, as at
Niğde, were hidden behind adobe walls, until our shouting,
chattering escort brought us triumphantly to a wooden gate set
in a high wall.

Mustafa alighted and pulled a bell, and after a pause the door
was opened a few inches to reveal a veiled head. Yes, it was the
right house, but Beria and her aunt were not there . . . they had
gone to the market and the old servant did not seem to know
who I was.

As we talked, a tall figure in pyjamas came down the steps to
the courtyard; Azim Yavuzalp, Beria's uncle, a grey-eyed man
with a melancholy Greco face and graceful hands.

'*Hoş geldinez*,' he said, advancing towards us. 'You are welcome.'

Mustafa and Cengiz could not stay, and after loving embraces
set off down the lane in a cloud of pale dust, followed by most of
the little boys. I waved to them with emotion, as to brothers or
childhood friends; then the door in the wall shut behind me.
Inside the courtyard, I was in a world where nothing had
changed for a hundred years.

Azim led me into a long cool room where a divan ran the
length of one wall and the floor was covered with *kilims*. I sat
down thankfully among the cushions while he welcomed me
again in halting English. He offered cigarettes and Turkish
delight, cold water and coffee, and instructed Gum, the servant,
to wash my hands and feet. With the dignity that comes from
quiet unselfconsciousness, he asked me to excuse his pyjamas,
since he knew Englishmen did not wear them in the daytime.

'But I am old,' he said. 'And I sleep a great deal.'

He asked for news of his son, for he was the father of Nazmi,

89

at Ankara, and listened with interest while I told him about our travels, only interrupting when I marvelled at the kindness of the Turks.

'Why not?' he asked. 'Why not? You are our sister.'

At the end of our conversation he spread a little mat on the floor.

'Now I will pray to God,' he said; 'My life is drawing to its end. I am making my peace with God before I die.'

Murmuring to himself, he carried out the ritual, ending with the downward movement of the hands over the face, to wipe away all traces of hypocrisy. A bow to the two angels who stand by during prayers. . . . Amen.

I sat in the white shadowy room with its honey-coloured beams, gazing through the iron-barred windows at the glare outside in the courtyard and savouring to myself the peace, the curious feeling of nostalgia evoked by this old house. Like the inexplicable sensation that comes in reading Proust or Chekhov, it was a nostalgia for a life I have never lived, the essence of summer in the country in a world of order and security, where the green reflections on the wall, the fruit falling into the long grass, all the slow, rich details of a tranquil life are the visible symbols of something my generation has never known.

In the courtyard, the old servant, blind in one eye, dressed in striped trousers and veil, continued her work, filling her metal pitcher, cleaning shoes on a broken Greek acanthus capital, driving off inquisitive little boys, who after peering through the gate at the fascinating foreigner had managed to open it and were trying to slip into the courtyard. When chased away they took up positions on the flat roof of the opposite house, where they could see down over the wall and could not be reached by the enemy. Patiently, determinedly, they waited there until hauled off by their mothers, fat veiled women with smiling eyes, who pushed open our gate to apologize, wishing me *hoş geldinez* and taking a good look themselves at the same time.

Then Beria returned with her aunt and cousin and I was enveloped in a warm tidal-wave of affection and attention; and after the kisses, the news, the exclamations, the preparations and the saying of grace, we sat down at the white-covered table, to a feast, distinguished not only by its quality but by its profusion, the splendours of a prosperous country table in high summer.

*   *   *

Bor has the air of rich serenity and quiet happiness often found
in country places where there is enough for everyone. Though
superficially there is little to distinguish it from other small
Anatolian towns, it is what goes on behind the high walls, in the
faces and voices of the people, the setting of their domestic lives
that gives it its peculiar quality. Perhaps the outward signs of
plenty, the vineyards and orchards and fields of grazing sheep
have so reassured them that they can afford to be relaxed, un-
hurried, mellow, enjoying a deeper and more subtle understanding of material prosperity.

In Azim's house there was comfort without luxury – beautiful
rugs, soft beds, fine linen, a splendid cuisine and a servant to
help, yet there were no modern conveniences. Charcoal replaced gas, oil lamps replaced electricity, water came from a
pump in the courtyard, meals were cooked on a primitive stove,
and washing-up done in a basin that must be emptied. In this
rural life everything takes longer to do, yet is infinitely better
. . . tomato sauce is prepared at home; vine leaves for *dolmas* are
not bought in tins but picked in the vineyard, laboriously
washed and prepared, *yoghurt* is freshly made each day and
bread baked in the kitchen from flour ground between stones in
the village mill, winnowed through sieves by the miller's wife
and daughter.

As an adopted member of Beria's family I had access to every
kind of household and visited many of the local women. Though
their houses and circumstances varied, they all emanated the
same exuberant hospitality. To some of us hospitality has become synonymous with expense, inconvenience, hard work,
competition, duty and exhaustion. The more money we have,
the further we remove it from its original concept, yet among
simple people and the very poor it is still a spontaneous gesture
of friendship, a desire to share or give. With them it is not yet
confused with entertainment as something special and occasional, but is as much a part of daily life as breathing and eating;
not to be set aside until there is enough money or enough preparations have been made but offered all the time. A chair in the
shade or a glass of cold water on a hot day can be as valid and
expressive as a fine banquet.

Though I had been living a harem life at Çengelköyü and
mixing with female Turks in the cities, I had seen little of the
lives and conditions of country women. Foreign travellers in

Anatolia often see them only as shrouded forms slinking about in the background, turning their faces away, pulling their shawls up to the eyes as strangers pass. They never sit in village cafés, never eat in restaurants. Whenever a crowd collects it is a male crowd. The women, curious and friendly, peer from doorways and windows.

But when you are accepted into their homes, in purely female society, you find they are not at all shy or down-trodden. With the shawl and veil off, revealing dyed hair and a direct gaze unlike their public shyness, they are eager to talk, to question and to laugh with a robust sense of humour.

Life for an Anatolian country woman can be hard and dreary, if she lives in a poor or isolated district. She spends the hot summer working in the fields and in winter is shut in by thick snow or roads turned to bogs; but in a prosperous area her life can be idyllic. Often surrounded by beauty, her material needs well provided for, she is peaceful, respected and secure.

Some of the women I met at Bor lived such lives, in settings like a Chekhov play. Visiting one of them, we came through a door in a wall into a rich garden where the light slanted through the poplars and the air was scented with hay. In an adjoining meadow a girl dressed like a stage peasant cut grass with a sickle. A square adobe house, the colour of the earth, stood among lilacs and roses and lawns of emerald green. Beyond was an orchard and vineyard.

Chairs were set under a great mulberry tree and when we were all seated our hostess stood up and came round to shake hands, greeting each one with 'Hoş geldinez'. Then refreshments were brought on a silver tray by a sunburnt smiling girl. As I sat in the shade sipping the home-made cherry cordial I was quite overwhelmed by the rural peace, the beauty and the extraordinary sensation of living in a story, yet I was intensely aware of the scents from garden and meadow, of the green shadows in the mulberry tree, and beyond the high adobe wall, the queer clattering of the storks in their nests, like old men with false teeth.

The women I met at Bor did not impress me as being discontented; they did not seem to be craving to join in the men's social life, which to my mind was far less desirable than their own. As usual, the centre of male activities is the café, and though the main square of Bor has a covered market and Ottoman *hamam* (Turkish bath) it is still hot and dusty. I wondered who would want to sit there, staring and fingering their beads, when they might be in a green garden or a cool shady house, cooking or sewing or entertaining friends.

There was the same tranquil atmosphere, even among the poorer women, although they work very hard. They scour wool in their courtyards, beating it with heavy wooden paddles, spin it on distaffs, card and dye it themselves. They do their washing at the *çesme* – which is usually on the roadside so that the clothes are covered with dust – thumping them with flat sticks as they lie bundled on the stones; and they draw their water from the same *çesmes*, carrying it in pewter or earthenware amphoras.

Some of them work on carpets. The looms are set up in a good light, near a window, and the women sit side by side on low benches. Bright coloured balls of wool lie in rows along the top of the frame and the downward threads, like the strings of an immense harp, are crossed and recrossed by the brilliant strands, woven so quickly in and out by the moving hands. A pattern on dog-eared paper is pinned up on the strands and the carpet grows from the bottom. The quality of a carpet owes more to the skill of the weaver than to her equipment. I have seen Anatolian village women weaving carpets of most intricate designs on primitive looms without a proper frame, where the balls of wool hung from a rope slung across the top.

This work has the advantage that it can be done at home with one eye on the children. One mother we visited had run a string from her foot to her baby's hammock and as she worked she rocked him where he lay, goggling with bright black eyes at the movements, the colours, the shadows in the simple room.

This well-behaved baby was typical of Turkish children, who by our standards, are extremely good. In poor families they work hard, helping in the fields, minding their little brothers and sisters, and in richer, urban families they sit contentedly among their elders or join in the conversation with a quiet self-possession. They are treated and they behave like adults and I have rarely seen them trying to draw attention to themselves by bad behaviour.

Most of the families we visited at Bor seemed to be prosperous or to have known prosperity, for their houses were comfortable and well-furnished, in the Turkish tradition. Built round courtyards, with banks of flowers, and a fruit or mulberry tree replacing a fountain, their whitewashed interiors are brilliant with rugs and carpets, with old carved chests and embroidered cushions. Though there are usually chairs there are always divans strewn with *kilims* and cushions, and despite a prevalence of crochet mats and doyleys the effect is charming.

Since Anatolian country men often do not put their money into banks but buy gold coins, which their women wear round their necks and foreheads, and carpets which become more valuable with age, it is not unusual to find splendid carpets in otherwise modest houses.

The women have their own kind of treasures, magnificent embroideries and ancient garments, such as wedding clothes, that have lain for years in wooden chests. When the women of Bor heard I was interested in such things they competed with each other in showing me their heirlooms.

One rarely sees such clothes outside museums – jackets of purple velvet embroidered with bullion; brocade *şalvars*, immense until drawn in at waist and ankle; pill-box hats and headscarves scattered with sequins; gorgeous materials woven in a hundred colours and patterns.

We passed the things round – a brocade dress of turquoise and silver; embroidered sashes for *şalvars*, veils and *yaşmaks* worked in gold and silver; a husband's bathrobe, ceremonial towels of handwoven linen encrusted with metallic splendour; a long, woven table-napkin bordered with coloured flowers on which the women wiped their mouths when they ate together. They were all exquisite, yet the richness of their embroidery, their elaborate detail gave a desolating glimpse of the long empty hours, the boredom and frustration of *harem* life, and brought to them a touch of melancholy as real as the faint and musty scent they emanated.

Our friends crowded round us, reminiscing, listening while an old lady showed us how to wear the clothes. Beria, dressed *à la Turque* in rose brocade *şalvar*, golden jacket and pill-box cap swathed with a white and silver veil was suddenly a different personality. No longer a modern, enlightened young woman she was a creature from the pages of Loti or Gérard de Nerval.

*   *   *

Beyond the town, by the river, is the vineyard where for generations the family have gone to spend the hottest months. Within a high wall are the vines and orchard, and old adobe house set round with long lush grass and mulberry trees. Entwined with grapes and roses, it seems to have grown up out of the earth. Inside are oiled wood beams and doors of natural oak, and open fireplaces and an upstairs platform where people sit on summer nights and watch the stars.

When we were in this enclosed world, scented with earth and leaves, we were absorbed, each doing as he chose. Beria doctored sick roses, grafting and binding up with ash bark, while her aunt collected vine leaves for *dolmas*. Her cousin gardened, inspected fruit and young grapes, and Azim, seated on a wooden chair beneath the poplars, dozed and dreamed and watched the river rushing by. I prowled through the empty house, absorbing the scents of trees and flowers, soaking in the peace and contentment of this sequestered place where all was green but for the colour of the roses and the late shafts of light that came across the wall and through the trees. Once more there was the sense of living in another age and world, where summer meant a fragrant green repose. The glare, the beach, the brilliant sea did not belong at all, nor the arid plains nor crowded city streets. Here, in this life, the long hot days meant people lying about in hammocks and chaise-longues, and ladies in white dresses with parasols, spattered with shifting shade; the damp smell of the river banks and the abandoned swing dangling from the fruit trees; and the sounds were not the wireless, the tyres of fast cars squealing on the corniche road but distant cries of children playing and the cracked voices of old women calling in the chickens, shutting them up for the night.

Outside in the twilight, teams of black oxen plodded past, drawing home their loads of wood.

At night, in the town house, I slept, sunburnt, relaxed, in a kapok bed set in a whitewashed room. The light of the full moon shone through the square panes, draining the colour from the *kilim* rugs, blanching the courtyard with its delicate iron balustrades and ghostly acanthus capitals lying among the shadows.

CHAPTER TWELVE

'VERY, VERY BAD IN THE SOUTH'

OUR departure from Bor was emotional, for Beria felt she might not see her old uncle again. Eyes were moist as we blessed and embraced and commended each other to Allah, and the crowd in the bus yard were moved to join in the fare-wells, patting us on the shoulder and murmuring good wishes, while newcomers stood on tiptoe to get a good look at us.

'Adana? They're going to Adana,' I heard people telling each other with awe and respect.

Adana is in south-east Turkey, on the Cilician plain, and to get there from Bor one crosses the Taurus mountains, the great range which shuts in the Anatolian plateau from the coast. I was full of excitement at the prospect, anticipating cool snow-clad peaks against dazzling blue skies, and a dramatic transi-tion from the enclosed world of the plateau to one where marble ruins were spread by a brilliant sea; but when late in the afternoon our bus staggered through the pass known as the Cilician Gates and we found ourselves among the olives and umbrella pines of the Mediterranean, we were both worn out with heat and alpine grandeur. I could take no more scenery, history or discomfort, and stared with distaste at Tarsus, when we stopped there, thinking it typical of St Paul to be born in such a dreary town.

Adana, on the Seyhan River, is miles from the sea, and after the peace and comfort of Göreme and Bor seemed intolerably hot and noisy. It filled us both with such despair that we began to bicker even before we left the bus depot.

I wanted to stay at the Park Hotel, which I had heard about, but Beria did not like the sound of it. She asked if Rüknettan *Bey* had recommended it and was very dubious when I had to admit that he had not.

'*Turkistik oteli?*' she said doubtfully as we stood in the noisy bus depot. 'Good? Modern? *Güzel?*'

'I don't know. Let's go and see . . .'

She turned to the grimy youth who was holding our bags.
'*Park Oteli? Güzel?*'

He made a grimace of contempt.

'*Yok. Eski* (old). *Çok uzak* (very far).'

'Ah!' She began to speak rapidly in Turkish, firing questions
at him; then she turned to me and said, '*Park oteli* no good at
all, very, very bad. Very old. Very long way. Good *oteli Pamuk
Palas*. Here. Right here.'

I didn't want to stay in Adana at all. There was a bus to
Iskenderun in an hour. Why couldn't we take it? When Beria
said No, we couldn't do that, I suggested that she stay in Adana
and I would wait for her in Iskenderun. She clutched my arm
with a disbelieving stare.

'Impossible! Impossible not go together!'

'Why?'

'Impossible I stay alone. Many bad men here . . . very, very
bad men in South. In South ALL men bad. ARAB!'

I could see Arab was as bad as Kurd. Hot, tired and thor-
oughly bored with Adana I gave in and agreed to go to the
Pamuk Palas.

'He say very good *oteli*,' Beria said placatingly, as we
followed our boy with the bags. '*De luxe . . . banyo . . . çok
güzel.*'

Pamuk Palas was entered from a hot and narrow street and the
first sight we saw of the *çok guzel* establishment was a party of
men wearing pyjamas, leaning limply against a small table in
the hall as though too bored or tired to sit upright. They waved
us on up the stairs to the hotel office on the first floor where we
found two little boys, both under twelve, who were handling
the bookings. The smaller child was smothered in a large apron
and seemed rather dazed but the older one was very businesslike, and before we could change our minds had booked us into
a double room with a bathroom.

The little boy led us along a corridor where doors opened on
each side to reveal male forms in pyjamas, prone upon unmade
beds. Even before we reached the chosen room I could smell the
bathroom and as we came into it the fragrance hit us with full
force, taking the breath away. The heat came out with the
smell and Beria turned pale. The little boys ushered us in and
escaped as quickly as they could.

Beria threw herself on one of the beds moaning '*Çok sicak* . . .

çok sicak' (very hot). Our room was on the western side of the building, its walls exposed to the afternoon sun. The window opened upon a brick wall, so close that you could touch it in comfort, and at the top of this wall was a frosted glass roof. Not only could fresh air not get in but all emanations from the bathroom must join these penned permanently in the bedroom.

It was the worst kind of bathroom, combining the faults of both east and west. There is nothing pleasanter than a clean traditional Turkish bathroom with its silver dipper and marble basin, its clogs and tiled floor, just as there is nothing worse than a European bathroom that is dirty and has faulty drains. *Pamuk Palas* had gone in for western fittings while retaining oriental plumbing and hygiene. All taps were covered in slime, the floor was ankle-deep in water which had oozed from the ill-fitting pipes of basin, bath and lavatory, and mixed with dust and dirt brought in by occupants to form a sort of bog; the seat of the W.C. had gone, taken perhaps for firewood or a souvenir; there was no hot water and the air was thick with the terrible smell of Turkish plumbing and cement that has never dried out.

I can take squalor if necessary but I prefer it to come cheap and picturesque. This was neither. Leaving Beria gasping on her bed I went to look for the little boys.

Trespassing through a room where men were taking showers and washing their feet, I found them in a sort of linen cupboard, and after a great deal of action, walking up and down the passage, blundering into wrong rooms and interrupting Moslems at their prayers and toilets, we came to rest in another room, much the same but not quite so hot. The manoeuvre was complicated by Beria's refusal to be left alone in the bedroom for an instant, assuring me that her virtue and perhaps life were in constant danger in this Arab community.

Installed in our second room I prepared to take a bath, but found there were no towels, no light in the Stygian bathroom and no hot water. This bathroom, a little cleaner and drier than the first, had a cosmopolitan touch about it. One tap was labelled *CHAUD*, the other *SICAK*, which is Turkish for hot, both, however, running cold.

I rang the bell for the little boys but this time a harassed young man appeared. Making myself heard above the sounds of neighbours clearing their noses and throats in preparation for prayers, I asked for a towel and another light bulb. The

young man went away and after a long time came back with
one small hand-towel and a step ladder which he set up in the
bathroom. Wavering on the top step while I held the two sides
to prevent them slithering apart, he screwed in the dim little
bulb he had taken from the reading lamp – a chromium pipe
with a chromium female figure doing the splits – which stood
on the bedside table on a sheet of newspaper.

Out in the street it was still very hot and we found our distaste for Adana increasing at every step. The people were rude,
the street boys cheeky and there was none of the gentle charm of
the people at Kayseri and Bor. Heat, flies, dirt, crowds, noise
and confusion seemed to be the general background, against
which unpleasant youths featured, conspicuous by their un-
Turkish lack of courtesy and co-operation. A number of them
spoke English of a sort, scraps learnt from the movies or American soldiers perhaps, since the favourite greetings were 'Hallo
sweetheart' and 'Hi baby!' Stopping at a street stall for fruit
we were abused by the owner because we would not buy his
under-ripe, over-priced apricots, and when I photographed a
couple of *haşlama*[1] men one of them pursued me with threats,
while the other demanded payment.

'No good at all,' said Beria. 'Very, very bad. Not *Turkish*.
Too much Americans.'

I said crossly that it was not fair to blame Americans for
everything; but when I told her that bad manners in Adana
are not a new development, and that as far back as 1914 Sir
Harry Luke was commenting on the rudeness of the locals to
strangers, she shook her head and said, 'Not Turkish. Armenian. *Yürük* (Nomad) *Arab*!'

Things were better in the back streets and we spent most
of our time in the bazaar, though even there the stall-holders
were more aggressive and commercial than elsewhere, trying
to force us to buy and making sarcastic remarks when we
refused.

Yet this bustling modern town with its factories and airport
descends from a city so ancient that no one is sure of its origins.
It could have been founded by the Hittites; it was constantly
swept by invaders. The Assyrians came down on it, the Persians,
the Macedonians with Alexander; the Romans, the Arabs, the
Byzantines came; the Seljuks, Armenians, Mamelukes and

---

[1] *Haşlama*, a cold herbal drink.

Ottomans; the French and the Americans. Yet no one seems to have left anything behind, unless perhaps it was the French army of occupation in the 1920s, who bequeathed a knowledge of their language. Adana is really a new city in spirit, very rich and busy with its cotton and agricultural products, its tractors and cement, its shops full of things we had not seen in the humbler towns, and its streets full of traffic.

Prejudiced and bad-tempered, we decided we liked only the *Ulu cami* (Great Mosque) not because it is beautiful but because it is so comic and eccentric. It has an elongated jelly-mould over one door with a cart-wheel nest on top, full of storks, and a number of fat little domes with tiny spires and crescent moons with horns; a courtyard with wide carpeted arcades where people pray, and inside, tiles and splendid rugs and sickly green paint with gold. There is an ornate minaret with loud-speakers and a small graveyard, and across the road a *medrese* with green-tiled domes, built round a courtyard with a fountain, and fig and olive trees. Here we found several young men in pyjamas, lying in bed in the open, who got up and wanted to show us round, pointing out the wavy roofs and towers and birds sitting on the crescents, some of which are so horned that they almost meet in a circle, and asking questions about us and our travels in an eager friendly manner.

That night we dined in the roof garden restaurant of the *Erciyas Palas* Hotel, where the air was cool, the food pleasant and the tables clean, under the vines and coloured lights. The company was mixed – American officers with well-dressed friends, prosperous Turkish people and a few foreigners. At another table were the driver and conductor of our bus, who greeted us kindly as we sat down. Still dressed in their grimy working clothes, it was pleasant to see they were receiving from the waiter the same tender attention as he was bestowing upon the richer clients.

Sleep did not come easily at *Pamuk Palas*. All night long the light from the passage shone through the glass door into our air-less room; a baby wailed; people snored and moaned. Every sound came to us, for it seemed that most of the patrons were sleeping with their doors open in a fruitless attempt to catch a vagrant breath of air. Inspired by the same idea I opened our bathroom window, but it did no good; we were shut in, for Beria refused point-blank to have our door open. For myself,

'INDOMITABLE'

'SPECIAL — TURKISH'

'THE LITTLE BOYS WHO RUN TURKEY'

'NEW TURKS IN OLD CLOTHES'

'THEIR EYES SMILE' (ÜCHISAR WOMAN)

'THE LITTLE TURK'

STAMBOUL

Bosphorus steamer · Siesta in Stamboul

Bosphorus houses

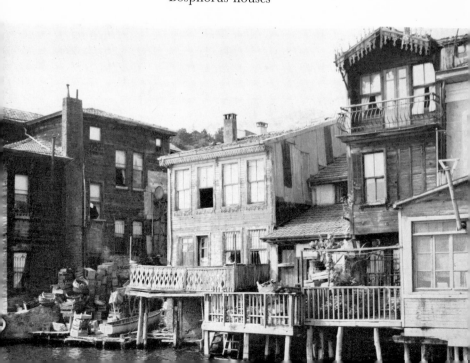

Basketmaker · Coppersmith

Haslama man · Samovar tea

Shoe cleaner · *Narghilé*

Prayer-time

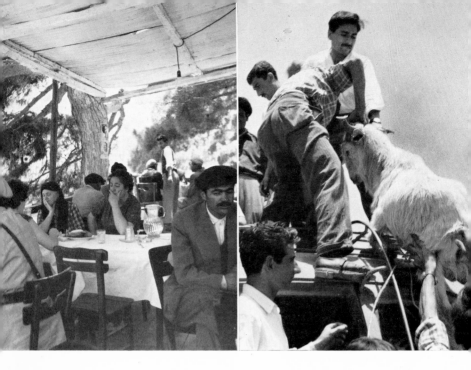

ON THE ROAD

Wayside *lokanta* · Cargo

The emergency

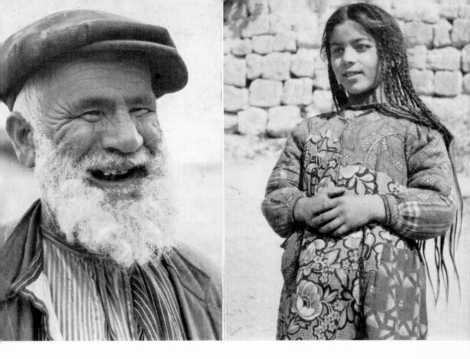

IN CAPPADOCIA

Countryman · Village girl

Göreme valley

CLASSICAL FRAGMENTS

Halicarnassus · Hierapolis

Ephesus · Telmessus

'ALL LOCAL COLOUR HAS GONE ...'

In Galatia   ·   *Kara Deniz* (Black Sea)

In Hatay

COUNTRY LIFE

Carpet weavers · *Tandir* (country oven)

Akseki: in the heart of the Taurus

Winnowing · At Bor

The swinging cradle · The village wedding—Üchisar

THE TURKISH COASTLINE

Kara Deniz (Black Sea)

Ak Deniz (Mediterranean) at Marmaris

rape by every Arab in the town seemed preferable to the slow torture of the airless room.

As soon as we could get on a bus next day we left for Iskenderun, Beria reluctant at the thought of encountering more Arabs, myself delighted at the prospect of reaching the Mediterranean.

Iskenderun, Alexandretta-ad-Issus, is at the point where the coast forms a right-angle round the sea, before continuing down to the Syrian border. Between Adana and the coast is the Cilician Plain, a hard hot land with few oases of charm, but in my optimistic mood I hailed each one – a stone bridge over the Seyhan River, where cattle drank; cotton, mimosa, oleanders along the roadside; some thatched villages, and then, dramatic, rearing up ahead, seeming to sail across the plain, Yilan and Toprak, ruined castles of Cilicia. The wireless in the bus played full blast and half-tuned in, and the Turkish music pounded through my head and made it ache . . . Ula-ula-ulaaa . . . Ula-ula-ula-ula-ula . . . the wailing, strident female cry . . . ula-ula-ula . . . the gramophone disc with the needle caught in the same groove . . . Ula-ula-ulaaa. The sticky syrup from a box of *baklava* seeped down through my basket, gluing together everything within reach. The heat soared, the hot wind blew in on us. Outside were dusty eucalyptus trees, aloes, prickly pear and olive trees.

From time to time we stopped for water, at streams or wayside springs; at other stops little boys overran the bus with *gazöz* and *ayran*, made from *yoğhurt* and water, and mineral waters from Afyon. Far off, the long green mountains stretched, changing, beautiful, and serene, beyond the heat and rushing of our life. Brightly-dressed gypsies squatted by the roadside; in the fields surrounding small settlements, people were building outdoor sleeping platforms, high, rickety, with brushwood roofs; then suddenly there was a ruined aqueduct and a glimpse of sea and ships and military installations, and finally Iskenderun, with the mountains behind and the Mediterranean ahead, very still and blue between its headlands.

*   *   *

In Anatolia, I always found it hard to believe the Turkish Mediterranean was the real Mediterranean, just as I found it hard at first to believe Greek ruins in Asia Minor were really

Greek. I thought of the Mediterranean in terms of Côte d'Azur, Greece, Italy and Spain, as I thought of Greek ruins in terms of Greece and Sicily and Calabria. This part of the world, this elbow-shaped indentation of the sea into the Turkish mainland was not Mediterranean, it was Middle East. The Mediterranean was wine and guitars and *bouillabaisse* and vine-hung *tavernas* or *ristorantes*, not solemn men in pyjama jackets and cloth caps, sitting on kitchen chairs staring into space.

Nevertheless, I was ready to like Iskenderun, even though its Mediterranean was the wrong one, because it was on the sea and because it was Alexander's city, founded after his victory over the Persians at Issus. I was thinking of Alexander, encouraging his men before the battle, and galloping into the river, leading the charge; of Darius, fleeing, leaving his mantle and shield behind, and the Macedonians pursuing him over a ravine filled with the bodies of dead Persians; of Alexander honouring Darius's women; so it was rather a shock to find, not Greek ruins or traces of barbaric splendour but a small grubby town, full of beggars, some of whom were deformed (which Beria assured me was not Turkish) and flies and heat of the most vicious kind, a special Iskenderun heat that broods and oppresses. The air, the sea seemed to be suspended, without life or movement; the people stupefied and apathetic.

Beria was in despair. Faint and sick, barely able to drag herself along, the moaned unceasingly that she loathed Iskenderun, had always loathed it, it was *çok sicak*, it was dirty, Arab, very, very bad. It was *not* Turkish.

It is not surprising that she had this feeling. There has never been much love lost between Arabs and Turks, and this area, known as Hatay, was annexed to Syria after the Ottoman Empire ceased to exist. It was not incorporated into Turkey again until 1939. To Beria, coming to Hatay was rather like going abroad, since it is naturally full of Arabs and Arab influence.

We had meant to stay a couple of days but within an hour we knew that we could not get out fast enough. With a hounded feeling we repacked our bags, checked out of the hotel and went to the bus station.

'Adana no good. Iskenderun no good. We try Antakya,' said Beria. She looked at me severely, for I was the one who wanted to go to Antakya (Antioch). 'If Antakya *çok sicak* we go back Stamboul!'

I dared not argue. I hoped silently that Antioch, beyond the mountains, near the Syrian border, would be cooler. Surrounded by flies and beggars we waited by the bus depot, eating *dondurmas* (ice-creams) and sipping luke-warm *limonat*. I do not care for Turkish ice-cream, which is made from sheep's milk; it is too sweet and soft, like frozen cotton-wool and gelatine, and it slides glibly on the tongue, but I ate on doggedly to please Beria and the proprietor of the shop, who ran in and out with cups of *ersatz* coffee, sticky cakes and quantities of cold water. Beria stocked up with *baklava*, Turkish delight and little local nuts embalmed in sugar, which were very good but indigestible. I was glad when it was time to depart.

Things began to improve as soon as we left Iskenderun. As we climbed into the mountains, the air grew cooler and the splendour of the scenery increased as the sun sank and the light shone out into the mountains, misty blue and purple. Beyond Belen, the Iron Gate of Syria, was the glittering lake of Amuk Golu, and away to one side of the road a medieval village on a ridge; then we were down in the plain and bowling along a straight road between pink oleanders, past fields where herds of black goats grazed and men in baggy pants worked with cattle, drawing loaded hay carts through the ripening corn. It was so lovely, so soft and mellow that the roadsick passengers cheered up and began to eat again.

We entered Antakya at full pelt, and as we alighted Beria and I turned to each other spontaneously and said, '*Antakya çok güzel*.' We felt the personality of the town and knew we should be happy there. High above us was a ruined castle on a hill and all around were winding streets. We quickly took an *araba*[1] and set out for our hotel.

To our delight and astonishment there were coloured umbrellas and fairy-lights set out in some of the gardens, and people were eating in the open air. By the end of the drive we were prepared to like everything.

The hotel did not let us down. Inside the solemn building were cool high-ceilinged rooms with French windows and tiled floors; everything was spotless; the young lady at the desk was friendly and spoke English. For a modest sum we were given a room big enough for a sultan. There were simple Turkish bathrooms with marble basins, silver dippers and *takunyas* and two

[1] *Araba*: Vehicle ... usually horse-drawn carriage.

kinds of *tuvalets*, a Turkish one with a carafe of fresh water, and a European one, erratic in functioning but very clean.

There was a restaurant in the rose-garden. The tables were set out by an artificial pool, and coloured lights hung in the trees. The air was warm, and beyond the garden-wall the Orontes River flowed slowly past. The food was good, and the waiters, in clean white coats, quiet and efficient.

Such comfort and peace were too good to be true; but lest I got too carried away from reality, the plumbing in the bedroom basin brought me gently back to earth. No matter how I turned the tap the water would not stop; the handle went round and round in my hands and a stream of pure liquid gushed forth, and when at last I gave it an extra turn in the hope of producing some result, it fell off and clattered into the basin, while the water careered down the plugless drain.

CHAPTER THIRTEEN

A HOT TIME IN ANTIOCH

OUR liking for Antakya continued, despite the hot weather. Here it was a different kind of heat from Adana and Iskenderun, drier and less oppressive, and at night a cool breeze blew into our high-ceilinged room. We ate breakfast on the loggia among the roses, where green plants were banked round a trickling fountain, and as we lingered there, enjoying the sound of the water and the scent of the flowers, the heat would mount and the haze spread over the hills.

During the day we went sightseeing in the town or into the surrounding countryside, sometimes staying away till evening, sometimes returning to take a siesta; and dinner at night in the moonlit garden, with the trees, the roses and the coloured lights reflected in the pond, was a perfect prelude to sleep.

We explored the country between Antakya and the Syrian border, though our Turkish friends told us this would be difficult. They said transport was almost impossible there and the people were unfriendly, speaking of them as though they were two-headed monsters and inferring that Syria was as bad as Greece. They admitted that buses did go to such places, but said they did not always come back – giving the impression that drivers and passengers were dragged into the woods and massacred by bandits – and we might have to wait for days in primitive villages for a bus back to civilization. In any case, they said, there was nothing to see there . . . just these *Alevi* (Shi'ite) people, and who wanted to see them?"[1]

I did, and I meant to; so we hired cars and drove about to Kislak and Yayladagi on the Syrian border, through landscapes of astonishing beauty, finding villages inhabited by friendly people in antique dress who overwhelmed us with hospitality and kindness.

[1] *Alevi.* A Moslem minority in Turkey. Most Turks are Sunnites and believe that the Caliphate should go to the man best qualified to hold it; the Shi'ites believe it should go only to descendants of Ali, son-in-law of Mahomet.

'You see?' said Beria, as a Kislak woman killed a fowl for our lunch, as the villagers begged us to stay the night with them. 'Good people . . . my people . . . Turkish!'

There is nothing left of ancient Antioch, apart from the ruined citadel on the hill, and walking in the crowded streets with their Turkish touch of hurricane and blitz it is hard to picture the rich and beautiful city built by Seleucis, Alexander's friend, or the temples, statues and public buildings that adorned it. Despite Beria's talk about Arabs and Bad Men, we made friends with a handsome young poet, like a harassed Persian princeling, who was of undoubted Arab blood. He gave us a volume of his poems and led us to a quarter where the old houses touched overhead, and where I found all the things I was learning to expect in Turkish back streets – ancient palaces inhabited by humble townspeople, hidden courtyards and fountains; delicate wrought-iron, roses and grape vines. Beyond these secluded streets was the bazaar, the streets of copper-smiths and shoe-makers and all the daily life of the town, but barely a sound penetrated the enclosing walls, or disturbed the peace of the jasmine and cypresses. Many of the people were Arab, they had Arab names and spoke Arabic but once Beria had adjusted herself to hearing this language spoken on Turkish soil she admitted that they were not after all very, very bad but really very nice. The majority were darker and thinner than the Turks, with quicker movements, and glittering penetrating eyes. Everyone was hospitable and we had many invitations. One was to a circumscision party which, after two days of singing and dancing and feasting and praying, culminated in a triumphal tour of the streets, with a band, and the circumscised boys riding in decorated cars.

Another evening we went with our Persian princeling and his wife to the engagement party of a neighbour's daughter. It was held at a roof-garden *gazino* with a view over the lights of Antakya and a stiff breeze blowing in from the mountains. The guests sitting at the tables by the railing were all done up in coats with scarves tied over the head, but there were festive signs in the form of coloured lights and a profile of Atatürk outlined in red fluorescent lighting. Hostile wooden chairs were drawn up to a long table facing the dance floor, and rows of similar chairs were arranged on the opposite side of the room as though for a concert. These were full of female relations and

children, little girls in satin with sausage curls and little boys in
overcoats and invisible pants, who very soon began to slide up
and down the floor.

The immediate families of bride and bridegroom were lined
up against the wall as though facing a firing squad, the un-
married sisters in pink and green satin. When all were assembled
the young couple appeared, the bridegroom very red and bashful, the bride clearly terrified. They were greeted with applause
and put into seats of honour. We gaped at them, while the bride
dropped her head even lower and the young man tugged at his
collar as though for air; then a lamentable band struck up and
the engaged pair rose and solemnly circled round the dancing
floor, while the female relations goggled and all the men stood
together at the other end of the room, looking embarrassed.

After this, everyone took to the floor, ladies dancing together,
young children weaving through the crowd in hysterical excitement, prim little girls pushed round backwards by old gentle-
men. Refreshments were served, very sweet sticky little cakes
made with walnuts, and sweet sticky lemon syrup. Since there
was a shortage of glasses you had to gulp down your drink as
quick as possible and pass your tumbler along so it could be
washed.

After a Master of Ceremonies had made a speech and been
applauded, the bridegroom moved to the microphone.

'A very musical family,' murmured our princeling as the
young man opened his mouth and gave tongue. A long, long,
sad, sad Turkish song came forth, a weary, weary wailing, oh so
sad and melancholy, with quavering cadenzas spiralling up into
the air.

'He is singing about the moon,' said Beria, who was leaning
back with half-closed eyes, enjoying the song, and suddenly, as
though hearing it through her ears, I found a charm in the
singer and his sad, gentle wail, something moving and poetic
which, apart from the night at Uchisar, I had never found
before in Turkish singing.

Saying good-bye to the engaged pair, I was struck by the
expression on the girl's face. With head still bent, she seemed so
crushed and petrified that I could only assume she wished no
part of the engagement. When I suggested this, Beria said it was
possible; the girl may have wanted to marry someone else; but
of course, she added, she will marry the one they have engaged

her to. When I asked if this might not be a mistake she explained that probably the parents had made the match and since parents usually chose well and carefully the young people would not question the choice, however much one or both of them might love another.

'In Turkey we fall in love after marriage, not before,' she said. 'Much the best way.'

*   *   *

Antioch was an early Christian centre. St Paul and St Barnabas preached and converted there and according to the Acts of the Apostles, 'the disciples were called Christians first at Antioch'. But in its earlier days it was a great place for pagan revels and festivals.

The most famous of these took place in the pleasure gardens of Daphne, a few kilometres outside the town at Harbiye, where worshippers of Apollo gathered to honour him. The festival, which was based on the myth of Apollo and Daphne (the nymph who became a laurel tree to preserve her chastity) had such a name for licentiousness that commanding officers forbade their soldiers to attend it; but plenty of other people went and had a very good time in the name of religion, chasing each other through the laurel trees which stood as a warning to reluctant females.

A splendid temple stood among the groves of cypress and laurel and within it was a golden statue of the god, encrusted with jewels. The sound of streams and waterfalls filled the air, and there was a stadium for Olympic games and summer villas for the rich; but after the coming of Christianty Daphne declined, until at last a Christian church and cemetery appeared in Apollo's groves, the temple was burnt and the golden statue destroyed.

When Beria suggested that we should go to Daphne at eleven o'clock one morning I was not enthusiastic. Ancient pleasure gardens, scenes of revels and gods and nymphs can be very disillusioning, and I feared a sort of dull *Kültür Park* with gravel walks and red-hot-pokers behind linked chains. I felt I would rather read about Daphne in its licentious gaiety than see it in decay; but I was wrong; for though the gods and revellers have gone, the trees are still there, the waterfalls and the view from the groves out over an Arcadian valley. Down the mossy steps, in a green gloom where gold lights flicker through the leaves, the sky is blotted out by spreading mulberries and oaks, and plane trees, and here and there is Daphne's tree, the bay tree, with its shining leaves. The planes of Anatolia are so noble and so splendid that it is easy to understand why Xerxes decorated one of them with golden ornaments and left an Immortal to guard it.

Water is everywhere, in pools and streams and cascades, springing from the earth and rushing down the hill, and the air is full of the sound of its movement.

In the gardens of the Alhambra, the ear and imagination are bewitched by the music of invisible streams running away in the darkness, but at Daphne it is more like a tap left on, though soothing at a distance. The air smells of water, of damp moss and ferns, wet earth and mouldering leaves, delicious smells of coolness, all the more welcome for the knowledge that beyond the sheltering trees the parched air tightens face and throat, the harsh light screws the eyes up in defence.

We plunged down the hillside, into the groves where the gods and nymphs had lived. The few gipsies washing their clothes and children in the pools, the fat ladies sitting on chairs with their feet in the water did not matter, even the *bekçi* (keeper) telling me which waterfalls to photograph. 'Not that one,' he said angrily. 'This one. All the tourists photograph this one!' These are the valleys where the sun never comes, where the damp chill rises round the ankles. Their offerings are more subtle than those of the world above, a shaft of muted light upon a silent pool, a slow, revolving leaf touching the water, a spider's web, and across the stream the jalousied lights filtering through the trees, the endless, endless green receding into its own depths, green upon green upon green. In the places where the Greeks have been there is an atmosphere of gentle happiness and divorcement from time, as unmistakable as the wild herbs that grow round Greek ruins, or the little lizards that bask on their stones.

At the top of the gardens we sat eating grilled chicken, drinking water from the spring and looking out upon a valley of olive trees. The scene before us was so Greek, so full of poetry that I felt no surprise when I heard the notes of a pipe, a sad and hollow sound, evocative, archaic, which might have come from a shepherd dressed in skins.

'*Kaval*,' said Beria. 'Shepherd's pipe. *Çok eski.*'

Under a plane tree by a stream a group of men were sitting, making pipes of hollow wood. As they cut they tested them, playing a few bars, so that the air was full of soft unfinished phrases. Among them was an old man with fine features and faraway eyes. It was he who had played the air I heard and when I approached him he repeated it, primitive, eastern, full of sweetness, his eyes straying over the distant scene as though remembering a youth spent there among fauns and goddesses.

'Play it again,' I asked, and he patted the earth beside him, inviting me to sit down. He handed me a pipe and began to play, signing for me to follow him, and I listened, enchanted but in despair because I could not do so. It was full of unexpected notes and shapes, and I could get no more than half of it before it was time to leave; yet though so ravished by the melody, not a bar of it could I remember when we reached Antakya.

*   *   *

The young lady at the hotel desk was very anxious that we should see the ruins of what she called the Port of Ancient Times. All the visitors went there, she said, it was much more interesting than peasants and villages, and there was a bus every day to Samandagi, about 30 kilometres from Antakya, from whence we could proceed to the coast.

This was Seleucis, a rival city to Antioch, and a great port. St Paul sailed from here on his way to Cyprus, only 130 miles away. Legend says that Seleucis Nicator, the founder, meant to establish his city higher up on Mount Cassius, but as he was sacrificing to the gods before building, an eagle flew off with the victim's flesh and dropped it on the place where the ruins now stand, a sign that the gods wished the city to be built there.

We obediently took the bus to Samandagi, travelling across the rich, black-brown earth of the *Büyük Kara Çay* (the Great Black River). Our fellow-passengers were all Arabs, speaking Arabic, the women in bright-coloured clothes with many gold coins jangling from their necks and ears, and eyes ringed round with kohl, 'to make them bigge, according to Mahomet's promise of women with eyes as bigg as egges in his imaginary paradise'.[1] Even Beria had to admit that they were friendly and good-natured.

---

[1] Sandys, George: *Sandys' Travels*, 1673.

'You must come to my house,' one of the women said, jangling her gold chains, speaking through an interpreter. 'There is
much fruit in my garden now.'

The Arab driver was friendly too. At Samandagi he told us
that a special bus was going shortly to the sea, to load some luggage. We could go in it, see the ruins, and return in it.

We accepted the invitation and looked round for food to take,
for it was midday and we were hungry; but since the bazaar
had just finished and everything had been cleared away, there
was nothing much available. Beria set off to look for fruit, and
led by the bus driver and an old gentleman wearing an eye
patch made of a bottle-top, and followed by most of the village,
I found an open-air shop where white *yufka* bread was being
cooked, taken from the oven on long poles and folded over and
over while still hot.

While I waited for our bread, I photographed the barbaric-
looking women in bright-coloured clothes, who, with long black
hair and babies on their backs, were all suspicious of the
camera. I was looking down into the focusing screen when
someone moved in front of the lens, blocking my vision. It was
a male back, and without raising my head I called out, 'Please
... please,' signalling with my hand for the owner to move
away. When he did not respond I looked up indignantly and
asked if he did not realize he was spoiling my picture; but the
policeman, as I thought he was, looked at me sternly and said,
'*Yok*, madame . . . *yok, yok*!'

'What do you mean "*Yok*"?' I said. 'You're in the way.
Please move.'

He did not move, but said again in a slightly threatening
voice, '*YOK*, madame.'

I looked again and saw that he was not a policeman but some
kind of soldier. I was about to expostulate when I noticed Beria,
surrounded by a crowd of excited people, waving her hands and
talking very fast, very loud. Everyone else was shouting so I
began to shout too.

'What are they doing?' I called. 'What is the fuss about?'

'No photographs,' Beria called back. 'Forbidden.'

I was irritated.

'But why not? I'm not doing any harm.'

The soldier came towards me and put his hand on the
camera. The movement annoyed me and instinctively I lifted

my hand to brush him off. Something made me pause. The crowd had left Beria and gathered round me and now I saw that she was signalling frantically to me to do nothing.

I looked at the soldier, now supported by a colleague. He was very angry and the people seemed disturbed. Their friendly curiosity had changed to a surly, suspicious silence. Beria was clearly worried.

'What is the matter?' I asked.

'Where is your permit?' the soldier demanded. 'How did you come here? What are you taking pictures for? Do you not know it is forbidden? You have no business in this area . . . you must leave immediately.'

'But we're going to the seaside,' I cried, remembering the bus and looking round for the driver.

'*Yok!*' It was forbidden to go to the seaside, and we couldn't stay here either; it was forbidden to be in Samandagi; photographs were forbidden, everything was forbidden and where were our permits . . . ?

Beria, who had got through the crowd to my side, cried, '*Basin carte . . . basin carte . . .*' nudging me to produce my press card. The soldiers scarcely glanced at it, renewing their questions angrily. In the middle of the argument, while I was expressing strong views about Turkish red tape and bureaucracy, the bus drove off and left us behind.

'Now look what you've done!' I cried, in English. 'We've missed the bus and there won't be another.'

The soldier looked at me blankly but before I could speak again Beria said, 'Ssh . . . ssh. *Militaire.* Put us in jail.'

As she spoke the soldier took my arm as though I were under arrest and began to propel me through the crowd, looking very stern and angry. Suddenly Beria cried. 'Wait . . . wait. Here is a man who speaks French.'

Annoyed and baffled, I turned to the newcomer, a middle-aged man in civilian dress who, it appeared, was the local mayor.

'What are you doing here, Madame?' he said. 'Why are you here?'

'But why not?' I asked. 'Why shouldn't I be here?'

He looked very serious and still speaking French said, 'I am asking you Madame, why are you taking photographs?'

'But why shouldn't I take them?' I cried. 'Is there a law

against it? I'm not doing any harm. And now the policeman has spoilt my pictures and made us miss the bus.'

This time he almost shouted.

'Once more, madame, *what are you doing here*? Why are you taking photographs?'

Beria was looking so distracted that I said, 'I'm a traveller. I take photographs because I'm interested.'

'Ah. And what will you do with these photographs?'

'I don't know yet. I take pictures because I am interested in people. I'm not doing any harm. I'm not a spy, if that's what you're worrying about.'

My interrogator uttered a cry.

'Ah! *Espion!*' He glared at me fiercely and all the people murmured together like a stage crowd.

'Now I've done it,' I thought. 'Why did I ever say anything so silly!' I could see Beria's eyes signalling black flashes of nerves, anger and fear. I thought of what would happen now ... of the Turkish prison, the long delays, the letters to the consul, everyone being annoyed with me, and worst of all, my pictures being taken away.

'*Espion!*' said the Turk once more, rolling it round his tongue with relish, '*Non, non*, madame. *Espionne!*'

I was so astonished at this anticlimax that I scarcely remarked it and went on talking. 'All right then, *espionne*. Anything you like.'

He fixed me with a steady eye.

'From what country do you come, madame.'

'From Australia.'

'Austria?'

'No. Australia.'

The crowd had stopped murmuring and were listening with dropped jaws.

'Australia? Ahhhh!' Once more the theatrical, indrawn breath. '*Alors madame ... vous êtes Anglais, hein? Vous êtes Anglais?*'

There was something so unnerving in the way he said this, something so sinister that I felt I was really in for trouble, but before I could stop myself I heard my own voice speaking.

'*Non, monsieur. Je ne suis pas Anglais. Je suis Anglaise!*'

For a second there was complete silence while he stared at me; then he threw back his head and roared with laughter.

'*Madame, madame,*' he said. '*Vous avez raison. Vous êtes Anglaise* . . .' and he went on murmuring *Anglaise* . . . *espionne* to himself with delight.

When I asked him where he had learnt to speak French, he said he had lived in Paris some years before, studying at the Sorbonne, and when he learnt that I had just come from there and that I had been living in the student quarter everything else was forgotten . . . my presence in Samandagi, the photographs, the espionage, the permit. He was dying to talk to someone who knew his old haunts, and we might have continued indefinitely had not the soldier come up and taken my arm again to lead me away to jail.

My friend recalled himself from the rue St André des Arts and explained to us. We had no right to be in Samandagi at all; no one could enter it without special permission from the police in Antakya. It was a military area, forbidden to civilians, especially forbidden to foreigners; certainly we couldn't take photographs, under any circumstances, and you above all, madame, for though you are Australian you have an *English* passport . . . so madame . . . I am afraid . . . I regret that I must ask you to leave as soon as possible. . . .

Then we all talked together, mayor, Beria, soldiers and I. We had not known Samandagi was forbidden; the people at the hotel had said that everyone came here; we did not know that permits were needed. We would leave at once, if we could find transport. . . .

'Come with me,' said the mayor. 'I will find you a *dolmuş*. You may wait in my office.' Telling the soldiers to release me he led us to a building in the square, followed by the police, the military and all the townspeople.

It was a pleasant kind of arrest and detention. The mayor seated us in his office and while fascinated underlings gazed in at us through the open door, gave us cigarettes and ersatz coffee made from nuts. It was brought by a charming young policeman, who, when I thanked him in Turkish, blushed and said shyly in a high voice 'Nothing!' in English, then was overcome with embarrassment.

For all his friendliness, the mayor still had some questions to ask; questions that all Turks ask. Why did I photograph only the poor people? Those in rags? The poor houses? The Turks did not like this. People came and took such pictures and sent them to *Life Magazine* and wrote bad things about Turkey. Why didn't I photograph new houses ... modern things ... people in good clothes? He appeared more or less satisfied with my answers but as though a few doubts still lingered in his mind, asked what I thought of the Turkish people.

When I told him, the air completely cleared, except for the officer who had arrested me and who remained a little suspicious, though scrupulously polite. I think I hurt his feelings when I referred to him as a *jandarma*, for he was in fact the local military commandant.

At last enough people were rounded up to share a *dolmuş* to Antakya and we were seen off with good wishes from the mayor and his attendants, more like honoured guests than suspects narrowly escaped from jail; but though the officials were kind, our fellow travellers in the *dolmuş* regarded me uneasily all the way to town; and when the car was stopped by Customs police and searched, they seemed to feel my presence was responsible; but Beria's loyalty to a difficult protégé appeared unshaken. She was prepared to stand all kinds of embarrassments and possible unpleasantnesses in the cause of my education. All the same she was limp with exhaustion and relief when we reached Antakya and the safe shelter of our hotel.

CHAPTER FOURTEEN

THE CITY OF TOMBS

I think Beria was surprised to get out of Hatay alive, for afterwards she always spoke of our day at Samandagi rather as the British speak of Dunkirk. She could not leave the district quick enough and eagerly packed up to move back to the hated Iskenderun and Adana, on our way to Konya.

Konya is on the Anatolian plateau, within the Taurus, and we were to travel there by train, which is a fairly tough proposition in Turkey at the best of times. Arriving at Adana we found it even worse than we expected, for the Express had gone and there was only the *Posta*.

You have to travel in Turkey to realize what this means. The *Posta* is a mail train that wanders slowly across Anatolia, stopping at every station for as long as possible and in between stations wherever it can. Its name heard on lonely platforms late at night or in the heat of a burning day – '*Motor yok*! *Posta*!' – is the signal for all hearts to fall. It is always late and nearly always crowded with luggage, animals, crates, peasants on local visits, soldiers, and the few foreigners crazy or desperate enough to travel in it.

Slowly, noisily it lumbers into Adana station, covered with oriental dust, worn out after its terrible journey from Aleppo or Teheran or some far city, and as it heaves itself to a stop a change comes over the forms waiting limp and hopeless on the platform. In the twinkling of an eye the train is stormed, foreigners mown down together with locals, friends and relations pulled through windows and luggage thrown in after them.

People go on milling in long after the train is full, packing the corridors with their rolls of carpets and cardboard suitcases, knocking each other in the eye with their bottles of water and newspaper parcels. Those who get seats in a compartment are constantly beseiged by the overflow from the corridor . . . kind smelly people with babies and string bags, who chatter and stare and munch, while from time to time the grimy glass doors are slid back to reveal blind beggars asking for alms in the name of Allah, or men selling every kind of food and drink or, as always, safety pins, shoe laces and watch-straps.

The interior of the train is encrusted with instant dirt. Soot blows in the windows when open and when shut the stench is intolerable. The lavatory, which must be reached by climbing over the nomads camped in the corridor, is usually an object of supreme horror where even the footholds have vanished, buried in the souvenirs of past passengers.

After leaving Adana, the *Posta* totters through the cotton fields and eucalyptus trees of the Cilician plain, to the Taurus and the Cilician Gates which lead back to the Anatolian plateau. It stops, panting, at countless little anonymous halts where people swarm distractedly all over the lines, ignoring the platforms, getting in on the wrong side, jumping on and off when the train is moving. Apart from the passengers there is a constant stream of food merchants, mostly under 12 years old. Even before the train has stopped the air is full of shrill little voices crying their wares. There is an air of panic about the whole performance, though at each halt there is time to write and pass crossed cheques through the Osmanli Bank.

I often wondered where Turkey would be without these little bullet-headed boys who help to run the country, driving tractors, managing petrol stations, minding sheep, cattle and babies, serving in restaurants and at hotel reception desks with grave efficiency and concentration.

As the *Posta* climbs into the mountains and the chill in the air increases, charcoal trays for *şiş kebabs* appear by the lines, and tea replaces the water and *gazoz* of the plain. The scenery becomes increasingly spectacular as the train penetrates into the heart of the Taurus. It dashes through tunnels and out again at such short intervals that from above the line must resemble a ribbon threaded through lace beading. Screaming with despair, the engine plunges into a tunnel, filling the carriage with reeking smoke, emerging without warning on the other side to reveal a gigantic abyss, wild and wonderful, but only visible for a second before you are in the next tunnel, from which you shoot out into more jagged peaks, rising sheer from each side. Another tunnel, another flash of staggering scenery, and so on, through thirty-two tunnels, through the heart of these legendary mountains.

Beyond the Taurus are the steppes, the bare bleak Karaman

I

country, serene in the grey light of evening; then as darkness
falls the *Posta* staggers into Konya, St Paul's Iconium, the
Seljuk capital, the sacred city of the Turks.

Half asleep, frozen and exhausted, I feared that Konya
Istacion had suffered not only the usual Turkish earthquake but
a tidal wave as well, for to the structural chaos and disorder
were added great quantities of water. Deep pools and puddles
lay everywhere; descending passengers waded ankle-deep to
reach the exit, while others clung and clambered over fallen
wreckage; but there had been neither earthquake nor tidal
wave. Reconstruction was going on at the station and it had
been raining hard for some time. Immediately we reached the
open air it started again, the bleak, black rain of the plateau,
driving down into the marrow of our bones.

In the days when I had to draw maps of St Paul's missionary
journeys, in divinity lessons, I little thought I should ever be so
insane as to come voluntarily to such places as Caesarea,
Antioch or Iconium, and this first view revived the resentment
that Kayseri and Antakya had lulled with their charm. The
visit to the ancient city was something special to Beria, as a
devout Moslem, rather like a good Anglican going to Canter-
bury or York, but I could see that even she was wilting at this
first impression. There was nothing visible but a bare, open
space with dreary buildings spaced out in the cold darkness,
and a long road, presumably to the city, leading away into a
murky cloud of mist and rain. Without warm clothes of any
kind we stood, teeth chattering, shuddering, wondering why
on earth we had come. We never recovered from this feeling
about Konya. By daylight all was drab. Through the streets
passed figures muffled in dark shawls and trousers, with
papooses on backs, *çarsafs* pulled across to protect their
faces from the wind. The only colour was an occasional gipsy
or country woman in brilliant red and yellow, or little painted
carts full of squatting figures, faceless and formless. Horse- or
donkey-drawn vehicles were everywhere; *arabas* outnumbered
taxis, and high black waggons, shaped like *caïques*, lumbered
about. There were few signs of open-air life in this bleak settlement, though street photographers, blue with cold, carried on
their work, taking solemn portraits before black velvet panels
painted with flowers, and inscribed across the top with
SOUVENIR OF KONYA.

Because we knew we were prejudiced we tried conscientiously to do it justice. We saw all we could of its life, its mosques and museums; we rode in taxis and *arabas*, in a school bus (which we helped to push each time it stopped), and we tottered all over the town with heads bent into the teeth of the gale. We explored, bartered for painted wooden Konya spoons and *kilim* rugs in the bazaar, bought almonds in paper twists and ate them in the street. We strolled slowly in the Aladdin park on top of the hill, picking up fragments of tiles and ceramics in peacock, jacaranda blue, turquoise, amethyst, chartreuse and imperial yellow, the glazes of the tiles in the tombs and museums. The *Vali* (governor) was helpful to us, the police were kind Beria's friends most hospitable, the hotel was comfortable, the food pleasant, the city full of fascinating things . . . yet we did not like Konya; there was something about it that we could not love, apart from the cruel wind that howled off the steppes, something we could not fathom.

Legends say that it was the first town to emerge from the waters of the Flood; in any case it is very ancient, dating from pre-Hittite times. It has known as many changes and conquests as Adana, and though it is quite different in character from the Cilician town, it disappointed us in much the same way, despite the fact that it contains so many treasures. I wish more Turkish cities could have grown as Syracuse in Sicily has done, where each invader has added something to the buildings of their predecessors, and the mixture of Greek, Byzantine, Arab, Spanish and Italian architecture gives a rich and complex character; but in Konya so much has been destroyed or pulled down that to the stranger it presents a rather dreary anonymous appearance. Many of the houses are built of adobe, with high walls concealing the gardens within, and the streets in the poorer quarters are rough and unfinished. The historical monuments that remain are so widely scattered that they are like little islands of the past in an indifferent present, and this scattered disposition prevents them giving any character to the whole. The real attractions of the city are indoors, in the mosques and museums; its works of art, its antiquities, above all its tombs, simple or splendid, Seljuk or Ottoman.

Of all who held Konya – Hittites, Phrygians, Cimmerians, Lydians, Persians, Greek, Romans, Byzantines, Arabs and Seljuk Turks – it was the Seljuks who brought it to its greatest glory, beautifying it with splendid mosques and monuments, making it a centre of art and enlightenment. In the thirteenth century, Mevlana Celaleddin, poet and mystic, was brought from Afghanistan by the Seljuk Sultan, Aladdin, and founded there an order of Dancing Dervishes. Konya is still a sacred city to the Turks, although the holy men are no longer there. The order was closed in 1925 by Atatürk, but the Dervishes are still very much part of Konya's local colour, even appearing on wooden spoons and stamped on envelopes for which you pay a few extra *kuruş*.

As at Kayseri, it is the Seljuks who have left their personality most strongly on the city. Here, in their ancient capital, they seem to be all round, gazing from museum walls with strange fat faces and slanting eyes, the most fascinating and mysterious of all faces. The long line of the brow continuing as a crease or shadow almost to the hair, the fat and padded eyelids, the small curved mouths make all other features seem insipid. Even the loveliest of flat oriental faces appear bony and monotonous beside these calm and sensual people with their strength and cruelty.

The tomb of the Sultan Aladdin and those of his family are in a small domed, whitewashed room adjoining the mosque that bears his name. With their tiles of heavenly blue and pious inscriptions traced in the same blue glaze round the coffin-shaped sarcophagi, they are extraordinarily simple. Their austere grace is a complete contrast to the tombs on the other side of the town in the convent of the Dancing Dervishes, where Mevlana Celaleddin is buried among his followers.

The convent, now a museum, is powerfully atmospheric, calm and dusky and withdrawn. The air is filled with music, relayed from the library, and it is not hard to picture the holy men gravely turning and turning on the polished floor while their brethren in the musicians' gallery played on the drums and flutes. Whirling in their high pointed caps and long pleated skirts, they danced with arms outstretched, one palm facing towards the earth, the other towards heaven, turning and turn-ing until they reached a state of ecstacy in which their spirits could achieve their desire to be united with God. The Dancing Dervishes were gentler and more tolerant than other orders, nor did they indulge, as did the Howling Dervishes in extrava-gant practices like eating red-hot coals or swallowing serpents.

As the stored-up excitement is received upon entering a theatre, so is the nature of this convent recognized even before it is visible. Even as you stand at the door, slipping off your shoes, thrusting your feet into the curious slippers provided, you are aware of a hovering scent, a solemnity and grandeur which, protected from the dissipating movements of the outer air, has preserved itself, magnifying and feeding upon itself until it is almost tangible. At first, coming in from the daylight, the eyes are a little blinded; then out of the dusk emerge the imperial purples that are almost black, the depths of submarine greens, the richness of the gold and silver embroidery. Behind a protecting barrier, in an enclosure hung with jewelled lanterns, are the high raised tombs of Celaleddin, his followers and family. There is something specially terrible about the coffin of his father, who is buried sitting up. On his deathbed he was visited by Mohammed and died as he was rising to greet the prophet.

These tombs are like a tremendous poem about death, about grandeur and decay and the physical death of kings. There is nothing of the spirit in their solemn splendour, it is utterly mortal, for everything recalls the mind to the pitiful body within, decayed, fallen to dust, hideous in its gorgeous trappings. The sense of mortality is emphasized by the personal touches, the dead man's turban, the use of perishable textiles, the shape of the coffin so clearly seen beneath the rich velvet with its glittering embroidery and golden fringes, tilted towards the feet as though about to descend into a grave, as though waiting for the prayers that will be said over it. All the loneliness of the physical death is in these tombs; they speak so eloquently of the slow dust gathering on the splendid pall, the tarnishing of the silver, the gentle discoloration of the white turban, turning from white to cream, from cream to brown; and most poignant of all, the occasional shaft of sunlight that penetrates from the outer world, through the shutters, to light upon a patch of faded glory.

Outside in the courtyard of the convent there is nothing of this sombre atmosphere. There, surrounded by the cells of the Dervishes, are flowers and fountains and birds, and above the cells many little round domes, like half-submerged bubbles, and rows of little pointed chimneys shaped like Dervishes' hats. Beyond them are the dome and minaret of the main building and the monument above Celaladdin's tomb, a fluted cylinder of green tiles, rising up above the smaller domes with a fluted Dervish cap on top, and above, the crescent moon.

It was not until our last afternoon that I understood why I did not like Konya. It was a feeling that the whole city was a tomb. I discovered that Beria, so balanced and practical, shared it, despite our cheerful friends and comfortable hotel. It caused a claustrophobia which made us slightly hysterical.

We were visiting a house where a strange Turk lived alone among antiques and *objets d'art*. Once in the house, the outside world was shut away. No sound penetrated the heavy tapestries and curtains, and as the hours passed there came a sense of being in a trap. It was impossible to leave, for our host was pressing, almost hypnotic. Beria grew frightened, I became restive; we felt there was something oppressive, almost sinister about the silent house, especially when we found the servants had gone out and we were quite alone.

'Maybe he's mad,' Beria whispered as he brought down scimitars and daggers from the wall. 'Maybe he murder us;' and then, as he turned away for a minute, 'Bad man ... no good at all. Looking at me in bad way.'

He certainly liked Beria. He made hedging proposals to her, stroked her arm, letting his hand rest on her shoulder. When the lights went out, and we were plunged into a darkness heavy with incense, for once she could not take command. Pretending that I did not understand his protests and persuasions, I led her firmly down the narrow stairs, and found with relief that the heavy front door was unlocked. Out in the street we shivered and giggled nervously with relief. Our courage returned a little, and some commonsense.

'It's just that he's lonely,' I said. 'He's just glad to have someone to talk to;' but Beria said, 'No good. No good at all. Very, very bad.' She shuddered and rolled her eyes. 'I felt I was in prison.'

But *buried alive* were the words in my mind; drawn down and submerged in the silent past of this city of tombs.

CHAPTER FIFTEEN

OVER THE TAURUS

WE had come a long way together, lived in each others' pockets, gone to the mosque together, argued, laughed and complained. We were like a husband and wife who long for freedom but are unhappy apart, and when Beria suddenly realized her time was running out and she must go back to Istanbul I felt both liberated and bereft. She had shown me so much, taken me behind the scenes of Turkish life in a way I could never have done alone, yet there was always the sense of seeing through a window rather than being part of the scene myself.

She went uneasily, convinced that I would come to a bad end without her, and our farewells were loving, tearful and protracted as between friends who do not expect to meet again. Whatever happened, she said, I must come back to Stamboul for *Kurban Bayrami*, the festival commemorating Abraham's sacrifice of the lamb. This is an important holiday; celebrations last for three days; the mosques are floodlit; lambs are sacrificed by every family who can afford them and shared out among relations, friends and the poor.

The Güneys had three sheep to sacrifice and Beria felt that I must see the performance since it was Special-Turkish. If necessary she would hold up the sacrifice until I got there.

'One day, one sheep cut; two days, two sheep cut; third day, wait you come.'

I said I would do my best, though I was not very hopeful, for I was going back to the Mediterranean, to Antalya, to travel along the southern coast where transport is almost non-existent; but I promised to fly home from Izmir, and with a final embrace we set out in our respective buses. I was glad to be travelling alone again, for only then can one shed one's personality and absorb, perhaps even reflect those of the people one meets.

For the third time I was crossing the Taurus, a two-day journey of extraordinary beauty and extreme discomfort. The

serpentine mountain road clinging to cliff faces gave the sensation of riding in a roller-coaster, and the zig-zags, increasing
altitude and erratic nature of the driving so upset the other
passengers that periodically we had to stop at roadside springs
to allow them to recover. From one of these I looked down into
a green valley, on a cluster of grey stone houses with thatched
roofs held in place by rows of stones. The silence came swirling
up the heights, encircling, enclosing, pulling down into a vortex,
bringing the treacherous insinuating desire to take off and float
gently like a feather into the soft green world below.

Higher and higher we climbed, into the very heart of the
mountain peaks, among stylized toy Christmas trees, precise,
vivid, with silver-tipped branches. The oblique afternoon sunlight deepened the brilliance of the colours, while in the distance
the snowy slopes turned gold. In the forest, spread thick under
the trees were violets, white and purple.

The bus was like an inferno; everyone was stupefied by
petrol fumes and the grinding noise of the engine, but towards
dusk we descended into a sunlit valley. The people working in
the fields straightened up and smiled as we rattled past into a
village built on the mountain slopes. In a vine-hung square the
bus stopped with a final flourish and clatter and stood shuddering all over. This was Akseki, where we were to spend the night.

I was petrified with exhaustion, heat and cramp brought on
by sitting too long in the same position on a hard uncomfortable
seat. There was a little chill in the air which I felt might suddenly turn into one of those bracing alpine winds and I
hastened to find shelter before this should happen. As I alighted
I saw right before me the magic word *OTELI*, with a staircase
leading upwards. Too tired to ask questions, I tottered through
the doorway.

I was only halfway up the stairs when I realized that this
hotel was not quite what I had hoped to find. The stairs were
murky enough but the landing was in pitch darkness. There
was no one to be seen, though I could hear voices murmuring
somewhere near, so I picked my way carefully over the damp
cement floor and pushed open a sagging door. Inside was a
kind of dormitory with five or six beds, and as I entered a
powerful smell met me, a rich bouquet of old clothes, old boots,
sweaty socks, human excretions of all kinds, antique, strong and
well-matured. It came mainly from the forms on the beds, which

I distinguished as those of old, old men, all lying fully clothed, except for their boots, on sleazy mattresses.

They looked at me with their rheumy eyes but said nothing; then a form came from the corner and asked what I wanted. I explained that I was from the bus and wanted a bed for the night. He looked blankly at me as though I had asked for something extraordinary.

'Haven't you got any beds?'

'Yes.'

'Where?'

He pointed to the only empty bed in the dormitory.

'Here,' he said simply.

I said, 'Haven't you got another room?'

He shook his head, surprised at my lack of enthusiasm.

'I'm tired,' I said. 'I want a room to myself. Do you understand?'

He looked perplexed for a minute, then beckoned me out into the hall. On the other side was a closed door which he pushed open.

'In here,' he suggested.

There were already seven women and children in the room, all gathered round what looked like a stove but which proved to be a bundle of luggage used as a table. Pots, casseroles and newspaper parcels were spread about and the smell of feet was here replaced by the more refreshing scent of the cucumbers which were being wolfed down by all hands. One woman was not eating; she had spread a mat in the corner and was saying her prayers.

'There's no room here,' I said. 'All these beds are full.'

The women round the table nodded in agreement. There were four beds, and even assuming that the babies being suckled at the breast were going to sleep with their mothers, there still wouldn't be enough to go round. I looked narrowly at the young man and realized that I was supposed to share not only a room but a bed.

'A single room,' I said firmly, and moved back to the hall where I stood waiting.

He cogitated for a minute, as though hoping I might change my mind, then he said, 'Here,' and opened the door next to the female dormitory. For a minute I could see nothing at all, for the cupboard into which I was peering had no window of any kind; then I saw dimly that wedged into this tiny den was a sordid bedstead furnished with a striped mattress. There was nothing else; there was no room for anything else, not even the door, which opened outwards.

'What is this?' I asked.

He replied without much optimism. 'Single room.'

I suppose I could have entered by taking a header from the hall on to the bed but I was really not in the mood. I lifted my chin and said '*Yok!*' and began to descend the stairs again, followed by the entire company. The old men rolled from their beds and padded to the door in their socks, bewailing the loss of their sleeping companion, while the women with the cucumbers and casseroles were insulted. Nor was the proprietor pleased, for he had not liked my saying '*Yok*' to his cupboard, and they all assured me loudly that I wouldn't find another bed in Akseki; that everything was full up. By the time I reached the street they had squeezed their way out to the upstairs balcony, from which they could follow my progress down the street, but there was no malice in their performance; it was only the intense interest of simple souls who have dull lives and nothing much to think of.

At the other end of the village I found a building marked *OTELI* perched on the side of the hill, where the proprietor, harassed and bewildered, rustled round fruitlessly, then flung open a door upon a room containing three beds.

'This room is full,' I said, as two startled faces confronted me, but the patron murmured in explanation, 'Spik Inglish ... spik Inglish.'

I apologized to the young man, who did in fact speak English, and backed out into the hall where the *patron* stood staring at me as though I were deranged, unable to understand why I would not turn in with the married couple when we all spoke English so nicely; but at last, with a resigned shrug, he led me to another room, snatched up the male belongings that were scattered about and invited me to make myself at home.

Remembering the advice my friends had given me for travel in Anatolia, I pulled off the sheets and pillowcases and handed them to him without a word, and while I waited for the clean ones I felt the bed for bugs, specially in the corners of the mattresses where they like to congregate.

In the chilly darkness I set off for the village *lokauta*,

followed by the usual group of little boys anxious to direct me, but there was no trouble finding it for a wailing dirge from the wireless led me straight there. In the hard, harsh light I saw the tables and chairs, the men in cloth caps, the staring faces which turned to me as I entered. The strident song went on and on, driven forth from some capacious Turkish female bosom with all the force of a steam engine, endless and monotonous, its basic thread interwoven with static and the sort of noises you get when a station is not properly tuned in.

I sat down at a corner table and looked about hopefully for service. In the opposite wall was a half-door from which sounds of spitting and crashing could be heard, and presently there came out a goofy boy in a dirty shirt. I asked for the menu. He stared in astonishment at my wild request. Too tired to explain, I made my way to the serving hatch and looked inside. There were several grubby men gathered round a stove and seeing one of them waving a skewer I ordered *şiş kebab*. I returned to my table to wait but had barely sat down before a soldier drinking *raki* in the corner began to hail me.

'*Madame, madame, parley Fronksy?*' he cried. And then '*Madame, madame, un peu . . . un peu . . .*' like a child repeating a lesson, his voice getting more and more blurred. It was impossible to read, for he was shouting to make himself heard above the female singer, and when the idiot boy came to the table and laid before me a plate of liver, which I hate, a large hunk of grey half-cooked bread, and a fork and spoon which he pulled out of his pocket, the gastric juices cascading about in my starving inside united into an angry soup and I said some bitter things in English. The boy was unmoved and went on laying out the loathsome feast.

'*Yok!*' I said fiercely, seeing the prongs of the fork clotted with dirt, and I handed the implements back to him. He took them philosophically, wiping them on a filthy handkerchief before offering them again. I picked up the liver and made for the serving-hatch, followed by the dumbfounded boy. The other diners had long since given up eating, the better to concentrate on their staring, and even the soldier had temporarily stopped his bleating cry of '*un peu . . . un peu.*' I pushed open the lower half of the serving hatch and scrambled through the aperture.

The men on the other side regarded me with oriental fatalism. This was not one of those cheery places where you are

welcomed into the kitchen and invited to choose what you want
to eat. It was definitely a closed book where morbid secrets were
kept from an apathetic public; but I was too angry to care, and
handing the liver to the first man I saw, I wormed my way
through the grimy bodies until I was face to face with the stove.

'Where are the *kebabs*?' I asked; but with an expressive
gesture they told me that they were finished, pointing to the
dead charcoal bed to convince me.

'*Şiş kebab yok!*'

There was nothing except what I saw on the stove. I turned
to the three cauldrons and lifted the lids, revealing a terrible
sort of bean stew, boiled scrag-end of mutton and a pilaff with
all the rice stuck together in a glutinous mass. In desperation I
ordered the beans and mutton, but when they came, ten minutes later, stone cold and swimming in grey congealing grease,
I could not eat them.

Seeing me look at my watch, the soldier now changed his
repetoire. '*Madame*,' he called, '*Kellaraytee? Kelleraytee?*' and
after saying this for some time lapsed into Turkish and asked for
my address. Fed up with the food, the noise and the soldier I
left the restaurant and returned to the hotel; but the day was
not yet over. I had barely taken off my sandals when there was
a loud thump on the door. Outside was the *patron* and beside
him the soldier from the café, very red in the face and a little
unsteady on the feet.

'*Madame*,' he announced. '*Je suis le Gendarmerie*,' and pushing
me aside he lurched into the room. The patron stood hovering
helplessly behind him.

The soldier invited me to sit down on the bed and taking the
chair for himself asked for my passport which he made a great
show of examining, until I pointed out that he was holding it
upside-down; then having spelt out a few words carefully to
himself he began to interrogate me pompously in Turkish. I
became impatient.

'Oh, don't be so silly,' I said. 'There's no need for all this.
I've got a *permis de séjour* and a *basin carte*.' and I brought them
both out.

He was fascinated. He took the press card and compared its
photograph with that in the passport, then he examined the
permis de séjour all over, saying 'Mmm' and 'Haa' with tremendous significance; he fumbled in his pockets for a piece of paper,

which I finally gave him, on which to write his findings, and called for pen and ink, which the *patron* scurried off to get. Then he demanded my address in Australia, and when I wrote it out for him, addressed me as Madame Sydney.

'Avoostralya,' he kept saying. 'Avoos*tralya* . . .' and then 'Gelibolu!' (Gallipoli) as though that explained everything. I stood him as long as I could, but finally, struggling to keep my eyes open, I said '*Bonsoir, monsieur,*' rather coldly. He jumped up with an eager smile, took my hand and shook it up and down, repeating '*Bonsoir, bonsoir,*' as though it were a new word, but making no effort to leave, so that in desperation I had to eject him by force, taking him by the arm and pushing him to the door, where he regarded me amiably through his *raki* fumes saying '*Bonjour, monsieur*' as I shut the door upon him. The last I heard was his hand thumping and his voice shouting at the door of the married couple who, no more cowed than I was, shouted at him to go away and leave them in peace.

I woke to find the sun shining into my whitewashed cell, lighting up the chair, the bed and the unstained wood table on which reposed a beautiful old *testi* or long-necked water jar. No bugs had materialized during the night and the one flea that had bitten me had barely disturbed my sleep. After some perilous juggling with a teacup full of water in the combined urinal-washroom, I dressed and went out to look for breakfast, but as I suspected, there was no breakfast in this frontier town. The café was shut and there were no fruit shops, only shoe shops and barbers, as in all Turkish villages, and bakers who produced that terrible, inedible Turkish bread. There was no sign of the mouldy curd cheese called *cimi*, for which Akseki is famous, nor of their special *yoghurt*, which, it is said, will keep for a year. The houses, built in tiers up the slope of the hill with a splendid view over the broad valley, are partly dug into the hillside, and many have the ends of logs protruding from the outer walls, like crude versions of the Casa de las Conchas at Salamanca.

I was glad when we left Akseki, taking the road where the nomads move with the changing seasons. In the sunny fertile valleys draped peasant women stood upright, motionless, like Russian *matrioshki*; then came a long descent down the mountains to a land of vineyards and oleanders, and suddenly ahead a brilliant shimmering blue shone out beyond the olive trees . . . the *Ak Deniz* or White Sea. . . . The Mediterranean.

CHAPTER SIXTEEN

THE WHITE SEA

'Do not worry madame,' said Ahmet. 'I will get you back to Stamboul in time for *Bayram*.'

'We have friends who can help,' said Errol. 'We shall get in touch with them.'

They hovered round my breakfast-table, young, intelligent, eager to help. I ate another black olive, some more goat cheese; I looked at the dew on the flowers, at the blue mountains across the water and I heard the fountain at my side, a gentle background to the young voices. I forgot all about one-sheep-cut. Antalya was beautiful. Why not stay where I was? Why hurry back to Stamboul?

'I've decided to stay on,' I said. 'It doesn't matter if I don't get back until after Bayram.'

The boys were delighted. Immediately they began to organize my stay in Antalya. Ahmet had a French-speaking friend who worked in the tourist office; he was taking a rich American tomorrow by taxi to see Aspendos, and would gladly take me as the rich American's guest. I must go to Side, said Errol; to Alanya, said Ahmet. It was ancient and beautiful, said Errol. Ahmet said he would buy my bus ticket himself and book me a hotel room.

I agreed to everything. Life at the Divan Hotel was demoralizing me with its baths and soft beds, its harmonious carpets and civilized meals, but even pleasanter was the atmosphere created by Errol, the proprietor's son, and his friend Ahmet, who handled everything and everyone with immense efficiency and good nature. During the summer, hotels and tourist offices in Anatolia are often staffed by such boys, students from the universities, good-mannered, well-educated and usually speaking English or French.

There was nothing Ahmet would not do for you. Within an hour of my arrival he fixed the wireless in my room, brought me a cold drink, sent a cable to Australia and was trying to get me a ship from Antalya to Istanbul. My decision to stay on gave him even more scope to be helpful. I left everything to him, and occupied myself with the beauties of Antalya and the unaccustomed comfort of my life there. The Divan is set in a rose-garden, on the edge of the sea. Over the water are the mountains, Climax and Solymna, which change and deepen in colour every hour, reminding me of the mountains across the lagoon in Suva, Fiji. As I ate my breakfast by the fountain they were mauve and grey; at midday they were cobalt; at night, as I dined in the garden under a new moon, they were black. In the evening, as the sun descended behind them, throwing its late light on the silky bay, the mellow light shone in on the trees and gardens, turning them darker, liberating the purple shadows that lie waiting in all green things. With no need to hurry I would walk through the park by the sea and take an *araba* into the town, clopping lazily along the broad road where the little shops were bright with fruit and vegetables, and people sat drinking tea under the trees by the ruins of Hadrian's Gate. Behind the Roman walls, narrow streets wind among old Turkish houses with lurching roofs and elegant painted decorations, leading down a steep hill to the little port. From here St Paul sailed to Antioch, and the Crusaders embarked for Palestine, but there is little traffic now, apart from the ships of the Turkish Coastal Line on their way from Istanbul to Iskenderun.

The sky over the town is patterned with an assortment of forms, a medieval clock tower, Turkish minarets, crenellated battlements and cypress trees; there are solid Roman walls and arches, Byzantine churches, the domes of Ottoman mosques and the pointed octagonals of Seljuk tombs. The museum is in an old mosque which was formerly a church. In the past the mosque gates were shut every Friday at midday because of a legend that the Christians would come back at that time to recapture the town.

Antalya was first named Attalea, after Attalus, king of Pergamum, who founded it, and later it was known as Satalia and Adalia. It was a Seljuk city for a time, and I hoped to find Seljuk buildings, for I knew that the Sultan, Kiliç Arslan (The Sword of the Lion) had a summer palace there. Though there are few Seljuk remains, there were compensations. One day a strange man I met in the street took me to his house and showed me an astonishing room where the divans round the walls were upholstered in purple velvet, curruscating with silver and gold embroidery. Thick carpets covered the floor and the light glittered from chandeliers. The ceiling was carved and painted, and velvet, clotted with metallic splendour, hung on the panelled walls. Shuttered against the daylight, it was a survival from another age, like an aristocrat who has remained concealed long after the revolution has passed. A palace, the family told me, smiling as I stood marvelling; a summer palace of the sultans; and going downstairs, through the outer room where nappies were airing by the fireplace, I saw the crest carved over the ancient door.

Always there is this secrecy in Turkey, this hiding away of rare or beautiful things. The loveliest gardens, the richest vineyards are beyond the highest walls, the most splendid apartments set in sombre buildings that give no hint of the wonders they contain, so that seeing them brings a sense of excitement.

*   *   *

I went with Ahmet's rich American to Aspendos, now called Belkis, which has a massive brown theatre like a warehouse, and which rather bored me; and to Side, which I loved at sight. Once a centre of pirates and slave traders, it is all silent now, with marble blocks and pine trees round a white beach and a ruined theatre with a view across the water. I spent a blissful, solitary day, sitting on sun-warmed marble, dozing on sun-warmed sand.

On this ancient Greek coast the Mediterranean stops being Middle East, the ruins seem really Greek and the air has the feeling of classical Greece.

Alanya, known as Corakesium, was also a stronghold of pirates, who worked with the pirates of Side, until the Romans wiped them out, and later it was a summer headquarters of the Seljuk sultans. Travelling along the coast to Alanya I met my first really drunk Turk. He was very anti-British, and showed me photographs of, so he said, his sisters, wearing very few clothes and employed, apparently, in Beirut, Port Said and Cairo dives. He was rather insulted when I asked if he were a commercial traveller and said coldly that he was a sailor, but by the time we reached Alanya he was trying to embrace me, to the shame and horror of the respectable passengers, who drove him off, apologizing for his discourtesy.

The first sight of Alanya, seen from the road, is arresting. Beyond a curving beach a headland rises, wild and free, and riding on its heights a medieval castle. The drama of the scene gives no hint of the grubby little settlement behind the hill and I was bitterly disappointed when we entered the modern town. Even the famous bay seems rather featureless after the changing and subtle beauties of Solymna and Climax at Antalya, and it was not until I had climbed the hill to the castle and explored the narrow lanes among the old houses that I began to feel Alanya's charm.

The hotel recommended by Ahmet was slightly institutional but spotlessly clean, run by a kindly Turk who spoke no French or English. My room with whitewashed walls and a view over the sea suggested summer in Britanny, and the washing facilities, though simple, were above reproach. With whitewash, olive trees and a blue sea little else is needed.

I ate my meals in a restaurant right on the beach, where the tables were set under grape-vines and where in the evening I could hear the *muezzin*, the voice of the sleeper, calling from a far-off minaret, and watch the sea as night came on, black and still with the faint path of a new moon, and the mountains dark against the brilliant stars.

I was among the Seljuks again at Alanya. Though its history goes back to the Greeks, it is the Seljuk personality that survives in the walled town high on the headland, and it was they who built the *Kizil Kule* (Red Tower) and the shipyards, which are still in use.

From the walls of the old city is a heavenly view over the blue bay and down upon the little houses among their olive trees, cypresses and prickly pears. Below is the *Kizil Kule* and a little quay running out into the placid water, like an arm bent at the elbow. Though the road itself is dazzling white in the hard sunlight, the houses and crenellated walls are the same red-gold colour as the town. Because the settlement is built on a steep slope it does not have the enclosed character of walled towns like Dubrovnik or Avila or Avignon and seen from above or from the sea, the walls give the effect of an outline or boundary rather than a defence. The modern town appears as a series of boxes arranged in rows behind the beach, which curves away into the distance with the bald and crumpled mountains behind. In the unimaginative light of midday they are uninteresting,

K

lacking the evening shadows that transform them to blue and purple velvet; but the sea is always perfect in fine weather, wide, becalmed, shining like a cat.

At the top of the hill is a medieval village with houses made from fragments of the old walls, so built into the ruins that they seem to grow out of each other. Among these red-gold cottages are deep narrow lanes and small enclosed gardens, where fig and olive trees and cactus grow among the rough-piled walls, and poppies and abandoned tombstones mingle with the vegetables.

As soon as I appeared in this place a crowd of children gathered round me and completely took me in charge. They led me to a mosque, slightly Byzantine in appearance but Ottoman in origin, with a white minaret and a pink-tiled dome, then up the hill again, crying shrilly that I must see the *kale* (castle) at the top. From here I looked down on the pink dome of the mosque amongst its olives and cypresses, and beyond to another wave of the descending hill where the town lay, its banal features hidden by greenery. Behind were the mountains of the Taurus, now assuming their subtle afternoon colourings, and spread out before us the curve of the calm blue bay.

The children were delightful. '*Kilise*' (church) they cried, beckoning me on, snatching at my hands to pull me after them. '*Kilise*.'

I followed them through the ruins of the castle into an open space where the remains of a little Byzantine church stand, its dome embellished with encircling arches. Beyond the church in the direction of Antalya a divine prospect of sea and hills opens out, like the view from Cape Sunion, where powder-blue mists were gathering over the water. The children were very excited at having brought me there, impressing upon me that it was a Christian church and looking at me expectantly as though hoping I might perform some kind of prayer to show them how it worked.

Returning from the citadel I was followed by several youths who stopped to stare each time I took a photograph, and who, when I sat down by the road to change a film and enjoy the deepening colours of the mountains, stood whispering and watching me. Finally, having finished their conference, they spoke, to my astonishment in a manner neither friendly nor polite.

'Get out,' they said in Turkish. 'English woman. Get out. No good.'

Uncertain how to take it, for it was my first encounter with any real hostility or rudeness, I pretended not to hear, but they came closer and shouted louder, making threatening gestures. When I turned my back a stone fell close to my foot, then another, hitting me between the shoulders, and finally a shower of stones, a large one striking the camera. I was so angry I started up the hill towards the boys but they fled, shouting as they went, and disappeared behind a rock, from which they threw more and bigger stones. I climbed up to the road through the bombardment, calling that I was going straight to the village to tell the policeman what was going on.

There was a pause, and after a panicky consultation the boys scrambled out from their hiding-place and ran up the hill. By the time I had reached the road they had disappeared and there was only one to be seen, a small boy with a donkey who, trembling with fear, piteously appealed to me for mercy.

'I didn't do it,' he said. 'It wasn't me. It was the big boys.'

He was very small indeed and I realized that he had probably just come along when the performance was in progress, but I was too angry to be reasonable and taking his arm I demanded that he come with me to identify the other boys to the police. With a terrified cry he twisted away so violently that his coat peeled off and I was left holding it, while he rushed hysterically up the road, babbling that he was innocent. The donkey remained standing blankly in the road, loaded with vegetables.

' *Tamam*,' I called after him. 'I'll go to the *jandarma* alone but I'm taking your donkey.'

He shrieked with terror when he saw me starting down the hill with his animal. He was in a terrible position. Innocent himself, he must face either trouble from the police or trouble at home for the loss of the donkey. I was sorry for him, but feeling my bruised ribs and shoulder I hardened my heart. I repeated that no one was going to hurt him and I only wanted him to tell the police the names of the big boys, but he was too frightened to take it in. He could only get the word *jandarma* and conclude that he was going to be arrested. He clung to his rock up on the hillside, crying piteously, and I began to descend the road with the donkey.

I had only gone a few yards before I realized what I had

undertaken. What on earth was I going to do with the donkey? I couldn't take it back to the hotel with me, and possibly the police would accuse me of stealing it; yet how could I back down now, having made so many threats? Besides, I didn't know how to get rid of it, it was following me in a strangely docile manner, almost as though it didn't quite realize what it was doing. I stopped to consider and at once it stopped too. Having done so, it refused to move again. For a few minutes I tried to shift it but I couldn't drag it, and it took no notice of my pleas, threats or blandishments. I tried everything I could think of, reproducing the sort of noises I had heard people making to donkeys but none of them were any good. The creature stood with its head hanging forward, its long eyelashes drooped over its eyes and its silky ears poked forward. It was too much for me and I began to laugh. My pride and anger vanished abruptly, leaving me shaking with laughter that became slightly hysterical when I looked up and saw the terrified boy still peering down at me from his rock. He was too petrified to see anything funny in the situation and looked at me blankly when I called up to him.

' *Tamam*,' I called. ' *Tamam. Jandarma yok*.'

He didn't understand or he didn't believe me, and stayed on the hillside staring as I waved airily and walked on down the hill, leaving the donkey in the road. Hours later, as I sat on the hotel balcony, he came creeping past, scuttling away in terror when I called out 'Good evening'.

'They are hooligans,' said the hotel proprietor apologetically. 'But,' he added sadly, 'there are many here who do not like England.'

I felt depressed and went down to the little quay below the *Kizil Kule*, where there is a café with tables and chairs set out on the very edge of the sea, and views across the bay and up to the walled town on the hill, and where I often sat drinking *çay* with friendly locals against a background of political broadcasts or the hard insistent rhythms that the Turks enjoy.

I walked out to the end of the elbow-shaped breakwater to avoid the noise. The setting sun was lighting the old houses and the coloured boats floating by the quay. In one of them a father and son were paddling about gently, as though out to enjoy the beauty of the evening, and as I watched, the man called up to ask if I would like to take a promenade to the old Seljuk shipyards. I accepted, asking what it would cost, for the boats were all for hire, but he shook his head, smiling, and said it would be a pleasure and an honour. I descended the stone steps and climbed into the boat. We rowed slowly to the foot of the cliff where beneath five pointed arches the shipbuilding yards were hidden, entering as though into a sea grotto. Inside, boats were pulled up on the shingly beach, ghostly in the greenish glimmer that shone down from the skylights.

For an hour or more we paddled about the bay, aimlessly, at peace, reluctant to terminate the outing. It was more than the beauty of the evening that brought this feeling; there was a *rapport* between the three of us, though they spoke only Turkish, a sympathy independent of words.

'News very bad,' said the father, as we floated quietly across the pallid water to the stone steps. He shook his head. 'Not good. Perhaps war.'

I looked at the peaceful scene in the gentle lingering light. The sun had gone and the mountains, deepening every minute, were visible in the sea, where pale reflections floated. The sky was streaked with pink and mauve. Such talk did not seem remotely real.

'Do you want war?' I asked. 'Do you want to fight?'

He lifted his chin and said '*Hiyer, hiyer*' (no) and made an embracing gesture to include me and his little boy, the sea and the mountains. No words could have expressed more clearly his attitude towards mankind, his understanding of universality.

CHAPTER SEVENTEEN

A WORLD OF FRIENDS

ALL the time I was in Antalya, Ahmet was working like a beaver among his friends and contacts to solve my transport problems for the next stage of the journey. I wanted to travel round the coast from Antalya to Bodrum (Halicarnassus) turn inland to the Meander Valley and Hierapolis (Pammukale) then back to Izmir for my plane to Istanbul. Everyone was extremely discouraging about my chances of doing the coastal trip and urged me to give it up and go to the Black Sea instead, but I refused to listen. This is a wonderful part of the world, the ancient lands of the Lycians and Carians, people who came from the islands to settle in Asia Minor. It is rich in legends and history and ruined classical cities, many of them liberated from the Persians by Alexander the Great; it is beautiful, with the Dodecanese strung out all along the mainland, so close that they might have broken away only yesterday; but it is not easy to travel there unless you have your own boat.

The main difficulty is the section between Antalya and Fethiye, for apart from the regular cargo-boat from Istanbul there is no public sea transport and no coastal roads to link the little ports together. I had just missed the ship and there would not be another for three weeks; but Ahmet and Errol, who were taking it all as a personal challenge, refused to be discouraged.

One evening I was called downstairs to meet a young man, studious, nervous, puzzled, who was introduced as Yilmez Günes, a student from Ankara University, working in the tourist office for the vacation. He spoke a little French and he had come in answer to Ahmet's summons to help me. He knew people all along my route, he said, he would write notes to those who could be most helpful – a local *kaymakan*, or district sub-governor, a policeman, a schoolmaster, a farmer, all of whom would look after me and shelter me if necessary.

I would go by bus via Elmali to Finike, the ancient Phoe-

nicus, then by motor-boat to Demre (Myra) where his friend
Naci, a theology student from Ankara University, would
arrange for a fisherman to take me round the coast to Fethiye
(Telmessus) and from there, presumably with another fisherman, to Marmaris and Bodrum. After that, transport would
be easy, or as easy as it can be in Turkey. All these things the
boys assured me would be made possible somehow or other,
though they admitted reluctantly that they might be *çok zor*
(very difficult).

Yilmez came to see me off on the Finike bus and confided me
to the care of a handsome green-eyed country boy called
Hussein who was returning from his military service to his home
at Demre, and who looked after me tenderly all through the
long hot journey. The inland area was ashimmer with heat, and
quantities of dust blew constantly into our eyes and mouth. In
the late afternoon we reached Finike, more tropical than
Mediterranean, a dirty neglected little town without trees or
flowers, with ugly boxlike houses on the water's edge. The
valley behind it, where oranges, rice and cotton grow, is hot and
airless, and though the setting of the town is beautiful, with a
sweeping bay, and mountains reaching back into the sky, the
hand of man has done nothing to show that he appreciates
them. The harbour seems dead, with no bright *caïques* tied
up or fishing nets out to dry; the best hotel is out of sight
of the sea, facing the hot valley, and in the *gazino* by the water
crude chairs and tables are lined up on a concrete slab by the
pier, with a coal heap and petrol drums at hand.

The Turks don't seem to have the same touch with sea towns
as Spaniards, Italians, Greeks and Provençals. Here, on this
southern coast, no one has bothered at all to make the best of the
exquisite settings. The locals look at the blue mountains behind,
the silky bay before them and say, '*Çok güzel*', but they make no
effort to enjoy them in aesthetic or even comfortable conditions.
The things I missed most in Turkey were not the mod. cons. or
comforts of travel but the little vine-hung places for sitting to
enjoy the view, to drink a glass of something or eat a simple
meal. I missed them bitterly and increasingly and I resented the
Turks' complete lack of understanding of what a sea town
should be like. Sometimes, at first glance, or from the distance,
a town would appear to have the white simplicity I loved, but at
close quarters it proved an illusion, a remnant of the Greeks who

lived along this coast for hundreds of years, until the War of
Turkish Independence. When Atatürk drove them away they
left behind their square white houses on the sea, or climbing up
the hill among the prickly pears, their Cyclades chimneys, their
domed churches, now in ruins; and though they are surrounded
with hot-looking Turkish additions, the Greek touch is still
there for those who recognize it.

I am sure the Turks really love their beautiful country and
would kill or die for it without hesitation, but in some ways their
love resembles that of a man for his old mum or his faithful
doormat wife; a constant unchanging fundamental emotion
that never bothers about compliments, birthdays or other
trifles that make life so pleasant. With the Turks it takes the
form of complete neglect of appearance. Beautiful places lie
covered with garbage and dirt, and new buildings are usually
hideous and unsuitable, giving the impression that no one cares
enough to co-ordinate them. People just run up any old thing
anywhere they like, as they do in Australia, where the same
lavishness of large-scale beauty is regarded in the same
off-hand way, or taken as a challenge to man's ingenuity to
spoil it.

Hussein, who was staying with friends, took me to the stifling
little hotel, where we found the owner, fat and unshaved, water-
ing the garden in nylon vest and underpants. He was not in the
mood for visitors and had to be persuaded to let me in, but
finally took me to a tiny room, clean but completely airless.
The tariff on the back of the door said:

	T.L.*	
	3.50	Single bedroom
	3.00	Two beds
	2.50	Three beds
	1.50	Bed on floor

* T.L. Turkish Lire.

I never saw him again. Next morning I paid my bill to a
baffled little girl of seven, the only other occupant of the
building.

Although it was early when Hussein came to fetch me, the
flat plain was already steaming gently. In the streets a few little
boys and shrouded women carrying food slunk back against the
wall and stared as we passed, and in the cafés and on chairs on
the pavements were men I had seen the night before, looking

exactly the same, as though they had sat up all night in their clothes for fear of missing something.

At this hour the bay was pale and silky, and across the water the mountains had receded into the distance in an early morning mist. In the harbour we found a kind of whale boat with an engine, floating at the quay, and a crowd of people climbing in, arranging themselves for the trip. Newspaper parcels, string-bags, sacks, baskets and bundles were being handed in, cucumbers, bread and bottles of water. The boat was very full when we started off, speeded on our way by shouts from those assembled to see us off.

Once afloat, most of the passengers prepared to be sea-sick while the rest began to eat, opening their bundles, handing round their bread and cucumbers. Hussein and I had a news-paper parcel of hot fresh *bürek*, a sort of savoury puff-pastry, oozing oil and smelling of onions, but when we offered to share them they were politely refused. It was like a mass picnic, but with little gaiety and no singing.

Hussein was conversing with our companions, answering their questions about me. Everyone was very interested and wanted to help with advice. When he told them I hoped to hire a *special motor* (launch) from Demre to Fethiye they fell silent and regarded me with awe and admiration, as though abashed in the presence of one so rich and powerful.

I crouched under a neighbour's umbrella, for the sun was already very hot, shining back brilliantly from the smooth water. The subtle mountains behind Finike and the receding town softened as we drew away; then we turned to the west and away from the rolling lines of the Chelidonian cape, close to a bare coast where grey-white rocks rose out of low bushes, Provençal, parched, relieved only by the darkness of the vegetation.

Hussein leant over and said 'Demre', pointing ahead. In a distant bay was a long white beach, where as we approached, a couple of men came into focus, wearing the semi-pyjama outfit of the country. With their cloth caps and thick trousers they were badly out of place against the brilliant heat of the sand, yet somehow part of the landscape. I suppose these staring Turks in their unsuitable clothes are the descendants of the turbanned, bearded figures that lean about in the foreground of nineteenth-century drawings of Asia Minor, with crossed legs

and long bloomers. Not specially aesthetic, they give scale to
buildings or backgrounds, creating a little human interest for
the eye dazzled by tremendous prospects.

Having unloaded some boxes from our boat, the men made
off over the sandhills and vanished, and as we proceeded along
the edge of the beach I wondered where Demre was, for there
was no sign of human habitation. Though I knew that the
original harbour had been silted up since the days when it was
the port of Myra, I had imagined the town would be near
the sea, but when at last we drew in to the shore again it was to
a beach, deserted but for one small stone hut. Further off, the
dunes disappeared into a white shimmering glare of heat. A boy
with a donkey stood on the sand watching us.

We drifted quietly into a corner where the sand gave way to
the rocks of a little headland. The quietness that followed the
noise and vibration of the engine was profound, so complete
that far distant sounds could be clearly heard. The water
beneath us was so transparent that the boat might have been
suspended in space above turquoise-tinted sand, and to the
alchemy of early morning were added a hundred unformed
thoughts of this sea and all it stands for . . . antiquity, oil and
black olives, Odysseus, gods, Greek ruins and wine.

While the captain handed out the cargo, which was piled
among the rocks, the passengers pushed over each other in their
eagerness to disembark, the Turkish ladies staggering among the
Aegean rocks in their high-heeled shoes.

Once ashore, the charm of arrival began to wear off, for I
found that we were miles from Demre, which lay beyond the
sandhills. The donkey, which I had assumed to be the fore-
runner of others for our transport, was for heavy baggage. We
were to walk.

Carrying our belongings like refugees we set out for the village. At first, believing it was just over the first sandhill, I
walked philosophically, even with pleasure, taking off my shoes
and paddling in the clear sea; but presently it became necessary
to walk at an angle of forty-five degrees on the sloping beach,
where the sand slid from under the feet so that each leg had to
be dragged forward to join the one in front; and once away
from the water, the heat rushed up from the sand into the face,
while the feet, in sandals, were burnt as though on an iron deck.
A fat lady with two children struggled beside me in high-heeled

shoes, dripping with sweat and exhaustion but making no complaint beyond an occasional semi-comic grimace and a gasping cry of '*Çok sicak*!' Hussein, with the other men, was loping ahead in a way that showed he had been doing it all his life.

'Surely it will be over the next sandhill,' I thought, as we came to the top of the first, and this thought sustained me as we plunged and lurched down into the soft heat of the valley beyond: but it was not over the next or the next. For an hour we plodded on, and still there was no sign of Demre.

A group of people suddenly appeared on the horizon, struggling towards us through the sand, led by a patriarch with a beard and round cap, bloomers and a long stick. Hussein started forward, scrambled up the last few yards of the burning sandhill and took the old man's hand, raising it to his lips and then to his forehead; but the father seized him in his arms and pressed his face to the boy's cheek while tears streamed from his eyes. Then several elderly women came forward and gave him the same greeting.

Hussein had not seen his family for three years, the fat lady explained to me with moist eyes, and when, visibly affected, he returned, saying apologetically that he must now leave me, we were all a little tearful. He had already confided me privately to this fat woman's care and as soon as he had gone she and her husband made it clear with signs and Turkish words that they were going to look after me.

I followed my new friends – whose names I never knew – along a track between hedges and fences, past huts and houses, orchards and fields all dried out under the fierce sun and covered with a white fine dust. In several front gardens camels were lying down, chewing, or pottering about among the bushes, and by every house was a fat lamb on a lead, the *Bayram* victim awaiting the slaughter. At last we stopped at a gate and my friends signed for me to enter. I followed them through a vine-hung loggia and into the house.

It was like entering a cave or a dairy or wine-cellar, any delicious, cool and restful shelter from the heat. For a few seconds I was blind in the gloom; then shutters were pushed open and I saw that I was in a white hall. Two women in white came forward and said '*Hoş geldinez*', and I answered '*Hoş bulduck*', as Beria had taught me, meaning, 'I am glad to be here'. Since one of the women was old and obviously the mother of my hostess, I kissed her hand and held it to my forehead. She put her arm round my shoulder and led me into the house, into a large whitewashed room where a green dusk from the orchard was reflected through low cross-barred windows. The floor glowed with brilliant *kilim* rugs, and *kilims* and embroidered cushions covered the divans under the windows.

The women sat on the floor by the empty fireplace and I was motioned to a divan. I was barely seated before my hostess returned with a pitcher and basin, signalling for me to hold out my hands. She poured the water over them, and while I wiped them, knelt on the floor and removed my sandals, washing and drying my feet while the older women looked on approvingly.

A little girl came in with a tray and handed me an ice-cold lemon drink. Silence fell over us. There were no thoughts in my mind, for I was absorbing my surroundings through the senses rather than the brain. There was a rare beauty in the white-robed women sitting quietly on the carpets, their fine thin features and dark eyes framed by their veils, in the green gloom shining on the bare white walls of the simple room; but it was the peace and silence, the lack of fuss and pretension that were most wonderful of all.

I sat, relaxed and tranquil. No one was going to make any demands on me; I was not even obliged to go out into the heat again, for a messenger had been sent to find Naci, Yilmez's friend, and bring him to the house. It did not occur to anyone that he might be too busy to help me; they knew he would come and if he were physically prevented he would send someone in his place. In my mind Naci was already an old friend.

Outside, the sun beat down ferociously on the orange orchard and the almond trees. A *Bayram* lamb wandered about in the garden and from beyond came the small sounds of farmyard life. From time to time a little bell sounded, a foreign yet familiar note, and presently I saw the camels coming down the lane, nonchalant, sloppy yet co-ordinated, their big pigeon-toed feet flopping down into the dust, their long necks swaying and their dark-lashed eyes gazing indifferently over the hedges. All day long the Demre camels plod along the streets, carrying firewood, bundles, vegetables; superior, aloof and curiously elegant, while their little off-key bells clank and swing with the dead, hollow sound which, like the donkey's cry, the conch

shell, the fragmentary notes of the guitar, can evoke a whole
world.

*   *   *

Although Demre is only a small dusty village and the sea-port
of Myra has gone, with most of its buildings, there are still two
relics which attract foreign visitors from time to time. One is
the Lycian tombs carved in the hillside, and the other is a
battered sarcophagus, said to be that of St Nicholas, a martyred
bishop of Myra. St Nicholas is no longer there, for his bones
were carried off to Italy in the eleventh century by some pious
merchants from Bari. The Bari merchants just got there before
a party of Venetians, who came for the same purpose, and who
had to make do with someone else's bones. When the Russians
came, later still, there was nothing left at all.

St Nicholas was born at Patara, near Myra, and was much
loved for his kindness to children, sailors, and virgins, to all
of whom he became patron saint. The sailors and virgins may
have forgotten him but the children still honour him as Santa
Claus.

The Lycians, says Herodotus, came from Crete, led by
Sarpedon, brother of Minos. They were a virile, sea-going
people who retained their own alphabet and language against
Persian, Greek and Roman influences and who were heroic in
warfare. When the Persians defeated them at Xanthus they shut
all their women and children up in the city and burnt it to the
ground, then plunged into battle, fighting until the last man
was dead.

In some of their tombs, still scattered about Lycia, a stone
sarcophagus stands on a base – narrow, upright, resembling a
sentry-box; in others the dead lie in chambers carved out of the
cliffs, with columns and studded doors, like a strange city of
cliff-dwellers.

*   *   *

People began to arrive. Naci, home on vacation from Ankara
University, small and dark, with a shaven head, gentle egg-
shaped face and diffident manner; a garrulous man who spoke
French; a few hangers-on and observers. They were at my
service, they wanted only to know how they could help me,
though they said it would not be easy. There was no public

transport, no steamers, no buses; there was the *posta* (a jeep) that would take me part of the way to Fethiye but it would take days to do so; and the French-speaking friend knew a *kaptan* in the village, a *bon garçon*, who had a boat. If I liked he would arrange for me to hire it. He was pleased when I accepted the offer.

Meanwhile, said everyone, they would take me to see the tomb of St Nicholas, Père Noël, Santa Claus, since that was the reason why foreigners came to Demre. The Lycian tombs could be visited when it was cooler.

It was two o'clock and the heat was at its height as we walked along the village street, but all the men had turned out to have a look at me, some in the café, others ranged along the road under the dusty trees, standing to gaze, open-mouthed. I smiled and nodded to left and right and said '*Gün aydin*' (Good day) as we passed and they nodded shyly and said '*Gün aydin*' in their sheepish gruff manner. I was wilting when we reached the neglected white church of St Nicholas. Since it adjoined the police station, all the policemen came out to see what was going on and having nothing else to do joined in and left the building emptied of staff, telephones ringing and murderers uncaught. They took possession of the expedition, helping me carefully down the broken steps, calling out warnings of crumbling masonry and treacherous footholds, for the church has subsided so much that the front door is below ground-level.

Inside the mouldering building they proudly pointed out the faded frescoes on the walls and ceiling ('*çok eski*') and the damp and dubious sarcophagus in a dark corner ('Santa Claus ... Père Noel ... *çok, çok eski*') with such possessive pleasure that you might think they had made them all, themselves.

After the moist dusk of the church, the street seemed hotter and longer than ever, and I suggested going to thc hotel for a siesta; but Naci now told me that there was no hotel and that I was, naturally, to stay at his house.

I was very tired as we walked through the orchards of fruit and almond trees, over which hovered the shimmer of intense heat. At the far end of the lane were open gates and signs of farmyard life. A dog ran out barking.

'Welcome,' said Naci. 'This is my house.'

There was a two-storied building set among smaller outhouses; a farmyard; a great tree, and beyond, an orange orchard. People came out to meet us, and Naci introduced his family – parents, grandparents, sisters and brothers, babies, in-laws. They smiled.

'*Hoş geldinez*,' they said. 'You are welcome.'

They showed no signs of surprise at the arrival of a strange foreign woman; their main concern was to give hospitality, shelter and welcome to the traveller. From the ranks of family a pretty girl with hazel eyes stepped out.

'This is Yürdagül,' Naci said. 'My sister.'

'*Hoş geldinez*,' she said, raising my hand to kiss it, then hold-ing it to her forehead, and she laughed with pleasure when I kissed her on both cheeks and said '*Hoş bulduk*.'

She took me into the house, kneeling down inside the door to remove my sandals. We mounted a plain scrubbed staircase to a room where one wall was still unfinished, so that the orange trees, the green plain and the purple hills were spread before us. On a ledge outside were trays of apricots drying in the sun and on another tray were the stones which, said Naci, would be split open and the kernel used for cooking. 'We are poor people. We must make use of everything!'

'Be seated.'

There was a divan built along one wall, many cushions and coloured *kilims* on the floor. I chose the floor, and packed round with cushions, lay back against the rough adobe walls, my eyes on the tranquil landscape.

'My sister speaks no England and no France,' said Naci. 'You must speak to her in Turkey.'

I agreed placidly. Relief from the heat of the road, the com-fort of the shaded house, the serenity of the landscape had induced a mood of unspeakable content.

Yürdagül appeared with towels and an amphora of water. She knelt and washed my feet, then brought a pitcher of lemon juice, beaded from the ice-cold spring, sweetened lavishly in the Turkish manner. As she filled the glasses Naci talked from the divan where he sat crosslegged, saying that I was to sleep till it was cooler, after which we would go, on small animals, to see the *çok eski* tombs and the Roman theatre. He added that there was a wedding that night in the village and asked if I would like to go. I forgot my tiredness when I heard there would be Turkish dancing.

Yürdagül spread a double mattress on the floor of one of the inner rooms where the window looked out into the branches of a great mulberry tree. Square, whitewashed, with little furniture beyond a chest and *kilims*, it was a haven of peace, order and tranquillity. This world of rural simplicity revealed to me by the people of Demre, Uchisar and Bor has no relation to the dirt, heat, disorder and squalor of urban life. Its existence is rarely suspected by visitors who know only the big cities. It is hidden even from those who travel in Anatolia but stay in hotels or inns. It is only seen in the homes of the country people and is independent of poverty or wealth.

I woke to feel a gentle hand stroking my cheek. Yürdagül was kneeling beside me, with a glass of lemonade. It was time to get up, she said; I had been asleep for two and a half hours, and Naci was waiting to take me to the tombs.

In the dusty café among the eucalyptus trees the Turks were still sitting silently in their cloth caps and waistcoats, some in striped shirts, others in pyjama jackets. At first glance they looked a rough lot with their dark unshaven faces and their constant, unshifting stare, but all murmured politely when I smiled, inclining their heads a little sheepishly but with a friendly glimmer in their eyes. Many of them were Turks from Macedonia who were exchanged for Demre Greeks when repatriations were made.

The French-speaker I had met that morning was waiting for me with a dark anthropoid character whom he introduced as the *kaptan* of the *motor* that would take me to Fethiye. Tea was brought and we sat drinking the sweet strong liquid in little hot glasses, discussing the deal, while Naci went to get the donkeys for our ride to the hills.

The linguist had already settled the affair with the captain but it was all done over again in French for my benefit. The captain did not actually speak but gave grunts, which my friend interpreted to mean that he was willing to take me from Demre to Fethiye, that it was a very good boat with a very good motor and that it would cost 200 Turkish *lire* (about £20). I had such faith in Turkish honesty that I did not think of bargaining or questioning this price and consented at once, only specifying that I should disembark at the village of Kalkan to visit the Xanthus Valley. The captain grunted again to signify that this was agreed and the linguist added that he would meet me at eight o'clock next morning at the café. A small animal would be provided for my transport to the boat, which was some kilometres away, at Andraki.

During the conversation an audience was gathering round us and now I found I was the centre of a large crowd of fascinated Turks. They stared and stared unblinkingly, their only sign of emotion being a sort of intaken breath when I agreed so naïvely to the astronomical price demanded by the captain. Turks are the most expert and accomplished starers I have ever encountered and I cannot imagine why Edward Lear said they never stare or wonder at anything. They might not show signs of amazement, since their faces are rather impassive, but definitely they stare. Turkish staring is done with such passion and single-mindedness, it is so free of inhibition and bourgeois convention, so far beyond embarrassment and petty self-consciousness that it compels admiration. It has nothing to do with rudeness, for they are a naturally courteous people, it is more a national pastime, like fox-hunting or drinking *slivovitz* or playing the guitar. In western society the accidental meeting of the eyes between starer and stared-at results in one party, usually the starer, looking away hastily; but the really experienced staring Turk cannot be abashed by the object of his interest for he is unaware that he is doing anything offensive. If any eyes are averted it is more likely to be those of the stared-at; so that now, when I looked round, not an eye fell bashfully, nor did a cheek redden at having shamelessly listened-in to my conversation; on the contrary, I had the feeling that I was before a theatre audience who were waiting for the performance to continue, and so accustomed had I become to providing the entertainment that I did not think of questioning the situation or the familiar catechism that now followed.

'What is she?' 'Who is she with?' 'Where does she come from?' 'What nationality?' 'Where is she going?'

Those who had seen me in the morning, and were now fully informed of my history, passed the information round. She was French, she was from *Avustralya*, she was *touriste*. She was staying with Naci, but had lunched with the So-and-So's. She came from Finike and was hiring a *special motor* to go to Fethiye, T.L. 200. She had already been to Istanbul-Ankara-Kayseri-etc., and was on her way to Fethiye-Marmaris-Bodrum-etc.-etc.

When all this had been explained, the watchers returned to their marvelling contemplation of how I wrapped my handkerchief round my little hot tea glass; of how I took no sugar; of my dress, my camera, my hat, my bag, my red toenails. Then a venturesome character asked if I spoke Turkish, and I answered in Turkish, as at Uchisar reciting most of my vocabulary. Speaking my halting Turkish, I always felt like one of those birds that win wireless contests, for the performance seemed to rouse in my audience the same simple wonder, the almost protective admiration that a clever budgerigar might inspire. A wave of affectionate amusement surged towards me from the men, and when Naci came back with the donkeys I was farewelled with a rousing chorus of '*Güle, güle*'. Looking back I saw the men settling down to the tables with more tea to talk the whole thing over at leisure, still chuckling and repeating my remarks.

The setting sun was throwing long shadows into orchards and green fields where veiled women stooped and gathered, or rode on threshing sledges drawn by oxen. Embedded in the cultivated earth were ruined walls and fragments of buildings, and ahead was the line of vine-clad hills, now changing colour in the deepening light.

Beyond a farmyard at the foot of the hills stood a great Roman theatre among bushes and fallen masonry. Leaving our donkeys, we groped through the broken archways and corridors, scrambling over the fallen stone blocks, where herbs grew wild, into the arena. Here all was derelict; in the centre some dried-up tomato plants, and all round the grey tiers of seats rising up, immense and slightly overwhelming in the way of Roman theatres. High on the cliff-face beyond the amphitheatre, through a tangle of oleander and a kind of wild laburnum, were the Lycian tombs, eerie entrances to the underworld.

Like mountain goats, we picked our way up the vertical cliff-face, squeezing ourselves against the rock when the ledges were too narrow, stepping back quickly when the path disappeared beneath our feet. All round us in their burial chambers were the Lycians, those who have been left in peace, for many of the tombs have been robbed and lie broken and empty. Golden-brown, carved like the doors of houses, some are elaborate, others simple, some so badly damaged they are only rough cave-like openings, others apparently untouched. I entered one or two, small rocky cupboards with a view of the plain, pleasant places to sit with a book on a winter's day, protected from harsh

winds and exposed to the westering sun, which beats on the hillside all through the afternoon.

Arriving at a stable point, we rested and smoked a cigarette,
looking out over the calm evening scene. With the death of the
sun, the heat had gone from the air but round us a warmth still
lingered, caught in the golden rocks. Far off, the sky was fading
to a paler blue before deepening into night, and purple shadows
spread across the plain, intensifying the green of the orange
groves and poplar trees. At this time of day in any country the
past comes back as it rarely does in the midday glare; tenuous
and intangible things are in the atmosphere and with the
subtlety of lighting imagination works more freely. I wondered
how different was this scene in essence from the days when the
Lycian men went off to fight in the Trojan war. The sea-port of
Myra is now a small inland village, changed beyond recognition, inhabited by alien people, but the evening tranquility
could not have changed. The sun had set in the way we had just
watched, and shadows had grown long on the sunwarmed rocks
of the mountain with this same slow movement.

Sounds came from the village, camel bells, dogs and voices,
and from time to time that most disturbing of all sounds, the
agonized cry of donkeys. I breathed the scent of the flowers I
had picked in the ruined amphitheatre and the wild herbs I had
gathered on the hillside. This was the Turkey I was growing to
love; a peaceful rural world I shall never forget.

CHAPTER EIGHTEEN

A WORLD OF FRIENDS (*continued*)

AT the house Yürdagül was waiting for us with tea and cold drinks, and she now asked, through Naci, if I would like to have a shower. When I gratefully accepted she led me out to the courtyard where one of her uncles awaited us, dressed in pyjamas. Together we proceeded through the orchard to a field some distance from the house, where a curious brick tank was connected with a long, open, elevated water conduit. The uncle disappeared into a subterranean grotto beneath the tank and presently an engine started up and water from a pump began to splash into the brimming tank, the surplus careering away down the open drain. I stood slightly confused, looking for something that remotely resembled the sort of bath I had come to expect in Turkey.

Yürdagül gestured.

'*Banyo*,' she said.

I saw no *banyo*. '*Nerede?*' (Where?) I asked.

She pointed to the tank.

'*Burada!*' (Here!)

I was still bewildered, but obediently climbed to the top of the tank, knelt down by the running water and began to wash as well as I could, but Yürdagül was distressed. Calling above the noise of the pump and using pantomine she made it clear that I was to take off my clothes and get into the tank.

I was slightly surprised. Turkish women are very modest and the tank was in an elevated position in the midst of an open field, without a bush or tree in sight; but since she continued to demonstrate by pulling imaginary clothes over her head, I meekly took off my own, and slid feet first, into the tank, holding my breath as the coldness of the water rose up around me. I could feel my skin tingling as I sank down until I was submerged. It was like bathing in iced soda-water. All the accumulated fatigue and discomfort brought about by searing

winds, hot buses, stuffy bedrooms, flies and dust fell away and
I felt restored and invigorated.

She now indicated that I was to wash myself with soap and I
followed her instructions. Uncle had come out of his grotto and
walked away into the distance, hitching up his pyjama pants as
he went. He called to his niece without turning his head, asking
her to let him know when he might safely return and stop the
engine. I could see him standing far off, gazing discreetly at
the mountains, awaiting his summons.

When it was time to come out she instructed me to haul
myself up on the edge of the tank, where I dried my top while
my legs dangled in the water. The warm evening air on wet
skin emphasized the coolness of the bath I had just left and
brought on a blissful sensation that was as much exhilaration
as relaxation.

As I dressed in clean clothes Yürdagül seized the things I had
taken off and washed them vigorously in the tank. Uncle was
recalled and performed the remarkable feat of walking towards
us with his head turned in the opposite direction until Yürdagül
shouted that I was now fully dressed. The pump was turned off
and we returned to the house through the orchard.

Upstairs on the open-air landing I sat on my pile of cushions
on the floor. Warmth and physical comfort following on the
stimulation of the bath brought on a heavenly drowsiness and
I lay tranquilly, looking out over the plain to the hills where we
had ridden a few hours before.

In the dusk Naci talked quietly from his divan, in tentative
English.

'You climbed the mountain very beautifully. You are very
light. Turkish ladies could not climb this mountain.'

'No? Why not, Naci?'

'Turkish ladies have very big stomachs. English, American,
French and Australian ladies do not have big stomachs because
they are very sportsman . . . tennis, cricket, baseball, football
. . . very good . . . but Turkish ladies play no sportsman.'

'But your sister . . . she is not fat . . . She is very pretty.'

'Ah, my sister . . .' he smiled affectionately, '. . . my sister is
perhaps a little sportsman.'

I was too indolent to disillusion him about the cricket, baseball and football, and we sat on in a peaceful silence until a
moving light shone from below and Yürdagül came up the

stairs with a lantern and a tray of food. All fresh, all beautifully cooked, it had been prepared by the little sportsman, but having served us she retired to eat below, while Naci and I, sitting cross-legged round the tray, ate with our forks from the same dishes.

By the time we had finished, night had fallen and the Lycians in their tombs had vanished into the soft darkness, but soon a grey light spread upon the landscape, muted, luminous, and in an instant a full moon rose from behind the dark line of hills, and shone in on us. All kinds of country sounds came through the sweet cool air, but absorbed though I was in the peace and beauty of the night, in my thoughts of the Lycians in the hillside, I was aware of a strange dull vibration that came from far away, filling and enveloping the night, dominating all lesser sounds; a drum, beating in a curious rhythm, at once muffled and penetrating, exciting, sensual, evocative, almost tangible.

'Listen,' said Naci. 'It's the wedding party. Shall we go, or are you too tired?'

Drowsiness was gone at once. Sleep was out of the question while that primitive sound travelled, searching, demanding, through the night.

There was a curious excitement walking along in the moonlight, a sense of liberation, of being anonymous, young, irresponsible. The blanching light threw dark filigree patterns in our path, and at times the hedges plunged the lane into shadow. Trees rose up around us, black and opaque, and houses were ebony blocks, lit by small amber squares. Occasionally, a voice called a greeting to us in the darkness, and we replied in unison, laughing for no reason.

The wide plain was covered by a softening web, and smooth surfaces glittered as though wet with dew. We turned into a narrow track where mud lay thick between the stones. The drum was now strong and insistent, accompanied by a melancholy, monotonous *zurna* (pipe). In the darkness a yellow light shone from the ground, a hurricane lamp, smoky and obscured, intermittently extinguished by the black forms that moved before it.

It was quite unlike the wedding celebrations at Üchisar. Naci had already explained that the men would be dancing in one part of the house and the women in another, and that when we arrived Yürdagül and I must not let the men see us, but go to the women's quarters as quickly as possible; but since the night was so beautiful the dancing was taking place out of doors, and as all the men were gathered at the gate it was impossible not to see them and difficult for them not to see us. We should have scurried past in the darkness but Yürdagül drew me back into the shadows and whispered to Naci that we were going to wait for a few minutes.

My heart leapt into my mouth with excitement. In the warm smoky light the men were singing and drinking, while behind them in the shadows the musicians pumped out their strange music. From time to time a dancer would step into a cleared space and sometimes alone, sometimes accompanied, execute the solemn movements of the Turkish male dance, the concentrated, drunken tottering which seems so clumsy and is so difficult to do well. They were so grave in their dancing, so deliberate, so unrelated to the stupified men who had stared at me blankly in the *café* and the village street that afternoon. Wine and *raki* had released them from their normal reserve and put poetry into their heavy limbs, giving them a new dignity, as the smoky lamp had translated their homely surroundings into something foreign and wonderful. The moving shadows in the yellow light, the lurching, graceful figures dark against the clear night sky, the blanching moonlight beyond . . . all wild and secret places were here, the mountains of Albania, the camp in the desert . . . remote and savage worlds beyond my experience, known only in imagination.

As the wine and *raki* went round, the men became noisy, singing in broken snatches, shouting hoarsely. Bursts of laughter rang out and echoed round the dark garden. At a sign from Naci we hurried past to the *harem* at the back of the house.

Unable to see or be seen by the men, the women were sitting on the ground in a triple circle. All in white, their veils flashed where the moonlight caught the gold and sequins. Round their necks and from their ears hung golden coins. Their ghostly forms were as striking as those of the dark gyrating men, but there was a world of difference in the atmosphere of this gathering. There was no music, and everyone seemed set for a good gossip on marriage and child-birth and jam-making. Babies were nursed and handed round for cuddling, toddlers stroked and petted, and older children ran about restlessly, stepping over the women or squeezing in beside them. After the colour and drama of the men's gathering this domestic, nursery atmosphere was dull and disappointing.

I sat down on the ground with Yürdagül, but she whispered that the bride was coming to welcome me, and presently a beautiful young girl, jangling with gold necklaces and ear-rings, with a gold-dusted veil over her head, came towards me, took my hand, kissed it and raised it to her forehead.

'*Hoş geldinez.*'

She called to one of the endless female relations paddling about in the background and at once a kitchen chair was produced and set in a prominent place. I was invited to sit on it, as though on a throne. I hate these rigid chairs, I hate sitting upright out of doors and I was perfectly happy where I was with Yürdagül, but I was lifted to my feet and obliged to sit on the hard unsympathetic wood, which, set on uneven ground, rocked each time I moved.

The musicians from the men's party appeared and took up their stand as close to me as possible, so that every blast and blow might travel straight into my ear. A hissing lamp was brought and held high to shine in my face, ostensibly so that I could see but also so that everyone could have a good look at me. There was much murmuring and persuading and then a young girl stepped into the centre of the gathering and began to dance. She moved sedately in a circle, lethargically swaying and moving her arms, without grace or charm, without a hint of oriental wriggles or convolutions. Everyone clapped politely, and after some pressing she repeated the performance.

She was followed by another young girl, then a reluctant matron, both of whom shuffled round in the same sheepish manner. There was none of the gaiety or vitality that makes country or native dances so memorable.

I was hoping things would liven up, but there was no sign of further talent or initiative and the first performers were followed by a long pause; then to my horror I found that the bride was standing before me, inviting me to dance. I shook my head, but everyone cried out and Yürdagül whispered ... 'Please ... it's a *kermesse* ... please dance ...' and fearing that refusal might seem rude or unfriendly I agreed if she would join me.

We stood up, the lamp was raised so that all might see and an explosion came from the band. I had not the faintest idea

what I should do so I raised both arms above my head and
began to move round sideways, rotating my hips in the way
I had learnt in Tahiti. The effect was gratifying. The women
broke out into shouts of delight, and encouraged by their
reaction I embellished the performance with impressions of
Turkish dancing based on local films and low class *bôites* in
Istanbul. This was greeted with even more applause, and
Yürdagül, smiling rapturously, sat down on the ground to
watch me, spellbound. I circled in the dust, enjoying the moonlight, the cool fresh air and the movements of my Arabian
hula, occasionally giving it a Spanish touch by snapping my
fingers like castanets. Everything was received with enthusiasm
and when I stopped the women crowded round, calling out to
continue. '*Çok güzel, çok güzel*, they cried, and once more
the music began, specially for my benefit.

The older women were the most excited. They shouted with
glee as though to say, 'This is how dancing was in our day,' and
one after another came up to me as I danced and made the
sign of a circle over my head, which, Naci explained later, was
the equivalent of crowning me or awarding me an Oscar. I
called to them to join me but they refused, though one or two
wriggled their hips nostalgically.

After me, no one else would dance, and the band soon returned
to the other side of the house where the men were drinking,
whence we heard the thumps and wails, the shouts and songs
mingling with the music. Yürdagül and I were both excited
and found it hard to sit still among the placid matrons. The
dancing, the moonlight, the rhythm had stirred us and I longed
to go round and dance with the men, though I knew it was out
of the question. As though sensing our mood, one of the older
women took us into the house, to an upstairs room where we
could hear the music and dance without being seen.

In the front garden the scene had changed, for the men had
had more to drink and were now quite uninhibited. The singing
and shouting were louder and the dancing had become wilder
and there was an impression of people dancing round a fire,
for the light seemed to flicker and move. Into this black and
orange setting two figures leapt – two men, supple and slight,
one with a black shirt and thick black hair. Together they
danced, so brilliantly, with such extraordinary precision that
all the other lurching figures retired, drew back into the

shadows, sank down to watch them. The boy in the black shirt was inspired. By his grace and genius the slow pedestrian Turkish dance was transformed. His leaps and turns were winged like those of a great ballet dancer and his limbs were so informed with lightness that he seemed to hover in the air before descending. All beauty, youth and pagan joy, he danced because he must, with no consciousness of being different from his companions, and with a shock I realized I was watching one who might have become a great artist, but who would live and die obscure.

'Who is it?' I whispered to Yürdagül as we watched from the shadows. 'Where does he come from?' and to my astonishment she replied 'It is Fikret, my brother, and he is dancing with Naci.'

As the two brothers finished their dance and retired into the circle of men, someone touched my arm. Behind me in the shadowy room a group of women had gathered and were now sitting on the floor. The woman who had taken my arm was fat and elderly but she moved with dignity and grace, seeming to glide. She drew me back into the room, and signing that I was to watch, she began to dance to the music, a wonderful sensuous dance such as I had never seen before. With the beauty of her movements her age and fat disappeared and she might have been a slender young girl. From the faces of the watching women it was clear that she was someone of importance. Presently she signed that I was to imitate her, and receding slowly across the floor, beckoned me to follow. Silently, in a circle, we danced round the room while the women clapped softly and the broken light from below flickered on the ceiling. Then the music stopped and she took my hand, kissed me on both cheeks and put her arms around me; but I kissed her hand and held it to my forehead.

Later, walking home in the moonlight through the sound of ghostly camel-bells, through the scents of grass and flowers, we danced among ourselves. Fikret flung himself into the air, turned and came down like a drifting feather, while Yürdagül and I essayed the movements that the old woman had taught us; but soon we became quiet, for we were all tired, and I was thinking of the two dancers I had seen. Past the houses, now in darkness, the darker trees and lanes, we walked dreamily, looking from time to time at the ever-receding hills, at the great white disk in the sky, feeling the scented warmth that still rose from the earth.

At the house a dim lamp had been left burning for us. Creeping carefully into the dark interior we made our way up the stairs to the landing where the moonlight poured in, blanching everything it touched. When the others had gone to bed I stood alone, looking out across the plain to the Lycians, listening to the little sounds, the creaks and rustles of insects, the tinkling bell of an animal moving in its sleep, the barking watchdogs and the lonely cry of a donkey.

CHAPTER NINETEEN

TO SEA IN A SIEVE

I SLEPT deeply, stretched out on the floor with Yürdagül beside me. I woke at five, when she got up, but she whispered that I was to wait until she called me. Outside, I could see a cool fresh morning and a green shade of fruit trees; below were the sounds of the farmyard – cows, roosters, children feeding chickens. Distant voices and camel-bells came clearly from the village.

We breakfasted on the landing, looking out on the flat plain where already heat was shimmering and a pale haze hovered before the tombs on the hillside. Everything we ate had been grown or made by Yürdagül – black olives from the garden, goat cheese, black bread, little sweet green apples from the orchard, and bowls of yoghurt and hot foaming milk.

Yürdagül accompanied us to the lane with affectionate farewells, then turned back sadly with the old dog while Naci and I continued on to the village. I was silent, for I did not want to leave Demre; and there was something else on my mind.

'Naci,' I said hesitantly, 'If there had been a hotel in the village I should have gone to it . . .'

He spoke before I could finish the sentence.

'Ah, no,' he said. 'Ah, no;' and the dignity and sincerity of his voice abashed me; yet I wanted to show my appreciation in some way.

'Perhaps there is something I could send from Istanbul?' I said. 'Some books . . .? You have all been so good to me.'

He shook his head, looking a little sad.

'Nothing. We have done nothing,' he said. 'Why shouldn't we be good to you? You are one of us.'

The repetition of his words on paper gives no hint of the quality behind them. There was no pride or resentment, only a gentle sadness, and my embarrassment at having made the suggestion was offset by the warmth that I felt each time I encountered this Turkish goodness and generosity.

In the village Naci led me to the café, where we sat down to await the *bon garçon*, the captain of my boat. Though it was so early a number of men were already there, sitting motionless on their chairs, so exactly as they had been the day before that the firelit dancers of the wedding party might never have existed.

The captain came at last and after several rounds of tea and much repetition of the previous day's conversation departed again to get his baggage, while Naci went for the donkey. The men gathered round my chair. One after another they came forward to take my hand ... my first Demre host; Hussein; his old father; the linguist; stray men from the wedding party. Each one wished to give me tea and the crowd became so carried away that complete strangers were coming forward to shake hands. The older men stood, four-square, staring like Hittite bulls; the young ones asked my name, where I came from and how many babies I had. They all spoke to me in Turkish, except the inevitable linguist who started off brashly by saying 'Spik Ingleesh?' or perhaps 'Parley Fronksy?' and who, when I answered in the specified language, stared at me in consternation or went off into shrill cackles.

By the time Naci returned with the donkeys I had drunk five or six cups of tea. I said good-bye all round, shook hands with my more intimate friends and set off for Andraki, followed by shouts of '*Güle, güle.*' At the police station, all the policemen crowded at the door to wave and call good-bye.

In the hot morning air the donkeys moved slowly, frequently stopping and refusing to stir so that we had to prod them with sticks. In the cornfields we passed a few peasants going to work with their camels, but for the most part all was deserted.

We were riding through a narrow valley, the dried-out mouth of the River Andriace. Beyond the parched brown stubble was a derelict Roman cornmill; then the ground became sodden and we found ourselves at a marsh, where the land takes over from the wandering, choked-up arm of the sea. We picked our way over stepping-stones to a mill-house where two coloured boats floated among the bulrushes and an outdoor privy was poised precariously over the stream. The Roman ruins and some scattered Lycian tombs were the only other signs of human existence; the only sound the slow splashing of the mill-wheel.

This was Andraki, the ancient Andriace. Where the sandy soil supports dry scrub, a harbour sheltered grain-ships; where the little mill-wheel turns, corn was loaded at a busy quay. Traffic coming from the east towards Italy called there, among it the ship taking St Paul to Rome. Now, the land has taken over from the sea, and Andraki has the still, abandoned feeling of such places, silent this morning in its foretaste of approaching heat.

The people in the mill-house welcomed us with drinks of water and chairs set out in the shade. Presently a handsome young soldier with a rifle appeared, announcing simply and affably that he was coming with me as far as Kalkan. After another long wait the *kaptan* arrived with two children and a great deal of personal baggage, mainly food, all of which with the children, the soldier and the gun were packed into a small open boat. As an after-thought my bag was handed in and I was invited to enter. I said good-bye to the miller and his children and embraced Naci, who farewelled me with moist eyes and many invitations to return to Demre.

The sun, now well above the mountains, shone down on the deserted cornfields. Slowly we moved over the suave surface of the river, attended by our own widening ripples, which travelled further and further until they reached the bulrushes and set them gently rocking. The cornfields gave way to swamp, with here and there a Lycian tomb, upright, like a high-class privy. Along the bank and in the sloping hills were scattered the grey stones of ruins; against the sky a ruined *kale* (castle) was outlined. Then came the Roman granary, built for Hadrian's navy, and beyond again, Byzantine walls and towers rising from weed-grown streets. Around us little black wild ducks skimmed gaily, and here and there small tortoises advanced slowly, stolidly into a stream so clear that every corrugation on the sand below shone separate and distinct.

At the wide and shallow entrance, sandbanks blocked our way. Suddenly the captain stood up, unbuttoned his fly, unwound a primitive sort of cummerbund from his waist and stepped gingerly out of his trousers, revealing long white cotton drawers, home-made, rather Persian in cut, with crochet round the ankles. These he tucked up carefully before climbing into the water, where he waded alongside, guiding the boat between the sandbanks.

A long island shelters the coast here, turning the sea to a gentle river. On the arid crags of the mainland the rocks are red, matching the castles that rise from them, but by the water they are white, stained by the tides. In the cornflower sea, where shafts of sunlight strike down to the depths, are rocky islets, thick with scrub, their parched stones seeming to increase the limpid coolness of the element around them.

Our boat was so small that we travelled almost within touch of the shore and our movement so quiet that we made only the barest disturbance on the surface. Beneath us all was calm and still, and the little islets appeared less as objects floating on the sea than as integral parts of the earth beneath it. The line of their foundations, like the roots of a tooth, could be seen going down among the submarine cliffs and deep strange valleys to the mountain tops whence they sprang.

'Tristomon,' said the young soldier suddenly, pointing to the mainland where a ruined castle stood out on a hilltop and an ancient town trickled down the sides of a rust-coloured spur. Below were white houses and olive trees, and at the water's edge, scattered Lycian tombs, ship-wrecked, lurching to one side, up to their necks in water.

The captain, mumbling about Customs papers and formalities, now steered the boat into the quay where he disembarked with children and baggage. An hour later he returned, accompanied by a bucolic character in pointed sheep-skin shoes, wool socks and cross-garters, who, he said, was having a ride to Fethiye. The villagers had done their best to entertain me, inviting me into their houses, bringing me glasses of strange sweet tea in which herbs had been infused, but I was cross, for Soldier-boy had told me this was the captain's village and he had been visiting his wife while I sat sweltering on the muddy quay.

At sea again, he spread a mattress on the tiny foredeck and solicitously urged me to lie down. Then he began to open the string-bags and bundles he had brought from his house, spreading the contents before me with the ingratiating manner usually associated with guilt. He wore the expression of one who has begun to suspect that ignorance of a foreign language may not be synonymous with stupidity and that perhaps I might be capable of realizing what was going on around me.

Before eating, he took off his trousers and lunched in his

crochet lawn underpants; afterwards, wrapping all the remaining food in newspapers, he stowed it away in an embroidered sack. Opening another bundle he took out a second-best pair of black-and-grey striped trousers, wide in the waist, baggy in the legs and low in the crutch, into which he climbed, carefully pushing down his crochet frills and lashing in the extra bulk with a scrappy cummerbund. He then stretched himself out in the bow and went to sleep, leaving the soldier at the tiller. His friend, grey in tone and covered with barnacles, curled up beside him.

Over the still, transparent water we moved, between islands and shore, steered by the soldier, who had become so engrossed in my Turkish-English dictionary that at times he nearly ran us aground; then the islets fell behind and we were on the open sea. The immortal coastline unfolded ahead and the little boat followed it faithfully, in the shadow of the rocks where Greeks had walked and climbed and cities stood and crumbled. The sense of antiquity, of a continuing past is so strong on this southern Turkish coast that it dominates all else, and the personality of the Greeks so informs the sea, the air, that neither time nor change can wear it away.

Suddenly the captain woke up and said something to the soldier, who looked startled and answered very firmly, '*Yok!*' The captain told him to ask me the same question and reluctantly, disapproving, the young man turned to me.

'Would you like to go to *Meis Ada*?' (Meis Island).

I looked up at him in astonishment, for *Meis Ada* is a small *Greek* island lying close to the port of Kaş. Thinking that I had misunderstood, I asked the captain in my pidgin Turkish if he were not taking me to Fethiye via Kaş and Kalkan.

He said, '*Evett* (Yes). Kaş – Meis Ada – Kalkan – Fethiye.'

It was strange; but suddenly thinking of Greek gaiety and lightness and the Greek way with beauty I had a longing to be again on a Greek island, even though I knew that Meis, which the Greeks call Castelorizo, is poor and its population half starved.

'*Tamam*,' I said. '*Tamam*.' (Okay).

He nodded and mumbled to his friend, who did not seem to care either way, but the young soldier, looking very alarmed, began to gather his belongings together as though he would jump out of the boat immediately. When I asked if he were

coming with us he shook his head violently and said, '*Yok!*'
drawing his finger across his throat and saying 'Boom-Boom'.
Since *Yunanistan* (Greece) was more or less at war with Turkey,
he explained, he would of course be killed as soon as he landed,
and I too, he added in pantomime, for the *Yunan* were *çok fenar*
(very bad).

I could not see why the Greeks should want to kill me any
more than the Turks but when I said this the soldier said No,
I should be safe in Kaş because the Turkish people were good.
I gave up and sat watching the misty blue island becoming
clearer and more substantial across the brilliant afternoon sea.
Never did hostile territory look less sinister than that little
island, the ancient Megista, floating like a sapphire before us,
and in my mind's eye I could see the white houses going up
the hill, the little port, the *caïques* and the coloured dinghies in
the harbour. Unable to convince me of my danger, Soldier-boy
washed his hands of me and by the time we entered the harbour
at Kaş was all packed up and ready to depart.

The little port faces into the afternoon sun, which glittered
on the windows of the houses and on the simple white buildings
on the hill. As I climbed ashore all the stored heat of summer
leapt at me from the village street.

A nineteenth-century traveller described Kaş as consisting of
three or four houses and a Customs House, and a large scorpion
which nearly bit him, but there is now a little more to it than
that. In a vine-hung café by the water's edge the male population were sitting on their chairs, with the women and children
leaning from their windows above. I smiled and nodded as I
went through the town and the people called '*Gün Ayden*'. A
Lycian tomb stood alone on the roadside, like a letter-box, and
on the opposite hill were a ruined church and the remains of a
Greek theatre and market place, for Kaş was the ancient
Antiphellus and has souvenirs of its classical past.

The captain had said that I must get official permission to go
to Meis, but when I made my request to the *kaymakan*, a friendly
man in slippers and pyjamas, he laughed and said in French
that as far as he was concerned we could go there any time we
liked so long as we didn't expect him to come with us.

'I suppose you realize,' he said, 'that if you go in a Turkish
boat you may not be very popular, for the Greeks do not like
us.'

M

While we talked, his wife plied me with lemonade and Turkish delight and poured cologne over my sticky hands. They were both horrified to hear what I was paying the boat captain. When I said I had agreed because I trusted Turkish honesty the *kaymakan* seemed as much despairing as pleased.

Escorted by his son, a bright little boy of ten, I went to notify the police, but it took some time to find them for they were all asleep or at home or in the café. Eventually the little boy led me to a kind of *caserne* on the edge of the harbour, deserted but for a very old man who was asleep in a blanket and striped nightshirt. Fighting back the nausea brought on by the heat and the intolerable stench of the W.C. I penetrated into the back of the building and found a dormitory, hideous in squalor and disorder, where unmade beds with sordid mattresses gaped and strange garments lay about on the floor or hung from pegs on the wall. The little boy was at a loss, and since the old man could not understand what I wanted, I pushed him gently out of the building with the words, 'Police ... Passport ... Quickly.'

He shambled away down the steps to the café and I prepared for a long hot wait in the room furthest away from the sleeping quarters.

After some time footsteps ascended the stairs and a gentle, closely-shaved bonehead in a thick woollen uniform appeared. He smiled at me disarmingly and asked what I wanted.

The little boy, whom I had expected to act as my interpreter, was suddenly stricken dumb and I had to explain for myself that I was on my way from Demre to Fethiye in a special *motor* and I wished to go to *Meis Ada*, now, at once. Having painfully studied every detail of my passport, Bonehead picked up my *permis de séjour* and began turning over the pages, motioning me to a chair as though there might be a long wait ahead. I sat down uneasily, for I recognized in his eye the look that comes to all semi-literates confronted with official documents which they cannot understand but which they feel instinctively are suspect. He read every line in the little booklet, spelling out the words to himself four times over, but finally, with a smile of extraordinary sweetness, he cautiously signed the card – in the wrong place – and said that it was *Tamam* and I could go to *Meis Ada*. I pattered thankfully down the stairs and into the street.

At the quay there was still no sign of the *bon garçon*, and I stood rather crossly in the heat wondering where he was. Time was passing and if we were to get to Meis at all we should have to leave soon. I was walking about impatiently when a small boy with a shaved head and pyjama jacket silently presented himself before me.

'*Hanim* (Woman),' he said. '*Polis. Motor kaptan.*'

I had suspected that something was wrong from the fact that the captain had not appeared, and now, when I understood that the little boy had been sent to take me to the police, I was angry.

'*Polis yok!*' I said, lifting my chin. '*Polis bitmek* . . . passport *tamam. Meis Ada tamam!*' But he kept on repeating that I must go to the police, even tugging at my arm.

I followed him back to the *caserne*, and up the wooden steps to the nest at the top. I could not believe my eyes when Bonehead rose from his table and, still smiling sweetly, asked for my passport.

'But you said it was finished!' I cried. '*Tamam Meis* . . . *Bitmek passport.*' He went on smiling and holding out his hand.

'*Gümrük*,' he said. '*Gümrük* (Customs).'

It was important, even necessary, he explained when I protested, refusing to hand it over. It would not take long – perhaps thirty minutes. I was to sit down . . . he offered the kitchen chair again. Nothing on earth would have made me sit down. I said I would go with him and my passport.

In the *Gümrük* office several people had gathered to see the fun and by the time I entered with Bonehead and the little boy and all the hangers-on who had accumulated and followed us in, there was not much room to spare. The atmosphere here was very different from that in the police station. There were things in boxes, files on the desk and behind it a rather bright-eyed unTurkish little man. When I asked him why I was being detained when the police and the *kaymakan* had all said I could go to Meis he answered coldly that he was the Customs officer and I must have his clearance before I could leave the country. When I protested that I wasn't leaving the country, that I would be back in a couple of hours he became annoyed.

'Madame,' he said. 'Meis is Greek, not Turkish. Foreign territory.' He thrust a bundle of forms at me and asked for my passport. It made no difference that I had no luggage beyond camera and handbag. I was told to sit down and declare how much Turkish money I had, where I had got it and at what rate of exchange, how much jewellery I possessed, how much foreign currency . . .

I filled in the form hurriedly, overlooking the foreign currency section, and handed it back, muttering to myself angrily. The lovely afternoon was slipping away and it would soon be too late to make the trip to Meis if we were to reach Fethiye that evening. I forgot all the kindness, patience and sympathy I had had from the Turks and when the official began to question me about how I had been spending my money in Turkey I lost my temper and told him what I thought of government red tape and the obtuseness and ignorance of officialdom, adding that I didn't wonder no one ever came to Turkey, that everyone went to Greece. In any other country I should have been put in jail but I was too angry to care, and when the *Gümrük* told me to open my handbag I emptied the contents all over his desk.

'Have a good look!' I said, seeing him fumbling through my letters, opening my compact and lipstick. 'Make sure I'm not smuggling anything!' but as I spoke he found my note-case and with a melodramatic cry pulled out a bundle of dollars which I was keeping for Bulgaria.

'Aha!' he cried, in the voice of one who has uncovered a spy-ring single-handed. 'Aha!' He fingered them. 'These are not declared on the Customs form, madame. Madame, this is a serious offence!'

I snatched at the dollars.

'No,' I said. 'You asked me about Turkish money and I told you. That's American money and it's nothing to do with you.'

'You have broken the law,' he said. 'You have not declared money. Do you understand, madame? And *Meis Ada* is Greek, not Turkish. You wish to go to enemy territory and return here. And you have broken the law!'

He was getting out more papers, filling in more forms. I saw, quite clearly, the inside of a Turkish country jail and smelt the lavatory. I gave in.

'All right!' I said in English. 'I won't go to Meis. Will that do? I won't go!'

He didn't understand but he realized I was disturbed.

'Meis *yok*!' I said, and I added, 'Now I hope you're satisfied!'

I glared all round and as I did a moaning cry rose, not only from the *Gümrük* but from the onlookers.

'Meis *yok*? Not go to Meis? Why not?'

'Because he's spoilt everything,' I said, waving at the *Gümrük* and speaking in the martyred, satisfied way of outraged children. 'I don't want to go.'

'There there . . .' they said. 'He didn't mean it.' 'Of course you're going to Meis . . .' 'But you must go to Meis now, whatever happens.' The *Gümrük* was as vocal as the others.

They were the most disarming people in the world. Over and over again in Anatolia, when I reached the stage of despair or fury, I was melted by some such kindness, some such childlike gesture. In a second all was forgotten and forgiven. I was patted on the back; invited to take tea in the café. I smiled and shook hands all round and everyone responded, even the *Gümrük*. As I left the building, followed by all who could be spared from their official duties, the others stood waving and calling '*Güle, güle*'.

Down in the café there was uproar. A loudspeaker fixed to a tree was disgorging a political speech with such force that it could be heard all over Kaş. I was led to a table immediately beneath the loudspeaker, where, seated on a rickety chair, I answered questions as best I could about my private life and activities; but in time the noise penetrated to my hosts and brought the conversation round to politics.

The most vocal of my companions was a man named Mehmet, a telegraphist who spoke reasonable English.

'We think,' said Mehmet, 'We think the reason why England always favours the Greeks is because of Mr Philip. Have you heard of this Mr Philip?'

'No, I haven't. Who is he?'

'He is a Greek man. And he is married with Elizabet. That is why England is so fond of Greece.'

Mehmet wanted to emigrate to Australia and get a job in the post office there. Earnestly, above the howls that came from the wireless, he exhorted me to use my influence with the Australian government to have things quickly finalized. Encouraged by his enthusiasm several others also decided to emigrate and I had a busy time answering their questions about prospects in Australia.

Carrying packets of sickly sweet biscuits and Turkish delight

which Mehmet had pressed upon me, I went down to the quay
to look for the captain.

He came at last, surly, baffled, scowling. The *Gümrük* had
made him pay for the ship's papers, he said. To get a clearance
for going to Meis he had paid forty *lire* and he wanted me to
reimburse him. Though I knew now that he was overcharging
me I hesitated to argue just as we were setting out to sea together in a small boat, and I consulted Mehmet, who was
puzzled by the whole thing. I told the captain I would settle
with him when we arrived in Fethiye.

'Good-bye,' called Mehmet, as we moved away from the
quay. 'Don't forget to ask your government about me coming
to Australia . . . and I will ask the *kaymakan* about the money . . .'
I did not hear the rest. I waved again and settled down in the
boat.

CHAPTER TWENTY

A MAGICAL NIGHT

AFTER all the fuss and drama, *Meis Ada* was rather an anticlimax. No one tried to shoot or even insult us. The most interesting thing about the detour was the way my shipmates and I were drawn together at the prospect of facing the enemy, yet how quickly, once ashore among the Greeks, I found the mainland reassuming the hostile, almost threatening character it wore when I first saw it from Rhodes. The enemy is usually the distant or unknown.

Far more dramatic were the results of the delay, for whereas we should have been in Fethiye before dark, we were still floundering about in the vicinity of Kaş when night fell. A wind came up, the sea turned rough, and beyond the shelter of the islands life in the little boat became disturbing. The awning, having flapped itself to rags, was taken down, so that night dews were added to sea-spray; water sloshed over the side and from time to time the engine choked, hiccoughed and stopped. I could take the dark, the wind, the rough sea, even the water coming in, but I did not like the engine failing when we were so close to the rocks. I said nothing at first but on the fourth failure I suggested we put further out to sea. The captain, annoyed about his forty *lire*, glared at me sullenly and refused to answer. His remedy for all the engine's ills was to pour in something out of a kerosene tin and peer at it with his little anthropoid eyes. It was unnerving. Lolling about in the trough of the waves the boat moved steadily closer to the rocks with each heave of the sea, and it was literally at the last minute that the engine was started up in time to save us from disaster. There was something extremely hostile about this ancient barren coast at night, it emanated the chill of the moon seen in daylight through a telescope, a grey dead stone hanging in space, giving off no light or life.

Apart from the *bon garçon*, my companions in the boat were the old man with barnacles and a youth of about eighteen who had replaced Soldier-boy. The old man was as silent and surly as the captain but the boy was friendly. He kept assuring me that all was well, misinterpreting my anxiety as a fear of rough sea or seasickness. No one was in the least concerned about the state of the engine or the possibility that we might end up on the rocks; I don't think there were enough brains between the three of them to imagine such a possibility.

'*Deniz güzel*' (Beautiful sea), the dopey boy kept saying to me. '*Çok* . . .' as we sloshed broadside-on towards the rocks . . . '*Çok güzel.*'

It was too dark to find words in the Turkish dictionary so I had to be content with replying vehemently, '*Güzel yok. Deniz çok fenar!* (Sea very bad)' at which he gave a delighted half-witted burst of laughter.

Since there was nothing to be done about the engine I lay down on my mattress to get what rest I could before the ship-wreck. Dopey covered me over in a solicitous manner and thrust a few sodden sweet biscuits at me. It was quite comfortable on the deck, apart from the fact that my head was lower than my feet, but when I reversed my position the sea washed over my face. As it was, there was a constant slow seepage going on some-where down my back. Lying in my damp cushions I made plans for the crisis, wondering what I should try to save.

Having arranged this in my mind I went off to sleep, waking suddenly as a wave came in over my feet. The wind was stronger now and the sea very black and angry. Oily swells of water heaved themselves towards the cliffs, sinking down with a sinister sucking sound or breaking upon the treacherous rocks which glimmered pale in the darkness. The night was thick, for the moon had not yet risen, and I lay quietly on the deck looking up at the sky. Dark and blue it hung over us, and suddenly I saw the stars, the same stars that the Lycians and Carians and Rhodians had watched as they set off to Troy; the stars that had guided Odysseus home to Ithaca and led the Argonauts up the Bosphorus on the way to the Golden Fleece. I forgot all about the imminent disaster and lay happily, thinking of these things.

'Kalkan,' said Dopey suddenly, pointing away into the darkness, where a few lights shone dimly. '*Köy* (village).' As he spoke the engine choked and stopped.

I sat up, feeling the time for action had come.

'Kalkan,' I said firmly to the captain, who was trying to thread a bit of string into the engine. 'Kalkan *şimdi* (now). Fethiye *yarin sabah*, (tomorrow morning).'

He looked at me lethargically and said 'Fethiye'.

I was determined. I had no intention of continuing this ridiculous voyage. I looked as threatening as I could and pointed out into the darkness. 'Fethiye *YOK*! Fethiye *yarin sabah*. Kalkan *şimdi*!'

He still looked blank so I added a few words about police, *basin carte* and *kaymakan* and seeing a slow, dim light beginning to move behind his primitive features I hurriedly said that unless it was Kalkan *şimdi* there would be no money at Fethiye.

There was nothing to stop him strangling me, or throwing me overboard and helping himself to the money but he was too dumb to think of it, unless it was just Turkish decency that protected me. The threat of non-payment woke him from his trance. He muttered about his two hundred *lire* and the extra forty for the *Gümrük* papers, and I repeated that he would be paid in Fethiye, but only if we put into Kalkan now.

Without another word he fixed the engine and turned the boat's nose towards the islets at the entrance to the bay. Perhaps he was glad of an excuse to put into port, for the prospect of eight hours more on that black sea was not a pretty one.

The engine was working beautifully as we entered the bay, and from the dark encircling hills its little puttering sound reverberated, that strange sound that is so much a part of the Mediterranean; then the captain extinguished it and we glided silently at the head of a lengthening triangle which folded back smoothly on each side.

Several *caïques* were lying by the landing-stage, knocking against each other in the gentle swell. In the darkness a number of people stood, waiting for us.

This was the village from which I should have set out to see the ruins of Xanthus, the Lycian city, if *Meis Ada* and the *Gümrük* had not prevented me. Waiting to disembark I felt resentful, but as I stepped ashore, carefully helped by the local *Gümrük* officer, my irritation vanished. The small and undistinguished fishing-village was, by the alchemy of darkness, marvellously changed. The long day's heat, lingering on in the earth, rose gently from the rocks on which we stood, strangely exciting in the evening air. A drowsiness hung over everything and there was a stillness on the land which, after the movement, wind and splashing waves was as soothing as the reassurance of one's own bed after a nightmare.

In this suspended stillness we moved slowly up the slope to the village where the male population of Kalkan was gathered, sitting on their chairs in the dark. All were affected by the same curious dreaminess, like people who have taken a drug or eaten the lotus. Movements were languid, voices lowered, a little flat and slow, and words came out tentatively into the warm dark air where they hung like tangible objects, as though uncertain whether they could ever spin themselves into a sentence. From the dark amphitheatre of the little town the waves on the open sea made a black irregular horizon against the sky.

From the darkness a figure came towards me.

'Madame Phelan?'

'Yes.'

'A telegram for you.'

Mystified, I took the paper held out to me. A lamp was brought and I read:

> 'Kaş. Mrs Naci Phelan
> *Kalkan gelicer*
> Avustralyah
> I spoke with little province And castum
> department employers The boat drivers Has
> NOT paid Money they Has paid only 40 Kuruss
> turkish mony until Best Wishes and you
> faithfully Stop i will stay At here two days
> Mehmet Telegraphist.'

My surprise at receiving a telegram was nothing to the surprise I felt at its contents. Mehmet must have gone straight to the *kaymakan* (the little province) and the *Gümrük* (castum) and asked about the captain. I longed to say something to show my appreciation of this thoughtfulness but there was no one to say it to, for the captain was certainly not the right one. With Dopey and Barnacles, he was standing in the shadows watching me with extreme uneasiness. He had seen me receive the telegram and since I suppose everyone in the village knew what was in it, had probably heard of the contents. His little black soul must have been shaking, for he came up to me with a desperate look in his eye and said, ' *Telegraf? Kaş?*'

I said, 'Yes.' I had no intention of telling him any more, and rather enjoyed his anxiety. He went back to his friends and they whispered together for a minute; then they approached the policeman and hustled him off into a corner where they stood plotting together, hissing like stage conspirators.

The *Gümrük* policeman asked if he could do anything for me ... *cay?* ... *limonat?* ... *su?* ... but before I could answer a voice spoke from the crowded square.

'My mother would be honoured,' it said in hesitating English, 'if you would sleep at our house.'

A tall slender boy came forward diffidently, a student home for the holidays, delighted to practise his English. *Gümrük* looked relieved, and announcing that there was no hotel in the village, said that I would do well to accept the invitation; although, he added, he would be honoured if I came to his house.

A party of guides now presented themselves and before I could demur I was whisked round the village, to the mosque, to an old Greek church and back to the square. As far as I could see in the dim light, Kalkan was in ruins; demolished buildings and piles of rubble lay about, and the earthquake effect was heightened by the howling of dogs in the narrow streets, like creatures abandoned by refugees.

As I reappeared, the village policeman detached himself from the corner where the captain and his friends were still whispering, and came towards me, looking rather sheepish.

'The captain says that you promised to pay him some money for the boat trip and now you are refusing to pay him.'

I was outraged.

'The captain is a bad man,' I said, 'I said I would pay at Fethiye. I will pay at Fethiye, not before. You tell the captain.'

The policeman looked relieved and sympathetic.

'*Taman*,' he said. 'Pay at Fethiye, not before.' But there was something else. 'Captain says you wish to stay here all night. Captain says he leaves midnight.'

I stamped my foot, as I had done so long ago at Izmir.

'Tell Captain if wind drops I will leave at three; if it doesn't drop I will leave at six.'

The policeman went meekly back with his message and I set off with my host up a dark rough street.

No lights showed anywhere around us but my friend's house

was brightly lit. I was welcomed by his parents and led to a balcony where several people were sitting in a deep and tranquil silence. There were brief introductions; a chair was brought, dried figs and *ayran* offered. No one spoke, but the atmosphere was warm with goodwill. They were so good to take me in, to give me refreshments and a bed, but best of all they did not want to talk.

In a shadowy corner a grandmother sat, her eyes dark patches beneath her white veil, and at her feet a little boy and girl. At one with each other and the night, with slack hands lying open, they sat as though listening; yet listening implies reception by one faculty and this was receiving through every sense. They were taking in the night in its entirety.

The wind had dropped and in the quiet air the moon had risen, throwing a white light on the sea. Far out the ocean sighed, heaving gently, as though moving in its sleep. The staring moon was drawing to itself some essence from the water; an invisible vapour rose to link it with the sky, and the blanching light had drained away all depth, all resonance. Objects had lost familiar dimensions, sounds become hollow, echoing ... the far soft sigh of the sea, a strange nocturnal bird, and in the darkness of the town, dogs barking, queer, insistent, in a high flat yelp. In the foreground a little mosque shone white, alien, insubstantial, and on the glistening bay black islands floated.

The moment was remote and ancient as the ocean, its beauty pregnant with the sense of witnessing a manifestation from a time before our time. Although these mysteries take place around us constantly we cannot always share them. We have allowed too many barriers to intervene ... apathy, sleep, and things evolved by our own cleverness, talk, entertainment, the ascendancy of reason ... which shut us in from nature as surely as the walls and roofs of houses.

I woke suddenly without knowing why; then I heard footsteps, shambling, stumbling up the stony street, and knew instinctively they were coming for me. It was not yet one o'clock and the room was hot. Outside, the strange dog with the high thin voice barked on and on. I had relaxed into a state of drowsiness that clung to me like a drug; I did not want to leave my flower-embroidered pillow; but the steps came closer, and fearing that the family would be disturbed I leapt up and pulled on my dress. A minute later there was a dull thump at the front door. The sound, falling into the dark deserted hall, brought terror. A summons in the middle of the night is always the unknown, always a threat.

When I opened the door I found the captain's barnacled friend on the step, just ready to hammer again. He said, in a thick sort of voice, that the captain wanted to leave, immediately. He sounded as though he had been on the *raki* and the thought of going off on a midnight spree with two drunken Turks and a half-wit boy in an open boat with a faulty engine was not enticing; but even while I protested I looked out at the sea and realized that I must go, for it had become so supernaturally beautiful that I might never see its like again. The moon was sinking; the shimmering was gone and the water was like black oil spread with a white path. In the air was the heavy stillness that comes in the hours before the changes ... before the sun rises, before the tide turns, before the moon sets. There was abroad a mysterious force that came from the earth and the ocean, from the universe itself, and this added richness was related to my drowsiness, for heightened receptivity is achieved only through utter physical relaxation; but such experiences come through the senses, not through the mind, and there are no words to bring them to life for others.

I said '*Tamam*', and leaving a note for my hosts I followed Barnacles out into the night. As I shut the great barred door behind me, I was suddenly glad, excited. There was a stimulation in the luminous air, in the shadowy steep streets, in the silence. Barnacles reeled away down the rough streets, swearing at the barking dog, whose voice now touched on madness.

The others were on the quay, half-asleep, talking in lowered voices. The sea slapped quietly against the stone wall, the dim shapes of the moored *caïques* rocked, their masts inclining towards each other; beyond, in the path of moonlight, the silhouettes of the little islands were black against white. As we cast off, as the guarded voice of the policeman called '*Güle güle*' across the water, this innocuous little departure became adventure in the most childish, most exciting sense. It was the unknown, the world of imagination, even though the reality, in cold truth, was not heartening.

Outside the bay the waves leapt round us, but the boat moved on as though drawn by the moon, straight into her white path. The moon herself, now yellow, tired, crept down towards the sea, then suddenly she hastened and was gone; and as though waiting for this moment a fresh wind sprang up and blew the spray gently into our faces. Round the boat came the mist, soft, damp, enveloping, and beyond were the iron cliffs and a deep and booming sound like a surf on a coral reef. On the salty mattress I slept and woke and slept again, while the stars, all clear and white, wheeled slowly across the sky towards the horizon where one by one they sank.

I was so happy, so at peace with myself and the universe that I wanted to tell the captain I was glad he had forced me to come, but since he and Barnacles were snoring their heads off I had to confine my remarks to Dopey, who was in sole charge of the boat.

'*Deniz güzel*,' I said, waving at the sea. '*Çok güzel*,' and he answered quickly, happily, like a pleased child, '*Evett . . . evett . . . çok, çok güzel*.'

The waves had grown very calm as though stroked into stillness, and slowly the night faded and it was day. The sun itself was hidden by the mountains, and light came diffused, revealing a coast so beautiful it might have been a dream. The pallid ocean round us, heaving lazily in great wide swollen sighs, reflected back the gentle sky, and colour floated, hesitant nacreous, upon the surface, as though waiting for light to, liberate it, to bring it strength and power to start a separate existence in the submarine depths.

Ahead, the Gulf of Fethiye opened out in the cool soft airs of morning, the lingering mists of night. Among the violet mountains in the sea were pastel islets; boats with triangular sails came slowly out towards us.

Barnacles, who had been awake for some time, had been periodically relieving himself over the side, an activity in which Dopey joined him, on one occasion handing the tiller to me so that he could dispose himself with more comfort. Now, as though called by an alarm clock, the *bon garçon* woke up, crawled forward, and kneeling in the bow like a figurehead gravely carried out the ritual; then he slid back into the boat and from under the thwart extracted the newspaper parcel containing his change of clothes. There were a sleeved vest such as Turks like for hot weather, shirts, trousers and underpants. He selected the day's choice and laid them on the deck. Though they were clean they had been very much squashed during the night but he shook them out with an air of satisfaction as though they were the last word in chic. He removed the sweater worn during the night and the stripey shirt beneath it, exposing a long-sleeved vest buttoning up to the neck. Watching him laboriously winding a cummerbund round his waist I felt a stab of pity for him. He was undoubtedly a rogue, in his primitive way, only protected from greater dishonesty by stupidity; but he was so thin and clumsy and poor that I could not help but feel sorry for him. What sort of a life did he have? I thought, watching him pushing the ends of the cummerbund down into the folded swathes. Here was I floating about without a care, free to move, to travel the earth, and made of money according to his standards; it was fair enough for him to swindle me if he could get away with it.

After fixing the cummerbund he took off his trousers – once more revealing the long cotton drawers with the crochet edging and the tape pulled in at the waist – and drew on the clean pair. He added a clean shirt; then rolling up the discarded garments and thrusting them into the newspaper he turned on me the dark, beadlike gaze of his little deep-set eyes.

'The money . . . You said you would pay me at Fethiye.'

I wondered why I had felt sorry for him. He was really a villainous specimen with his ape-like skull and small receding forehead, his dark unshaven jaw and surly, taciturn expression. My dislike returned and I said, 'We are not at Fethiye yet. I'll pay you when we get ashore.'

He looked at me sullenly and said no more, and in this silence we proceeded up the lovely gulf towards the town of Fethiye.

CHAPTER TWENTY-ONE

STRANDED IN FETHIYE

THE engine was turned off and we floated to the quay. It was eight o'clock and a fine morning with heat already in the air. Once more the captain turned to me, but I stopped him before he could speak.

'Ashore,' I said.

There were a number of men sitting on the quay outside a wooden shed, not drinking or smoking, just sitting on their chairs. Several were in uniform and looked like officials of some kind – the policeman, the customs officer, the postmaster; the others were local citizens in cloth caps and striped shirts or pyjama jackets, with yellow *tesbihs* (prayer-beads) in their limp hands. They all stared with great interest as I came ashore from the boat.

I suddenly realized that I was very tired and a little weak in the legs. I had not had much to eat the day before and very little sleep during the night. In this state of physical exhaustion it is easy to burst into tears if something happens to upset you, and the first thing to happen was very upsetting.

There was no bus to Muğla, the next town I must reach. One bus had just gone and there wouldn't be another until the following day. I was stranded in Fethiye.

Something of my delicate condition must have communicated itself to the men, for they set themselves at once to cheer me up. Fethiye was a nice town, they said; I would like it . . . full of charms and antiquities. There was a *çok güzel lokanta* and a *çaybache* (tea garden) and the *çok eski* (Lycian) tombs on the hillside which foreigners came to see. Someone even suggested I should sail across the Gulf of Fethiye to Marmaris with his relations, if they went there for *Bayram* (which they didn't). They were all so kind and charming that I was even closer to tears.

'You must have some tea,' said the customs officer, who spoke a little English. 'You are very tired after being all night in that boat.' A small boy was sent off for tea and when it came

I sat on my hard chair drinking and smiling at my audience, who smiled back at me when they caught my eye, for the rest of the time gravely and silently watching.

The *bon garçon* and his accomplices, who were lurking in the boat, had been unloading something rather furtively, as though they did not want me to see and perhaps realize I was being charged for an already commissioned trip. Presently the captain climbed out on the quay and beckoned to me. I ignored him. He thought deeply for a minute and then reluctantly approached the group and addressed me in his usual grunt. My companions pricked up their ears to listen.

'*Tamam*,' I said opening my bag. 'I'll pay you now.' I took out some notes and counted them into his grimy paw. 'This is the 200 *lire* you asked for bringing me here from Demre ...' the audience drew in its breath to a man ... 'and this is the 40 *lire* you say you paid to the customs officer at Kaş, which you want me to pay.'

His hands closed round the money, but I continued: 'But I have this telegram from Kaş which says that you did not pay 40 *lire* at all ...' and into the customs officer's eager hands I put Mehmet's message.

Never was there such a pathetic disclosure of small-time plotting. The captain's beady eyes quivered in his head with childish guilt and for a second he looked as though he might even run away. The customs officer finished spelling out the message to his friends and suddenly they turned on the captain and attacked him so violently that I was tempted to interfere and protect him. They tore into him and took him apart, abusing him for his dishonesty, for such behaviour to a visitor, quoting the Koran at him and threatening to tell the *kaymakan*. The disgust on their kindly faces was undisguised, and finally, covered with guilt, he handed everything back.

'No, no,' I cried, ignoring my friends' protests and returning the 200 *lire*, 'I said I'd pay you this ... Keep it;' and shoving it into his pocket he ran quickly back to his boat, bending down as though the angry words pursuing him were stones.

'*Çok fenar*,' said the customs officer indignantly, still rumbling with disgust. '*Çok fenar!*' And the words were echoed by everyone present.

That was the last I saw of the *bon garçon*. As soon as I had finished my tea my new friend the customs officer, named

N

Hussein, swept me off to the *Palas Oteli* and installed me in a hot, cleanish room which opened upon a verandah where a number of Turks were sleeping in striped pyjamas. He would come back, he said, when I had had a siesta, and show me round Fethiye and guide me to a *çok güzel lokanta*.

I slept immediately, drugged with heat, dirt, exhaustion and weakness brought on by hunger, and woke to find that Hussein had come to show me the sights.

Outside, the heat was formidable. Lying at the far end of its Gulf, almost in an enclosed bay, Fethiye seemed to be cut off from any breeze that might have relieved the torrid atmosphere. For all its classical associations as the ancient Telmessus, and the charm of its modern inhabitants, it was not enticing, resembling one of those little towns in the Middle East through which victorious armies have swept. There was the familiar Turkish air of catastrophe, blitz or hurricane, with ruined buildings open to the sky and jagged walls leaning weakly up against each other in the heat, and rubble and masonry lying about in the dust. There was also the impression that the mains had been bombed and the water supply run loose in the streets; but this time the disaster had really happened. Fethiye is subject to earthquakes, and these ruins were the souvenirs of the last visitation. Like the boy who cried, Wolf, when you come upon genuine earthquake scars in Turkey you find them hard to believe, so indistinguishable are they from the normal appearance of so many places.

Hussein glowed with pride as he conducted me along the street, pointing out the more spectacular ruins as though they were architectural gems.

'One year,' he said over and over again. 'One year . . plenty houses finish. Twenty people *kaput*.' He took a childlike pleasure in the fact that Fethiye had been so distinguished by nature. 'Plenty earthquake,' he assured me. 'Plenty earthquake Fethiye. Plenty houses finish,' and he laid them all out flat with a smart gesture of his hand.

It was quite true, there were plenty houses finish. They lay where they had fallen, with doors and windows gaping. In one part of the town streets of little wooden boxes had been set up like a wartime settlement, and people were carrying on in these. They were so close together that you could barely squeeze between them, and rather surprisingly in the middle of a row was an upright Lycian tomb with a top like a fireman's helmet. The hillside behind the town was studded with doorways to other tombs, carved from the rock, as at Myra.

People were up and about now, and the streets were full of the dark unshaven faces described as so typically Turkish by those who have never been in Turkey. (I have long since given up wondering what a typical Turk looks like.) On all sides grimy lambs were led about on strings, petted and loved and decorated by the children, unsuspecting victims of the slaughter that would begin on the first day of *Kurban Bayram*.

Everyone stared at me, for the story of my arrival and the captain's *çok fenar* behaviour was now well-known. We paddled along the hot streets in the dust while Hussein prattled to me of the beauties of the town, its distractions, its antiquities. It became hotter and hotter and I longed for someone to rescue me from such exhausting kindness, but he led me relentlessly to the *çok güzel gazino* where I sat on a kitchen chair in an arid, fenced-in patch of dust, surrounded by men in cloth caps, striped shirts, *tesbihs* and unshaven chins. The heat beat down on us, flies swirled slowly round and settled on our arms and faces and the wireless poured out angry political speeches. As at Kaş, against a background of broadcast disapproval I sat quietly, fêted and entertained by those who had no cause to like me.

Free at last, I waded through the dust towards the steep hillside where the tombs of the Lycians stand in irregular rows. By trespassing through gardens and orchards and climbing over walls I reached a grassy slope dotted with olive and almond trees where I sat down in the shade. From here I could see the heavy stone portals above my head and the bay below.

The tombs look exactly like the photographs, like Texier's tidied-up drawings. Most of them are much grander and more ornate than those at Myra, yet softer and more graceful, with columns and curved architraves, like fine doorways on elegant villas. They are more scattered about than at Demre, where the effect is of a cliff-dwellers' town, and at this time of day the afternoon sun shone full upon them so that the rich-coloured stone glowed almost orange. Below were the houses and gardens, the town and the fields, once a swamp, now drained and culti-vated; across the landlocked bay were chrome works, and beyond, the mountains, all softened in the sickening, steamy heat. It was not a disagreeable sight, despite the factories, though very different from Texier's drawing with its neat mosque and buildings, and its foreground of moustachio'd, turbanned Turks in bloomers.

In the waters of the Gulf, through which we had sailed so early that morning, is the island of Makri, now a picnic place, once the home of snake-men who foretold the future, for the people of Telmessus were famous in the ancient world for their gifts of prophesy and clairvoyance. Alexander the Great's soothsayer Aristander was a native of the town, and many people came here for interpretation of dreams and omens. One of them was Gordius, whose knot was cut by Alexander, and who was the father of King Midas.

It was very pleasant sitting on the hillside among the fruit and almond trees, thinking about Telmessus and its soothsayers, and the Lycians in their desirable home-units up above. Down on the plain the shadows were growing long and the purple light had come into the green of the evening landscape. There was a smell of cultivated earth and the gentle sound of olive leaves turning over in the breeze. The cry of a donkey came up from the fields. As the light faded Fethiye became very beautiful, the harbour like a lake or lagoon, with its islands and misty mountains reminiscent of Port Vila, in the New Hebrides. The town itself was a blaze of lights, ten white, four red and two green outside the cinema, several in the houses and at least four in the *gazino-çaybache* on the hillside, fading and glowing as the power fluctuated.

Back at the hotel, undressing in my stifling room, I was suddenly plunged into darkness, either because the proprietor felt the light had been on long enough, or because all the lights in the town had been extinguished at the mains for the night.

On the last morning Hussein collected me and put me on the bus for Muğla where, he said, I could get a bus to Bodrum, if any were running. He brought fruit[1] from the market for my breakfast, rounded up the proprietor, who had gone out just as I was about to pay him, and led me to the bus station where in the booking office we found the official stretched out on the table, fast asleep, his immense stomach rising and falling like a gasometer. Our bus, of the type the *Guide Bleu* calls *très*

---

[1] The fruit in Turkey is the most beautiful I have ever tasted and in summer one can live on it.

rustique, was waiting in the yard, and I climbed in, after photographing and exchanging addresses with Hussein. He had made himself my protector and guide in Fethiye, but in the gentlest, most chivalrous way imaginable; his attentions had been quite guileless and came from goodness of heart, though he told me innocently that he liked walking in the streets with me because he thought I had a pretty face. Long afterwards I sent him the photograph I took that morning and received in reply a letter which someone else had written for him in French.

'I would never have believed that a passing traveller, in a little Turkish port, would remember a humble *douanier* who tried to be helpful,' he said, and concluding with his humble respects, he enclosed a photograph of Fethiye before its destruction by earthquake. It is just such simplicity and lack of self-esteem that makes one remember Hussein and his fellow Turks.

CHAPTER TWENTY-TWO

A MARBLE HOTEL BY THE SEA

MUGLA, which lies in Caria, is almost a day's journey from Fethiye, inland, beyond the mountains, and I cannot believe anyone would go there except to catch transport out of it. By the time I arrived, I had decided that if there was no bus to Bodrum that day I would go first to Marmaris. It is on the sea and therefore must be preferable to Muğla, which is a torrid prosperous town with wide streets protected by hills from any hint of breeze; but my instinct to leave as soon as possible was checked by a sinister absence of buses in the depot yard, nor was there a waiting passenger in sight.

The man in the bus office was civil but not deeply interested in my plight. The prospect was not promising. *Otobus* Bodrum . . . *yok*; Marmaris . . . *yok*; *dolmuş* . . . *yok*. In a couple of days there would be an autobus to both Marmaris and Bodrum, but meanwhile *Yok*.

Tired and hot after eight hours on the road, and desperate at the thought of staying in Muğla, I sank down into a chair and said helplessly, 'Is there nothing I can do? No way at all? No *dolmuş?* No lift in a truck? I am willing to pay.'

He raised his eyes from his papers and looked at me; then he asked kindly if I would like some water or lemonade or *gazoz*? While I sipped, I told my saga in tottering Turkish. He sighed. It was very sad. Normally there might be someone going to Marmaris . . . but today there was nothing. Everyone was far too busy getting ready for *Bayram* tomorrow.

As we talked, steps approached the office and the figure of a man appeared in the door. He was small and seedy, with a sharp, dark-brown face and glittering black eyes. Under his little black moustache his short brown teeth were all chewed away, and he wore a pinstripe suit with nipped-in waist and sharply padded shoulders that stuck out from his bony frame like wings. With it went two-tone shoes and an open-necked shirt, and a hat of plastic panama was carefully perched on his oily hair. His fingers glittered and flashed with rings. He looked like a Middle East bounder of the worst type, though his string bags and newspaper parcels gave him a homely air.

'Any bus for Marmaris?' he asked.

'*Yok!*'

'A *dolmuş* then? Anyone wanting to share a *dolmuş* to Marmaris?'

The bus man looked at me doubtfully. Our new friend was not prepossessing, but I did not care. I nodded, and the newcomer at once rushed away, telling me to wait till he returned. Ten minutes later he rushed back saying that we must go immediately for he had organized a lift in a *pikâp* (utility) which was taking some workmen to Marmaris in five minutes. I said good-bye to the busman and rushed after Panama Hat, whose name was Mustafa, and who walked incredibly fast with his toes turned out, pattering on ahead with my luggage as well as his own.

The *pikâp* did not come in five minutes; in fact, we waited over an hour for it, sitting cosily in the gutter, since there was nowhere else to sit. By the time it came Mustafa and I were very friendly and so were all the other people who had gathered round to stare. Muğla was quiet at this time of day and any diversion was welcomed by the residents. The only visible activity was the women moving across the square, carrying armfuls of branches for *Bayram*, and the pathetic lambs out for their last walk with the young lords who would be eating them so heartily the next day. Mustafa was not a bad sort at all, and Marmaris, he said, was *çok güzel*, much more *çok güzel* than Bodrum; and when he said there was a *çok güzel* hotel right on the quay, I began to have fantasies about high white rooms over a glittering sea, long cold baths, cool breezes, breakfast and dinner on the *terrasse*. Mustafa was a cook by profession and we got on very well, except for a bad moment when I said I liked the Greeks. He was enraged. His little black eyes glittered like beads, and he looked so murderous and fanatical that I quickly added the Turks were very brave, very good soldiers, very kind people, and like a parrot said over and over again that Anatolia was *çok güzel*. I don't know if I would have calmed him down in the end but at this moment the *pikâp* arrived, and simultaneously the police came to inspect my passport and ask what I was going to do at Marmaris. Everything became very confused, for the driver of the *pikâp* did not want to hang about but the policeman would not be hurried. He sat himself down on the pavement with my passport and *basin carte* and began to write laboriously in his little book, while the driver hooted impatiently, the onlookers shouted and Mustafa ran back and forth between me and the car, vainly trying to get us together. This irritation cancelled out the previous one and united us against the policeman so that by the time I was allowed to go we were friends again.

The little wagon had room at the back for ten people, with two in front beside the driver, but there were twenty-one men packed in behind, all sitting on each others' knees, and five more double-banked in the front. Canvas blinds were lashed down at the sides so that nothing could be seen and no air could come in, and in this sweltering gloom I sat squeezed in between two fat workmen with my knees touching those of the man opposite, a plump red person, rather drunk, who fixed me with an unsteady eye and said over and over again, ' *Madame, madame . . . je suis . . . je suis.*'

I could not wait to get to Marmaris. I was so sure that comfort and peace awaited me there that I hugged my heat and tiredness, the better to savour the joys of my marble hotel by the sea.

'Marmaris,' said one of the men, and the drunk stopped saying ' *Madame, je suis – je suis*', and changed to 'Marmaris, *çok güzel, çok güzel*'.

I peered eagerly out through the crack in the tarpaulin at the white houses scattered below in the valley; then suddenly we were among them, running along narrow cobbled streets. Incredulous, I saw the ramshackle buildings, the garbage in the streets, the squalid cafés, the familiar air of cyclone, earthquake or blitz. Where was Marmaris? The truck stopped and we all fell forward upon each other.

' *Tamam*,' said Mustafa, and he began to grope for my luggage.

I still stared rather blankly, and the men, all waiting politely for me to get out, stared back.

'Marmaris?' I said.

' *Evett* . . . Marmaris!' they cried in a reassuring chorus.

It was too cruel. I said good-bye and climbed out after Mustafa who, with an encouraging smile, was waiting for me to follow him.

'*Marmaris?*' I said once more, faintly.

'*Evett*, Marmaris. *Çok güzel.*'

Since he refused to leave me, I accompanied him wearily through the hot smelly streets, trying to keep my mind a blank, to expect and hope for nothing. We rounded the corner and came out on the quay.

'*Oteli,*' said Mustafa, jerking his head to the west, and I hurried after him.

'Where?'

'*Burada!*' (Here). He set down the bags and wiped his grimy forehead with a dirty handkerchief.

'Oh, no!' I said 'No!' The cry was forced through my lips before I could stop it. His startled face pulled me up. 'But you said it was *çok güzel*,' I cried helplessly. 'Where is the *çok güzel* hotel?'

'*Oteli Ak Deniz*,' he said, as though that explained everything.

It was a bleak grey building on a corner, with a dreary fly-blown café underneath. I knew without crossing the threshold what I should find inside, I had been in too many others like it to have any illusions. There would be no baths, no cool white rooms, no breakfasts in the garden or dinners on the quay, watching the little boats. *Yok, yok, yok.* There would be impossible lavatories, no washing facilities, flies, dirt and an all-pervading smell of urine.

'*Tamam*,' I said at last. 'Come on.'

He led me into a dark courtyard where people were chewing away at scraps of bread. The smell I had anticipated came to meet us; the flies circled round us lazily, as though knowing they had plenty of time to enjoy us. A couple of figures emerged from the murky interior and began a conversation with Mustafa; then I was led up a dark flight of stairs and into a hall where a number of unshaven men were snoring on unmade beds. The landlord stopped at a door and threw it open, revealing a small room in which three beds were crowded together. It seemed that Mustafa and I were to turn in together, unless I preferred to sleep in the hall with the snorers. Of the three beds in the room, I was to pay for two, in the Turkish manner, but Mustafa, realizing that I did not care for the arrangement, said ingratiatingly that he would move the extra bed out into the hall so that I only paid for one. When I explained that it wasn't the extra beds I resented but the fact that he proposed to occupy one of them, he said soothingly that he would accompany the bed out into the hall and sleep there. I looked at him, and my irritation melted. He was the most villainous-looking character imaginable; rat-like, a Middle East spiv, with his sharp yellow face, ferrety features and a ghastly little moustache. His mean little body and swarthy Arab countenance, his weird combination of urban and casual dressing were terrible, yet beneath them his heart was as golden as his rings and his fillings.

'Why is everyone asleep?' I asked, and he replied that it was *Kurban Bayram* tomorrow, leaving me to guess whether they were recovering from the effects of premature celebration or preparing for the holiday. Marmaris was full of visitors, not only with friends and relations of the residents but an influx of butchers come to slaughter the sacrificial lambs. Most of the butchers were in our hotel and most of them sleeping outside my door, so I had to keep it shut all the time, which meant that the room was like a hot-box. After Mustafa had gone with his bed to join them in the corridor, I pushed open my window to let in some of the hot evening air. The pane swung back and hit the next-door window, at the same time giving an intimate and revealing view of the people in the house across the street, who were all in their pyjamas.

Apart from its two beds, my room contained two sheets, two quilted covers full of sand, two table-napkins spread over the pillows instead of pillowcases, one chair, one table covered with newspaper, one glass and carafe containing dust, and two ashtrays made of sardine tins. There was also one peg to hang clothes on and one small looking-glass so high on the wall that I could not see into it. Like most rural mirrors in Greece and Turkey it was wavy and greenish, giving one the illusion of being at the bottom of the sea. The late ardent rays of the sun shone in the window and the walls gave out the heat they had accumulated during the day.

The men of Marmaris were already celebrating *Bayram*. Turks are abstemious people but when they take to drinking they cannot contain their liquor. From sober, solemn and measured men they turn into sloppy bestial boors. They drool and vomit and slobber about, growing more and more befuddled until they finally fall asleep with open mouths dribbling, emitting drunken, strangling snores.

The streets were now filling up with these people and for the
first time in Turkey I found myself hailed at every step. All the
habitual reserve had gone, the silent stares were replaced by
cries and whistles and in the narrow lanes men came up close
to brush against me as they had never done before. I was
irritated rather than afraid, irritated because they were making
such a spectacle of themselves, but unafraid because I believed
in their decency and kindliness; but they were not a pretty
sight.

I found a restaurant on a roof-garden and after a long wait
a plump young man in a stripey shirt appeared, shining with
perspiration, and asked what I would like. I ordered fish and
white wine and after another long wait he brought the food,
then sat down and engaged me in conversation.

'Good evening,' he said, as though noticing me for the first
time. 'Where are you going? What is your name? I am called
Naci.'

I told him my name and that I was going to Bodrum. He
smiled.

'I am Naci. I am conservatoire, Ankara. I am trompette . . .
piano . . . Chopin, Bach, Rock-'n-Roll, mamba, rhumba,
cha-cha-cha.'

'May I have my wine?' I asked, rather ungraciously when
he had finished his recital, and he sprang up at once, saying,
'Yes, yes, I get it for you.'

He rushed away and came back, beaming, with a bottle of
red wine in his hand, but he was so naïve that I could not
complain. I told him to get another glass and join me.

Together we drank the wine and struggled with the dictionary. He was tremendously polite and his rimless glasses gleamed
on his pale perspiring face as he assured me that he could
organize my transport to Bodrum.

'Too-morrow,' he said with a pleased smile. 'Too-morrow
I am *otobus*. Too-morrow I am you *otobus* . . . Marmaris . . .
Muğla . . . *gazino* . . . play trompette . . . Chopin . . . Bach,
Rock-'n-Roll . . . drink one *bira*. After I am jeep you Bodrum.'
This was accompanied by expressive gestures; hands pressed
to the chest to indicate himself, to the lips to indicate the
trompette, towards me to indicate my part in it. Deciphering
his meaning I asked how much the jeep would cost from
Muğla to Bodrum.

'Nothing . . . nothing,' he beamed. 'I am jeep. Too-morrow, too-morrow . . . I am jeep you Muğla . . . Bodrum.'

By the time we were half-way through the bottle it was all over town that I wanted to go to Bodrum and everyone was mobilized to get me there. Some *raki* drinkers at the next table left their conversation and came over to tell me that someone called Mustafa was going to Bodrum by *kamyon* at five o'clock next day; that I could find a sponge-fisher to take me in his boat; that I could hire a special *motor* to take me; that I could get an *otobus* to Muğla and another to Bodrum. To all this Naci smiled confidently and repeated, 'Too-morrow I am *otobus* . . . too-morrow I you am *otobus* Marmaris–Muğla . . .' adding each time that he was to play trompette, Bach, Chopin, cha-cha-cha at Muğla *gazino* while I drank one *bira*, after which he was jeep Bodrum.

'But why *otobus*?' I asked. 'Why not go in your jeep Marmaris–Muğla?'

Then suddenly it all became like a demented dream. Naci didn't have a jeep at all; he was offering to find me one at Muğla, and on being pressed, admitted that it would cost two or three hundred *lire*, as much, if not more than a special boat. No one could have been more polite or well-meaning or at the same time more baffling and exhausting. He was dying to escort me round Muğla, to show me the sights, buy me one *bira* at the *gazino* and let me hear him playing trompette etc. etc., but for factual information he was a dead loss. Every time I asked him 'When?' 'How long?' 'What time?' his answer was the same: 'One, two, three, four, five, six . . .' I never understood what it meant, unless it was his custom to give all the English numbers he knew and you chose the ones you liked; in any case after an hour of *I am otobus . . . one, two, three, four, five*, I was so confused and worn out that I had to go to bed. He was still at it when I left him.

I woke next morning feeling sick and stupefied, and in this state groped my way to the outer air, stepping over the gargling forms and disordered bedclothes on the landing. Most of the butchers had already vanished, up early for the day's slaughter, but one or two were still sleeping off the *raki* and the cloistered air was faintly spiced with the smell of aniseed.

Within its landlocked bay the little town slumbered, drugged by its nocturnal humidity. At the quay, fishing boats were reflected in the placid water, their crews, wrapped in old sails, asleep among the nets. On the hill behind the town are the ruins of a castle, and on the slopes, white houses and clumps of cactus, relics of the departed Greeks, which give a faint look of the Aegean islands.

Marmaris is in the land of the Carians. They were sailors and sea-warriors who came from the islands, according to Herodotus, though they claimed they had always lived in Asia Minor. After the Persian occupation they gradually disappeared and modern Marmaris gives no indication that they ever existed.

At this hour the muted light gave to the dreary little buildings more grace than they possessed, and across the dreaming bay, green misty headlands and blue hills were pleated into one another. People were up already, preparing for the holiday. Little children in their best clothes followed me about on my walk or embraced, dry-eyed, the sacrificial lambs, so tenderly petted during the last weeks, now meekly awaiting execution. The air smelt greasy and bloody; flies buzzed excitedly. From time to time bare-chested men would hurry out from sinister side streets with spattered hands and clothes, some carrying pathetic fleeces or pairs of horns, like trophies, or loops and coils of entrails.

As the morning wore on, the butchers became busier and busier. They walked about the streets with their knives dripping blood, and the coiled entrails appeared in a less orderly fashion, dropped into the gutters where dogs tore them apart and fought over them. The thought of all this innocent blood so quietly shed behind high walls, the timid, bewildered bleats of the animals hustled to their death was odious and unnerving.

Though barely seven o'clock, the holiday was in full swing. Families were crowding into launches, to visit a mosque across the bay; the cafés were full of men busily getting drunk. I looked, without much hope, for a cleanish place where I might find breakfast but before I had gone very far I was hailed by Mustafa. Resplendent in his pin-stripe suit and two-tone shoes, he was sitting with friends on the quay getting stuck into the *raki*.

He was in good form. With his gold teeth gleaming he regaled his friends with the story of my adventures, showing me off as though I were an exotic bird in his circus, shedding fame and lustre upon him. At the end of the story I was astonished to hear him passionately condemning the *Ak Deniz Oteli*.

'*Çok fenar*,' he said, over and over again. 'Dirty, noisy, disgusting, very bad.'

'You said it was *çok güzel*,' I said in bewilderment, but he shook his head and I realized he was saying it to please me. All his companions knew I wanted to get to Bodrum and they all had suggestions to make, including a rather dumb, beefy-looking man who offered to take me in his boat for T.L. 200. The boat was called *Allaha Korusun*, meaning God Preserve Us, which I hoped was not an omen in view of my last experience. After much bargaining, and tea and *raki* had been washed down by both sides he reduced the price and agreed to leave at five next morning, though shocked at the thought of putting out to sea at *Bayram* when he could be ashore in Marmaris drinking *raki*.

I left them all at the quay and wandered away gloomily. A long insupportable day stretched ahead in this terrible little town, and after that a hot and horrible night. The hotel was too hot and smelly to be endured; I could not walk about the streets all day, even if there had been any attraction in them, and there were no shady *tavernas* or *lokantas* by the water where I could sit and read. The cafés were dark and noisy, full of men slapping down tric-trac dice and radios blaring out Turkish music or political meetings.

As the day wore on the smells of lavatories and slaughtered sheep mounted and mingled in the sickening heat with the noise, the flies and the increasing number of drunks lurching about. I spent a miserable afternoon on the quay, trying to read, on an upright chair, closely watched by a little boy who stood hugging a raw leg of lamb. *Kurban Bayram*, so far, had not impressed me as an aesthetic treat, and the colour, enchantment and gaiety described by Gérard de Nerval and others were all noticeably absent from Marmaris.

Allaha Korusun was very busy all afternoon ferrying people back and forth across the bay, and from time to time I caught glimpses of the captain reeling about the town, flushed and stupefied. When I mentioned this to Mustafa he assured me that all would be well in the morning and the captain would be as sober as a judge. I had little confidence in any of them. It was obvious that the captain was going to feel terrible in the morning, but there was nothing I could do but wait, beating off a drunken sponge-fisher who followed my every move, begging me to come in his boat to Bodrum, and a little boy who cried continually, '*Comment-allez vous?*' like a parrot.

By evening the air was saturated with blood, and the silence which had fallen while people slept off their lunch was once more broken by distorted radios, the crackle of static and the slapping of dice. Only a few little groups strolled or sat on the quay. Life in Turkish sea towns takes place in the back streets rather than by the water.

I found Mustafa ensconced on the quay with his friends, unsteadily consuming glasses of *raki*. He still wore his pin-stripe, but there was a wild look in his eye and his hat had moved to the back of his head. As I talked with him the captain came past, reeling gaily.

'Eight o'clock in the morning!' he cried. 'For Bodrum!'

'Five o'clock!' I said firmly, and he answered, suddenly looking sullen, that he couldn't go till eight, he had another engagement. I told Mustafa to cancel the deal, for if we didn't leave at five we shouldn't reach Bodrum before dark, and finally, annoyed, I moved away; but Mustafa, after a hurried conversation with the captain, rushed after me to say it would be five o'clock.

'Will you put up an awning for the sun?' I asked the captain, who, recovering from his sulks, waved his arms about and said, 'Awning ... anything ... anything ... food ... *ekmek* ... *şarap* ... *raki* ...' Everything he had was mine; and while we were about it why didn't I come and sleep the night at his house? His old mother would welcome me as a daughter. Plenty of room ... beds on the floor ... anything I wished; then we could start off early together in the morning. We would go to Bodrum (*çok güzel*): to Rhodes: to *Sonbeki Ada* ... His gestures and his hospitality were expansive and as he reeled off into the night Mustafa murmured that he was a good captain and the boat was *çok güzel*. I seemed to have heard that before at Demre but I did not argue. Wearily, in the breathless night, I made my way to the *Ak Deniz* and once more stepping over the exhausted butchers on the landing I fell upon my bed and passed into a stupefied slumber.

CHAPTER TWENTY-THREE

'ISMET, *ÇOK IYE KAPTAN*'

MY doubts about *Allaha Korusun's* captain were not unjustified. During the night a message came to say that he would not take me to Bodrum until it suited him to go. I sent back word that the deal was off and angrily spent another day in Marmaris before I found a new captain, named Ismet, who was agreeable to starting early. He was a thin, quiet, thoughtful-looking young man and had a fine strong boat called *Ayyildiz*, which is Turkish for the moon and the star.

'*Ismet çok iye kaptan*,' said the customs officers, who had helped me find him. '*Allaha Korusun çok fenar*[1],' and they nodded and glanced at each other in such a sinister way that I felt I had been saved from something horrible.

At four o'clock on the appointed morning I was up and dressed and waiting on the quay, hungry and unrested. It was the third day of *Bayram* and not many people were in a state to get up early, but a few stray figures had begun to drift about the streets and presently I saw a familiar form advancing towards me, walking in a purposeful manner quite unlike the sloppy mooching of the locals: Mustafa, dashing in his pinstripe suit, two-tone shoes, plastic panama hat and a jade-green, open-necked shirt. He carried a bulging string-bag in one hand and a newspaper parcel in the other.

'Good morning,' he said as he came up, and his gold fillings flashed in the morning sun.

'Good morning,' I said. 'Where are you going?'

'Bozburun. *Çok güzel köy*.' (village)

'You? Leaving Marmaris?' I exclaimed. 'I thought you'd come for a week?'

'*Yok*. Marmaris *pis*!' (dirty) '*Çok fenar. Çok fenar. Bozburun çok güzel*.'

'How are you going to get there?' I asked, and he smiled as though about to give me a great treat.

[1] 'Ismet very good captain. *Allaha Korusun* very bad.'

'*Ayyildiz!*' he said.

He began to unwrap his newspaper parcel. It was full of cucumbers. I turned away, knowing he was going to offer me one. He did and, when I refused, applied himself to it, which was almost as bad as having to eat it myself, for Turks eat cucumbers like bananas and with much noise and gusto. We waited on the quay for a very long time while the sun rose and the captain drank tea and negotiated with the customs officer about ship's papers and it was after eight when we finally got away.

I had no sad feelings about leaving Marmaris; I was so glad to see the last of it that my spirits rose as soon as we got aboard *Ayyildiz*. As we moved away from the quay the full beauty of the land-locked bay was revealed, and the charm of the town straggling up the hill towards the ruined castle. Our own widening wake was the only movement on a sea so clear and blue that I could see down through it to the bottom, and floating round us were small green islands. All the same I was glad to be going.

There was almost an air of picnic on board. Mustafa was in a gay mood, anxious to please, to entertain. Lions and tigers, he said, pointing up into the hills; lions and tigers lived there ... wild beasts that tore you to pieces; and he bared his brown chewed-up fangs ferociously, clownishly. He was ingratiating, showing me off to the others, boasting of my travels, my exploits, my experiences with the *çok fenar* captains – for *Allaha Korusun* had now been relegated to the company of the Demre captain. He began to eat his cucumbers again and the boat smelt like a bus. I had asked for an awning to be fixed up to protect me from the sun and lay under it in the bow, couched upon old sails and decayed mattresses. I was very happy leaning over the side watching fish, the shadows, the blue depths moving past, while the others talked together in the cockpit ... the captain, quiet and calm, an old man in a knitted nightcap and a plump person in a flowered shirt and solar topee.

Outside the harbour a strong wind was blowing. The decks heaved and bounced and unattached objects rolled about noisily. The men stowed things away and Mustafa, with his cucumbers spread round him, bellowed at me.

'*Tamam?*' (Okay?)

I nodded, though my bed was in the most exposed part of the boat, and relieved, with an encouraging smile, he gathered up

o

his goods and scrambled back to the cockpit, moving so clumsily that I expected him to go overboard.

I didn't want to go in the cockpit but even if I had there was no room for me. It was very crowded and all the men had put on sweaters and oilskins as though we were in for a big blow. The sea and sky were brilliantly blue but the wind was increasing every minute, and as we worked our way out of the shelter of the headlands it came to us from the direction of Rhodes with tremendous force. We were sailing very close to the coast and at times it looked as though we were going to be washed against the white rocks, but unlike the Demre boat, *Ayyildiz* showed no signs of breaking down, and I had confidence in Ismet. In any case these situations are never so alarming when the sun is shining and the sea is blue.

As the wind increased, my companions made frequent surprised and flattering references to the fact that I was not sea-sick. 'Turkish woman,' they cried gaily, impersonating someone heaving over the side; 'Australian woman . . . *yok!*' with a gallant shake of the head. They were so fascinated by my continued good health that they completely ignored my increasing physical discomfort, for though my spirits were high my body was taking severe punishment and was soon covered with bruises. Each time *Ayyildiz* met a big wave she rode bravely to the top, hovered briefly, then descended heavily into the trough beyond. As she mounted the wave my mattress and I were raised almost into a sitting position, and as she came down we were slapped heartily up and down on the deck, at the same time flung from side to side with great force. Since she was taking the waves at a slight angle, each descent was accompanied by diagonal rollings; yet no matter how high the wave or deep the trough her crescent-shaped body so protected her that lying in the bow, in one horn of the crescent, I was completely dry.

Just outside the harbour we encountered a boat returning to port. It was *Allaha Korusun*, riding in comfortably on the waves like a surfboat, loaded with people dangling their legs over the side. The *çok fenar* captain waved gaily as we passed, and we all waved back. Mustafa crawled perilously towards me.

'*Çok fenar kaptan* . . .' he said virtuously. '*Çok fenar, Sonbeki Ada*, KAHVE (coffee). *Çok fenar.*'

So that was it. *Allaha Korusun* could not take me to Bodrum because she was going over to the Greek island of Symi (Sonbeki) by night for contraband. She was now returning home with a load of illegal coffee and all those happy people on board were probably going to have some of it. It was so long since I had had any coffee that I found Mustafa's goody-goody attitude rather irritating.

We were on a high winding deserted coast, where the rocks are white among the dark-green vegetation, and keeping within its lee we battled against the headwind towards the point where we must turn. On the map this peninsula resembles a bunch of coarse, ragged seaweed spread out in the sea. One trail stretches towards Rhodes, then comes an indentation to Bozburun; a deep gulf takes the sea back almost as far as Marmaris again, then beyond Datcha the land runs out in a thin, long streamer. This is the Triopion Cape, on which lie the ruins of Cnidus, and behind it is the Keremic Gulf, where Cos, like a big fish, swims stationary at the entrance, looking across to Bodrum. The whole peninsula, a graceful protuberance of the coast, stretches out towards the Greek islands, like fingers trying to clutch back what they have lost.

Although there was no sign of a village and according to the map we were miles from Bozburun, I noticed that Mustafa was packing up his cucumbers, stowing away his spare hats and shoes in his string bag and in general showing signs of imminent departure; then *Ayyildiz* turned towards a row of barren islets close to the shore, slipping behind them out of the wind. The engine was turned off and we glided silently into a hidden bay where the sea sparkled into aquamarine as it neared the shore, and the high enclosing hills created a hot stillness. Lying off a dazzling crescent beach was a small coloured *caïque*, almost motionless on the transparent water. A little boy grazed a few black goats on the arid hillside.

Mustafa scrambled towards me with a gay smile. He wished me luck, he said, for the rest of my journey; he was glad to have met me and hoped I would continue to enjoy my visit to Turkey; and now, good-bye, for he was leaving us.

'I thought you were going to Bozburun?' I said, and he answered, waving his hand towards the hill, that this was a short cut to his village.

Alongside the *caïque* he waved once more, and with all his

string bags and cucumbers, boarded it in a flying leap. Climbing over its far side he descended into a dinghy which had been floating out of sight, and rowed himself to the beach. We watched his small wiry figure scrambling up the hill among the goats, turning to wave from time to time; then the engine started and we headed for the open sea.

It was hard to picture a more incongruous sight than Mustafa's plastic hat and pin-stripes against a background of ruined Carian towns, or imagine anything more uncomfortable than a long hot walk across rough country in such clothes, but I soon forgot his plight in the pathos of my own. As we emerged from the shelter of the islets the wind caught us again, stronger than ever, flinging the boat up into the air with such violence that I cast around for a rope to tie myself to the deck. After a cursory enquiry, the captain, reassured by my shout of '*Taman*', offered me a cucumber, and waving into the distance cried, '*Rodos Ada. Çok güzel.*'

It was indeed *güzel*; across the glittering, beaten-up sea Rhodes floated like a low blue cloud. The cobalt waves, now tipped with white, shone in the brilliant sun and the sky was yet another shade of blue. As on *Meis Ada*, I remembered the day I first looked across to Turkey from Rhodes and the faint sense of panic I felt, the unreasonable fear with which one regards all new countries from those which are familiar. I had almost decided not to come to Anatolia that day; and now, here I was, so much at home with the Turks that those thoughts seemed absurd. How could I have been even vaguely nervous about such homely souls? Already their deep inherent decency, their honesty and kindliness had bred in me such confidence and trust that I would have gone anywhere with them; as at the moment I seemed to be doing. It was worth making the journey if only to learn this truth.

We wanted to be at Bodrum before dark but were so slowed down by the headwind that by afternoon it was clear we should never do it. Though the sun still shone, the wind was increasing in violence, but *Ayyildiz* ploughed on through immense blue seas, battering her hull against the waves while my carcase, synchronizing, was battered against the deck. The captain and crew, charmed that I was still cheerful, still not sea-sick, peered up at me, waving and smiling encouragement, still unaware of my now pitiful condition. As well as my bruises

I was cold, and from time to time the wind blew heavy spray over me. Wrapping my head in a scarf I slid down under a bundled-up jib and surprisingly went to sleep.

Waking from a snooze, I found we were sailing through the narrow passage between the Turkish coast and Sonbeki (Symi), a brown bare island with pallid islets scattered all about it in the leaf-green sea. Suddenly I saw the port, the little boats in the harbour, and above, the domes of churches and the square white houses going up the hill. I called to the captain.

'*Sonbeki Ada.* Can we go there?'

He shook his head. '*Çok fenar.*'

Disgusted, I lay down again, thinking of the silliness of human beings. The people on Symi are sponge-fishers like those of the village opposite on the Anatolia mainland; their boats pass each other constantly, they do the same work and breathe the same soft air. Compared to the white town on the island, the little Turkish settlement is poor and pathetic, with nothing but the barest essentials for survival. On Sonbeki there is coffee and *retsina*, quayside *tavernas* to drink and relax in; but inherited distrust hangs like a curtain between Turks and Greeks and prevents them sharing these pleasures. As for us, we must sail past the island with its white churches and houses, a little nervous of going so close to the enemy, while the enemy, sitting in their vine-hung *tavernas*, watch us with suspicion and uneasiness.

I soon forgot my annoyance, for Ismet had told me that sponge-fishers of this area had brought up a bronze statue from the bottom of the sea, a goddess who now languishes in the museum at Izmir, and I began to think that we might even now be passing over the tombs of such lost beauties. I wondered what else was strewn along this fabulous coast, ships and amphoras of wine gone black, jewels, cargoes, bones of Greek sailors, mythical animals and gods, deep below our passing shadow, all covered over with the moss and slime that grows in those hidden places.

Beyond the shelter of Symi the wind was alarming. From time to time Ismet put up the sails to steady the boat but had to take them in because they would have blown to rags. I suggested that we might put into Datcha and stay till the wind dropped, but this was taken as a joke, as much out of the question as going to Symi. Apparently only shipwreck and sea-sickness were adequate reasons for putting into port.

The afternoon passed, rich and brilliant. The hot yellow sun descended the sky, the wind became a gale and slowly Symi drew away, her bare shoulder turned to us, her white town gone from sight. I lay under my jib, chewing a piece of bread, thinking of the three ships that set out from Symi for Troy under Nereus, the King's son, 'the handsomest Danean that came to Illium, excepting only the flawless son of Peleus'.

I did everything I could to keep my mind from my discomfort and despite the movement of the boat I dozed uneasily. Across the sea the islands turned a deeper blue, receding into their evening mists as the sun went down behind the mountains. With the fading of light and colour a bleakness came into the air and the scene was almost menacing. I slept again and woke confused. It was night. There was no wind and with barely a ripple the boat was puttering across a sheet of water. There were no lights, no sign of town or harbour. The men were standing up as though preparing to land.

'Is it Bodrum?' I asked, sitting up.

Ismet shook his head. The wind was very bad, he said; the sea was growing worse. We should wait in this bay until two o'clock in the morning when he hoped the wind would drop.

A couple of *caïques*, dark and deserted, floated at anchor off the shore. As we glided towards the rough landing-stage a little light moved down the beach towards us.

Ayyildiz was brought alongside the anchored *caïques* and I climbed over their spars and nets to the landing-stage. Ismet and his friends followed me; but this was no ordinary beach I was landing on, for suddenly, out of the night came a fragrance, released by the dark, a heavenly smell of herbs, the herbs that grow wild round Greek ruins, the scent of Greece, of antiquity. I stood on the beach, as though in a dream, inhaling it slowly, absorbing it, and a figure with a lantern came up to us and spoke.

'*Hoş geldinez.*' We shook hands, and Ismet kindly suggested I might like to use the *tuvalet*. There was a mumbled reply which I took to mean there wasn't one, then the man with the lamp said, 'Come with me.'

I followed him into the darkness while the others moved

towards a small lighted hut set back from the beach. He guided
me to a broken stone wall and indicated its shadows. I thanked
him and took advantage of them while he waited further off,
shielding his lamp. There was something immensely atmospheric
about this lonely place, the black hills in the background closing
us in, the silence, the scent of the herbs. There was no sound
but the night birds in the darkness, the lapping of the water.
Close by I could see the *caïques* riding at anchor, and at the
entrance to the bay an islet silhouetted against the moonlit
sea.

I was tired from the movement of the boat, and hungry, for
I had had nothing since dawn but a piece of soggy bread. It
would be nice to be able to write: 'We landed in the middle of
the night at a lonely bay and since it was *Kurban Bayram* the
men were just sitting down to a freshly-roast lamb, cooked
with herbs over an open fire; but unfortunately no one was
sitting down to anything, and when my guide led me into the
small hut I found the occupants standing about blankly or
leaning over a tric-trac board. One by one, other men crept
in out of the night to stare at the new arrivals, until there were
twelve or more gathered round, regarding me with their dark
unblinking gaze, as on that night at Üchisar. They were gauche
and shy, unshaved and rough in appearance but when I smiled
and said good-evening they answered courteously, pulling out
a chair for me, offering me tea or coffee. I had the feeling of
being in a pioneer's hut at a frontier or goldfield for there was
the pathetic rough tidiness that men achieve when they live
together without women. Everything was neat and clean but
strictly functional, with no attempt at adornment to soften
the bleak building, beyond a bloated, dehydrated fish hanging
from the roof.

A little man behind a primitive stove began to clatter about
with a *jesbah* (Turkish coffee-pot) and presently two glasses of
ersatz coffee were produced. I sat under the hard light of the
lantern sipping my drink, with the strange sensation that the
ground was heaving under my chair, and everyone stared at
me, smiling back shyly when I caught their eyes and smiled at
them. It was some kind of factory or timbermill and this was
the workers' recreation room, where they spent their lonely
evenings. As I listened to the conversation, to Ismet telling
them my story and describing my itinerary, one of the older

men leant forward and said kindly, 'You are tired? You wish to sleep?' and when I nodded there was a murmur of sympathy, and at once Ismet put down his glass and stood up to go. All the men escorted us back to the landing-stage and stood waving and calling '*Güle güle*' as we crawled across the swaying *caïques* to *Ayyildiz*.

Ismet and his friends unwrapped their cold stuffed peppers, goat's cheese, cucumbers and bread, and I brought out my fruit and tomatoes. Gastronomically it wasn't much of a meal but in other ways it was one of the most memorable I have ever eaten, sitting crosslegged on the cabin roof in the moonlight with the three fishermen, the black hills round us and the little island shining dark against the silver sea. Beyond the headland the wind still roared, but here it was calm and still. Then we prepared to sleep. I wrapped myself in the old sail and lay down again in the bow beside the whiskered fisherman, who, swathed in a blanket, gave out an acceptable warmth. The others curled up in the cockpit and soon the gentle air was filled with their peaceful snores. I lay looking at the white stars, thinking of the past of this country, its legends and history and people, so vividly evoked by the drenching moonlight.

*   *   *

I woke at two o'clock to feel the boat moving. The old fisherman had risen from his wrappings and the others were stirring in the cockpit. I watched the mysterious bay recede, the hills draw back and the little islet approach. Beyond the headland the sea shimmered, as at Kalkan on that enchanted night. At these times it seems to become solid, as though one could walk on it, a wide white plateau stretching to the end of the world. There are no familiar lands beyond these seas; they lead into a world we do not know, and the light on the water, the smoothness of the path are an invitation to voyage towards it. But *Ayyildiz* was no magic barque. Solid, handsome, safe as a house, she pottered through the haunted night, through the ghosts of the hollow ships on their way to the Trojan war.

'*Çok güzel; çok eski*,' Ismet said suddenly, gesturing towards the land.

Clear in the moonlight, its harbour and its white stones weirdly glimmering, were the ruins of Cnidus, the home of Praxitiles' Aphrodite, the loveliest statue in the world. The

Triopion headland reared above us, the sea sucking in against its rocky base. The tempest was over but the cliffs remained implacable, forbidding. Triopion has always been a place of violence and menace. St Paul's ship, trying to round it, was blown right off her course and had to shelter in the lee of Cyprus; but more absorbing than this thought was the sight of Cnidus, at three o'clock in the morning, all its ruins scattered about in the gloaming, lit by the sinking moon, whose light had turned to yellow, richer than the silver-whiteness of the earlier hours. Once more, as on the coast beyond Kalkan, there came the strange sound, the slow surge and muffled roar of a sea breaking on a far off reef; and on this sea without a surf, without a coral reef, it was mysterious, ominous. I pictured the black water welling into the grotto below the cliff, booming against the green encrusted walls, dull, reverberating, sucked back and down in silence; and I thought of the deep-down hidden swell below this oily surface where we slowly rocked, so easily drawing down a frail boat to the sinister depths.

The moon vanished, but the stars were still white, and once more I lay and watched them as Cnidus and the Triopion fell behind us. Colder, smaller and more remote than the stars of the tropics, these were the most magical of all; but now their brilliance was fading, for our voyage was nearly over. The sea was calm around us and in the distance the islands of the Dodecanese still wore their nocturnal black. Slowly the sky paled and from the darkness came more islands, hills and headlands, and finally the sun rose and shone out upon the island of Cos so that it glowed all gold, the big fish Cos, swimming for ever towards Turkey and never reaching it. Its houses were pale among the dark trees, its coast was clean and bare, with white-washed towers and ruined windmills.

Ahead of us, beyond a pale sheet of water, was Bodrum, beautiful in the suspended light of fading night and strengthening day. Across the bay came the boats of the sponge-fishers, going out to work, perhaps to bring up another goddess from the bottom of the sea, to find a sunken shipload of Greek wine. One boat was full of singing women and the sound reached us across the water, floating behind them as they passed.

'Bodrum,' said Ismet, pointing ahead, and now I saw a headland dotted with ruined windmills, round, like those on Rhodes. Where the sea was sheltered from the sun a little haze still hovered. Across the bay was the castle, ravaged and magnificent, and, beyond, a white town against lion-coloured hills, fresh and lovely in the morning air. Entering the little port, tying up in the shadow of the castle, I knew I should be happy here.

CHAPTER TWENTY-FOUR

THE BEAUTIES OF BODRUM

ISMET seemed to feel that his responsibility did not end with bringing me to Bodrum. After photographs had been taken, addresses given, money paid over, farewells made and hands shaken, I found that he had instructed the friend with the solar topee to escort me through the customs and find me a hotel. The customs officer gave no trouble, though he raised an eyebrow at my passport with its exit permit to *Meis Ada*, and as soon as I was cleared Topee took my bag and set off through the streets.

After Marmaris I was prepared for anything, but even from a casual glance it was clear that Bodrum was quite a different proposition. Whereas at Marmaris the general tone had been grey, here it was dazzling white, and where the sunlight at Marmaris had been an enemy, showing up the squalor, here it was welcomed by the limewashed buildings and echoed all round the town in a brilliant blaze. On the flat-roofed houses, grapes and vines grew over trellises, sometimes with chairs and beds set in their shade, and down by the water were open-air *gazinos* against the sparkling sea. It was as though the inhabitants were less bewildered, less taken on the hop than usual at finding themselves living on the coast.

The *Ege* Hotel, to which Topee conducted me, was spotless, run by a green-eyed Turk named Sali and his German wife Sara, a strange pale creature with dyed red hair. They were not young but they were clearly devoted, contagiously happy together. They lived downstairs in a kind of salon full of shawls, for there was an exotic tzigane touch about Sara, chuckling and whispering like conspirators, immensely amused at everything I did, but benevolent, protective and *simpatico*.

I was glad I liked the little town, for Herodotus was born there. A chatty, marvelling, Pepysian person, he has cheered me through many inexplicable waits in Anatolian buses, and nights when bugs prevented me from sleeping. He has a nice story about a Carian priestess near Halicarnassus, who grew a beard whenever a great disaster threatened, and one about Queen Artemisia of Halicarnassus, who fought for Xerxes against the Greeks.

Chased by a Greek ship during a naval battle, she outwitted her pursuer and saved her life by ramming one of her own allies. Though Xerxes saw it happen he assumed it was an enemy ship she sank and said admiringly, 'My men have turned into women, my women into men.' Luckily for Artemisia there were no survivors to correct him.

*   *   *

Bodrum life was very restful after my marine activities. During the middle of the day everyone slept, but early in the morning, in the grey light of dawn, the square outside the hotel would be full of people, all gathered to catch the bus that ran from Bodrum to Aydin and Izmir. At odd times during the day camel trains would slop through the streets, chewing, nonchalant, and women wrapped in black-and-white bedcovers would smile as I passed and ask me into their houses. Those who did not wear bedcovers wore striped towels, or so it seemed, with European dresses and well-wrinkled salmon-pink wool or art-silk stockings. On the whole, dressing was rather gay. Most of the women had dyed hands, red halfway up the palm as though having just done murder, and the mens' suits were often a bright green, worn with striped open necked shirts. Shirts with coloured checks were also popular and went with pinstriped suits. There were few collars, the majority favouring a single stud at the neck-band, and ties were never seen. On the head was a little woollen pillbox or the usual greasy cloth cap worn back to front so the wearer can touch his forehead to the floor when praying. Aesthetically, these grey caps are a poor substitute for the fez. The Turks fought more bitterly against Atatürk's prohibition of the fez than against his abolition of the Caliphate or any other reform, yet it was not originally a Turkish article of dress. It was brought from Austria by Greek and Venetian merchants, and chosen by Mahmud II as the uniform headdress for citizens of the Ottoman Empire.

I don't know whether it was their clothes or the people themselves but everyone seemed altogether brighter, more vivacious than usual, except of course the gathering of old men in the café facing the square, the same old men, who, all over the country provide a permanent background in Turkish villages. They get up at all hours to do it and I have often seen them at dawn, arranged in rows, as though at the theatre, a perpetual audience waiting to be entertained by life.

Everyone was very friendly and eager to be helpful except an anti-British character in the post office who was cold and even hostile. One day I dropped my key-ring on the counter, a present from Beria, with the moon and star on one side and Atatürk on the other. When the Anglophobe saw it he picked it up and pressed it passionately to his lips saying, 'Mmm . . . Mmmm . . . Mmmmm . . .' After that he was very effusive.

Bodrum is another of those Turkish towns now slumbering after a spectacular past, but with few buildings, apart from the castle, to show that this past ever existed. Legends say it was founded by the son of Poseidon, the sea god, who came there from the Peloponnese, with a band of Dorian colonists. It was a member of the Dorian Hexapolis, competing in the games in honour of the Triopion Apollo, until expelled in disgrace. One of its athletes took his trophy home and refused to give it up, instead of dedicating it to the god and leaving it in the temple.

The Dorians were overcome by the Carians, and then the Persians came and held Halicarnassus until Alexander the Great drove them out. It was a long and bloody siege, and when it was over, Alexander was visited by a woman named Ada, the ruler of nearby Olinda. She came to surrender her city, hoping in this way to save her people from destruction, and also to propose adopting Alexander as her son. They took a liking to each other and Alexander accepted her proposition. When he moved on he left her in charge of all Caria.

Nothing remains of these heroic times but odd scraps of marble lying about the streets or on the quay . . . a broken column used to tie up boats, or on its side used as a doorstep . . . sights familiar all over Turkey, a country which has classical fragments as other countries have mice.

The most famous of all the ancient town's buildings was the Mausoleum, the tomb built by another Artemisia for her husband, who was also her brother, King Mausoleus, and which was one of the Seven Wonders of the World. All that is left of it now are fragments found in the castle, for the Crusaders and the Turks before them helped themselves to its ruins for building their fortresses.

Modern Halicarnassus is built on two semi-ciricular bays, one facing east, the other looking out towards Cos, in the west. In the western bay, on the hill with the windmills, was the fountain Salmacis, vainly loved by the son of Hermes and Aphrodite. It was said that all who drank or bathed in her waters became hermaphrodites, but I could not verify the legend for the spring has disappeared.

In the days when the Greeks lived in Bodrum, their quarter was in the eastern bay, and here, beyond their ruined church, the houses still have vines and flat places for sitting on the very edge of the sea. The whiteness, the domed church, the Greek-looking chimneys, and the buildings going up in tiers to a background of bare hills, are reminiscent of the Cyclades.

Between the two bays is the peninsula where the castle stands. Ever since men have lived in Halicarnassus there has been some kind of fortress looking out from here across the water to Cos, for the fifteenth-century castle stands on the site of an old Turkish fort, which in its turn was built on the acropolis of the Dorian city. With the fortresses on Rhodes and Cos, the castle gave the Crusaders control of this coast in their fight against the infidel.

The castle is a wonderful place for long solitary afternoons at the time of year when the sea is smooth and the sun not yet too hot. It is full of things to stir the imagination: sinister holes through which bodies could slide silently into the water; alien stones, pieces of the Mausoleum, in the golden walls; inscriptions and coats of arms left by the Knights. There is a lion crouching high on a tower overlooking the sea, and down by the port a statue in an alcove with no head and all his right leg gone except the foot, another ghost come back to the sun after centuries on the ocean bed among the fish and weeds.

Because of the alchemy at work on the water, most sea towns are at their best in the early morning and at evening. Their days start with the death and birth of the sea; the death of the half-lights with their hazes and mists, and the birth of colour which comes slowly, hesitantly, as though waiting its cue from the sky. To Sara's and Sali's amusement I was always down on the quay at dawn, yet because it faces west I found Bodrum almost more beautiful in the evening. As the sun sets behind Cos, throwing the island into shadow and dazzling the smooth sea, the golden light falls on the castle, bringing out all its grandeur. Each evening, from the headland with the windmills and the cemetery with its crooked trees and turbanned headstones, I would watch this slow conflagration, the towers taking colour, the walls glowing orange and in the town the white houses stained pink, the *caïques* in the harbour gilded by the same rich light. Below me was the white quay with its flashing light, and far out, the Dodecanese, blue against a hyacinth sky, fading as the mountains darkened, disappearing into opalescent mists.

Then the light would go from the scene and the full white moon shine down on the castle and on the boats coming home, their engines subdued and people singing. Away in the mist were the last white sails. As I walked home in the twilight, the women and children dangling their legs over the quay, where the men worked on their *caïques*, would call to me, smiling, patting the ground at their sides. We would sit together, watching the deepening sky, while the moon, which had now found itself in the water, a luminous white stone at the bottom of the sea, made the first shimmering pathway on the surface, with Cos, receding, going back to Greece as evening folded round.

CHAPTER TWENTY-FIVE

THE LIVING AND THE DEAD

THERE is a bus from Bodrum to Aydin, in the Meander Valley, and from there trains run to Denizli, a market town within taxi distance of Hierapolis.

This is simple travel, compared with other areas, but I was sad to leave Bodrum and the Mediterranean, and Sara and Sali, who got up at four o'clock in the morning to make me tea and put me on the dew-drenched bus. We had to push it to make it start, and though the passengers were kind and a soldier held up everything till he had bought fruit for my breakfast, I felt aggrieved.

At Aydin there was no ceremony. Because the bus was going on to Izmir we simply stopped at the side of a hideously hot and dusty road, and the driver shouted that passengers for Aydin must descend at once. It was so uninviting that for a second I thought of staying where I was; but driver and passengers were looking at me with slight reproach, as though I were depriving them of a promised treat, so I climbed out, shouted to the boy on top about my luggage and was finally left behind in a swirl of dust. A dishevelled family descended with me and stood hot, dirty and distressed, surrounded by immense quantities of luggage, all done up in newspaper parcels, string bags and wooden trunks dating from the Ottoman Empire. They were waiting for a tram, they said, which would take them to the railway and which, they inferred, would come at any minute.

No tram came, but quantities of hot dust blew along the street, driven by a parching wind. The sun glared down with venom. I picked up my bag and walked to the corner to seek a taxi. A couple of youths in ill-fitting clothes appeared, drawn by the possibility of something unusual. As we talked, a battered car came down the street and one of the boys hailed it, installed me and my luggage inside and climbed in after me. 'What about your friend?' I cried, seeing the second youth left blankly on the kerb, but my escort shrugged him off without a pang. 'And the others?' I added, waving at the family with the Ottoman trunks; but they, through pride, diffidence or fat-headedness declined to join us.

At the smart new station, the youth, well pleased with his car ride, bustled about, enquiring the times of trains to Denizli, trying to find me a bus; but the news was not good. There was no bus at all and I should have to wait six hours, until ten o'clock that night, for a train.

This was the sort of thing I had hoped to be spared. Hot, tired and dirty, I felt I could just hold out if immediate trans-port to Denizli came along and moved me painlessly to my destination, where I should find food, a bath and bed; but things were not really so black after all. Within a minute of my first horrified cry, I was drinking tea in the office of the Director, surrounded by his executive staff. My story was told and re-told; I took photographs; I was pressed to leave my baggage in the Director's own office; escorts volunteered to guide me round the town; entertainments were devised to pass the waiting hours, and dinner at the new restaurant upstairs was recom-mended.

The Director was a dark, handsome man like the Shah of Persia, who seemed concerned that I was going alone to Denizli. Nothing was too much trouble for him. When I left his office, rested and refreshed, one of his young assistants, a simple, charming youth, was detailed to show me the sights and guard me from wolves. He led me through the hot and crowded streets, to the bazaar to buy fruit and finally to a park where hundreds of chairs and tables were packed close together, and people lay back limply, fanning themselves and murmuring 'Çok sicak'. Here we sat, drinking *gazöz* and eating pistachio nuts, while my friend gave me statistics about the railway, about Aydin's trade in dried fruit and cotton, and details of the other products of the rich and beautiful Meander valley. He asked me if I played football.

Presently, we were joined by a couple of his friends, one of them an admirer of American life who seemed ashamed of being Turkish. He spoke fluent, eccentric English with a phoney American accent and his whole outlook and manner were inspired by the movies. A little contemptuous of my companion, he was anxious to show the foreign woman that all Turks were

P

not so unsophisticated, talking across and above the head of my gentle friend in a way to exclude him. When he, crushed, had excused himself and left us I decided that I had had enough and that I too must leave. It was hard to get away from Smarty-pants, who wanted to tell me about his love life, but I finally shook him off and hid in the ladies' room at the station until he had moved away.

As I emerged from my hiding-place, I was hailed by a friendly voice from across the railway line. On the opposite platform several chairs and tables were set out under a tree, and here, as though on an island, sat the 'Shah' and three of his col-leagues, drinking tea.

'Come and join us,' they cried, and the 'Shah' descended to the lines to escort me across, while chairs, tea and cakes were offered by the others. I sat with them, smiling and sipping my hot, sweet tea, answering questions about Avustralya, and once more admitted that I did not play football.

'Do ladies play football in Aydin?' I asked, intrigued that I should have been asked this question twice in one afternoon.

'No, but Dutch ladies do,' they answered, which left me even more puzzled.

They were eager to know about Australia and what the Australian people thought of the Turks. Ashamed, I could not tell them that most Australians never thought about the Turks at all, or if they did, pictured them as blood-thirsty savages. I was relieved when the subject was dropped, and as though realizing that I was tired, the men began to talk among themselves. My brain wandered away from the conversation and I sat peacefully, thinking about nothing in particular, until the vehemence of the voices suddenly brought me back again. They were talking politics. The 'Shah's' kindly handsome face had become so transformed with fanatical anger that he was almost unrecognizable. I felt an instinctive physical fear at the expression in his eyes.

'We hate the Greeks,' he said. 'We always hated them. And we hate the English too. They helped the Greeks; they always helped them.'

'Oh dear,' I thought. This district was a hotbed of fighting between Greeks and Turks, during the troubles. It is no wonder they still hate each other. Hoping that no one was going to ask my views, my heart sank when one of the colleagues turned to

me and said, 'England is bad . . . bad . . . bad. England is bad
like Greece. My grandmother was killed by Greek soldiers; all
of us have suffered in this district because of the Greeks, and
England helped them; England supported them. All English
are BAD.'

It was an unfortunate moment, and I wished I were some-
where else. Taking the bull by the horns I said, 'But I am
English. Am I bad?'

There was a shocked and embarrassed silence. The 'Shah's'
eyes, still glowing with hatred, bored into me.

'You are Avustralyan,' he said.

'Yes, but I'm British too. My passport is English. Am I your
enemy? Do you hate me?'

The colleague who had lost the grandmother was silent,
angry and baffled, but the 'Shah' had greatness in him. After
a short struggle with himself the frightening look left his eyes.

'No,' he said gravely. 'We do not hate you. You are our
guest.'

He said it so simply, presenting it as the solution to the world's
troubles – as indeed it was – that I was almost overcome. I said,
'You are a good man,' and he bowed rather stiffly. I returned
to my tea, sweating slightly with heat, reaction and emotion,
while the bereaved grandson excused himself politely and left
my empested presence. The others, watching me carefully,
continued their conversation, but after the nobility of the
'Shah's' speech I no longer felt any embarrassment.

*   *   *

A fast, proud *Motor* (diesel train) runs from Aydin to Denizli,
through the valley of the Meander, the river that is said to
trace every letter of the Greek alphabet in its wanderings.
There is nothing meandering about life in the valley. Yellow
tractors bowl along the red earth roads, and cars and jeeps are
a common sight. Everything flourishes – orchards, gardens,
cotton, corn and cattle, and the people look prosperous and
happy.

The 'Shah' put me on the train, after his henchmen had
found me a seat among a noisy crowd of soldiers and peasants,
and I was so tired that I went to sleep at once, sitting upright.
I woke to find my head on the shoulder of a swarthy soldier
who was regarding me benevolently and protectively. When the

crowd thinned out, he ordered people off the seat so I could lie down, promising to wake me at Denizli.

A quiet little man took my bag and carried it to the door. We got out of the train just in time, for it shot off into the dark as we alighted, leaving us alone on a deserted platform. It was one o'clock in the morning.

There was no sign of life beyond a sad old horse in an *araba* (cab) waiting in the station yard. My friend asked where I wished to go. I replied that I wished to go to the nearest hotel, and in the creaking *araba* we tottered through the sleeping streets, to a dark back lane where we stopped. There was a sharp dispute between my escort and the driver, who said it was too late to go any further; then another struggle, this time with me, about who was to pay. I could not see why a total stranger who had gone out of his way to get me a hotel at one o'clock in the morning should also pay for the cab, but he did not see it that way. I was his country's guest, he said with finality.

Even in my twilight sleep I could see that the *Denizli Palas* was not a four-star hotel. The prevalence of brown leatherette, the light-bulb hanging like a yellow pear on the end of its fly-blown flex, the fine coating of dust and the general air of out-of-date vaudeville posters and seedy commercial travellers could only be called sleazy. It was a sad hotel that had either come down in the world or had bitten off more than it could chew, and its gloom was not lightened by the sleepy man behind the desk, the air of waiting up for the last train, the voices lowered for the benefit of those who slumbered above.

The bower to which I was conducted was not so much sad as nasty. As the door opened a sort of hot flush overcame us all. Heat, waiting behind the door like an insolent captive, emerged, and we were enveloped. It did not rush out like a fleeting hot wind but sauntered, for it was there to stay. It was mature heat with a richness and ripeness that gave it a tangible character; it had been there a long time and during its sojourn had absorbed many strange elements, individual contributions from passing wayfarers, human emanations, with sweat predominating, old socks, stale hair oil, mingled with the inimitable smell of greasy bed-clothes and the anonymous contents of cheap lumpy mattresses.

It was not enticing, but I had reached the state where criticism is a luxury. I said good-bye to my worried escort, wrenched open the window, turned off the light switch outside in the hall and lay down on the burgundy-coloured cover.

Denizli is a cheerful sort of town, full of people and cars. The marks of prosperity are everywhere – dress shops, stores selling wirelesses and refrigerators, and here and there agreeable restaurants or cafés set in gardens. The richness of the valley has changed the lives of the inhabitants, who not only dress differently from their rough slow countrymen in Anatolia but seem altogether smoother and brisker. The women are so bedangled with gold watches and jewelled rings and permanent waves that I felt very rural by comparison.

There could be no greater contrast to all this get-up-and-go than the ruined pleasure city of Hierapolis. This spa, built by the Kings of Pergamum, and a fashionable Roman resort, is now chiefly remembered for its spring festival of Astarte, when people crowded there to honour the Syrian goddess with music and an orgy of bloodshed, the eunuch priests slashing themselves with knives and frenzied bystanders castrating themselves with swords specially provided for the purpose.

As novices, the priests were castrated with pieces of Samian pottery, which Pliny says was the only way to avoid dangerous consequences.

Unlike Daphne, where silent echoes hover in the groves and waterfalls, and all the air is gentle, these ruins emanate sterility and desolation, final and complete. Even in their setting, the softness of living trees and flowers has been replaced by a freakish form of death, as glittering and merciless as the transformation of Lot's wife.

Driving to Hierapolis I stopped to see the ruins of Laodicea, the city which God threatened to spew out of his mouth for being neither hot nor cold. My taxi-driver bitterly resented my getting out to look at these scattered stones and bustled me back into the car as though Hierapolis were a cinema that would close at any minute. He had been promising me so many wonders that I felt sure I should hate the place, and when at last I saw it across the hot plain I wished I had not come.

For centuries the mineral streams which made the city famous have been trickling across and over the edge of the rock plat-form on which it stands, petrifying all they touch, turning everything in their path to a glistening unreal white. In some places the water still lies in terraced pools with sculptured borders, like fantastic rice-fields; in others it has hardened into solid greasy planes like ice; but from the distance it is ugly, like a great scar on the mountainside, a quarry down which candle-grease has spilt. The Turks call it *Pammukkale*, Cotton Castle.

It is not until you are almost within touching distance that the beauties of this ice-cream world emerge, for there are strange colourings in the waxy white cascades, chemical greens and yellows that glow in the shaded areas or glitter in the sun. In some places stalactites drip down from the borders of the terraced pools, like frozen water-falls; in others shallow pools resemble scalloped saucers, and on the slopes, where no pools have been formed, the white cliffs glisten as though made of sand.

Among the ruins of the city is a pool of the famous waters, welling up from a spring, trickling away in channels to the candlegrease cliffs. On the grassy banks, pink oleanders grow and marble columns lie like submerged stepping-stones; but the pool itself, glittering, with all the uncanny beauty of chemical manifestations, outshines its graceful setting. Its brilliant colour does not lie on the surface, a reflection of the sky, but is an integral part of the water itself, going down into the depths, even to the shadows where the sun does not penetrate; and its piercing clarity reveals not only things that are there but those that are not, changing illusions that drift and merge. Behind them the shapes of the banks are visible, the darkness of wet velvet, a green that is almost black, and lying on the bottom are fluted marble columns, stained greenish by the water, preserved for ever in a beauty greater than that of their terrestrial life. Watching them down there, among the weeds and ferny, subaqueous plants that wavered around them, I saw the sun strike clear to the bottom, light on the marble and illumine with miraculous richness this mysterious, stained-glass world.

On the hill, above the streets and tombs, is the ruined theatre. In the arena, dazzling in the sun, lie stone blocks, flung down anyhow, with marble carvings here and there . . . a laughing mask, a sculptured fish, a winged creature—woman or lion or sphinx. Beyond the entrance, a little fig-tree with its hard frustrated fruit might be symbolic of this silent world where once the crowds had danced and sung and held their festivals.

Below, by the welling spring, is some illusion of vitality; but here, among the headless figures tossed in upside-down, the Greek inscriptions overgrown with weeds, is total desolation.

* * *

Some days later, when I returned to Aydin, I found the 'Shah' waiting to hear my adventures. He hustled me off to his apartment where I was swallowed up by his female relations – a wife, a sister, an aunt, several young daughters and an antique mother. They welcomed me, stroked me, washed my hands and feet, sprinkled me with cologne, fed me with Turkish delight and jam and tea until my head swam. They were so warm, so kind, so demonstrative, so pressing with their invitations for me to move into their household and stay with them.

The old mother, wrapped in veils, sat on a wide divan, with her feet drawn up beneath her, watching me silently, with deep dark eyes like her son's, deferred to by her daughters and her daughter-in-law, occasionally uttering a comment which was passed on to me ... 'She says you have fine eyes' ... 'She asks why you do not eat' ... 'She wishes to know how many children you have.'

Seeing the 'Shah' among these women, like a benevolent *pasha* in his *harem*, I found it hard to believe he was the man who had looked so murderous at the tea-party. I liked and respected him for his nobility that day, yet I could not forget that crack in the gentle façade, the glimpse of hatred and violence beneath.

CHAPTER TWENTY-SIX

SO MUCH FOR XENOPHON!

M Y seat on the plane from Izmir to Istanbul was a last-minute affair, the result of combined *basin carte* and Turkish good nature, and when I landed at Yeşilkoy airport I realized the Güneys had no idea I was back. My Turkish was not up to a complicated telephone conversation so I had to take them by surprise.

There was no one at the apartment and after shedding the nylon dress I had been living in, and soaking in a bath, I set off to Çengelköyü, where I found Beria and *Anne* in the garden. They enveloped me with warmth, kisses, embraces and cries of delight, swept me into the house and began to feed me, convinced I had eaten nothing since we had last met.

The house was cool and fragrant with its views of the Bosphorus and the scents from the garden, and sitting in the chair with the best view I told my stories. Friends and neighbours came to listen, and everyone marvelled at my adventures, laughing at my dubious Turkish.

For several weeks I was glad to be back in a comfortable house, glad to be done with travelling. It was pleasant to loaf, to eat in good restaurants, to visit antique shops and book shops, to drink martinis on the Hilton *terrasse* and eat *gateaux* at the Divan Hotel. I swore I would never travel in another country bus or eat another grey anonymous pilaff; but presently I found myself thinking of Anatolia again, of the grimy unshaved faces and the solemn staring eyes, and though I tried to dismiss the thought, I knew it was time to move on. Istanbul is not Turkey. In this great cosmopolitan city I was looking through the glass window again.

*   *   *

The Turks were always asking me if I had been to the *Kara Deniz*, and if not when I was going. They are so proud of the Black Sea coast that they could not bear to think of a visitor leaving the country without seeing it. It is indeed beautiful, with a history that goes back into mythology. To the Greeks, who knew it as the Euxine, it was mysterious, the home of weird races ... Hyperboreans, Issedrones, Androphagi ... people who ate their fathers or had goat feet or slept six months of the year. For all its beauty it is a cruel sea, to be feared as much as admired. The Argonauts, pioneering into it on their way to Colchis, seeking the Golden Fleece, were apprehensive of what they would find, for legends told of its 'rocks and shoals, and fogs and bitter freezing storms', all of which are still there in abundance.

Now it is no longer mysterious, and along the Euxine coast are a string of holiday towns where the Turks go to cool off in the heat of summer, enjoying the beaches, the swimming, the fruit and the scenery. They love these resorts, but even more popular are the trips made up and down the coast by passenger ships of the *Denizli Bankasi* (Turkish Shipping Line). Everyone urged me to go on one of these, especially since my *basin carte* gave me great reductions on coastal shipping.

The ports of call are usually Sinop (the ancient Sinope), Samsun (Amisus), Ordu (Cotyora), Giresun (Cerasus), Trabzon or Trebizond (Trapezus), Rize (Rhezus) and Hopa, near the Russian border, so I decided to go by sea to Hopa and come back overland. I thought it would be fun to follow the route of Xenophon and his Ten Thousand in a Turkish bus, at any rate as far as Samsun, where I could turn inland across the plateau to Ankara, through Bogazköy, where Texier discovered the ruins of Hattushash and the Hittites. How innocent I was, how unsuspecting of what awaited me.

I could find out nothing about bus travel in the *Kara Deniz* area; so few people ever go that way when they can take a comfortable ship that those I asked for information regarded me with astonishment and horror. Even Rüknettan *Bey*, accustomed to my eccentricities, looked anxious and asked why I must leave a perfectly good ship for the horrors of the road, and Beria, though pleased that I was going, did not really believe I would be so insane as to return overland, especially since I was to travel in the *de luxe* suite of the *Ak Deniz*, the new luxury ship of the *Denizli Bankasi*.

She saw me off affectionately, sure I would change my mind, but she did not realize the depth of my insanity. Though the weather was atrocious, life aboard *Ak Deniz* was as splendid as the brochures claimed, my suite luxurious, and the rich fat passengers as friendly as the humble ones beyond the plate-glass windows; but it was clear that if I stayed on board I should see nothing of the *Kara Deniz* behind its angry waters. Sinop, Samsun, Trabzon, seen in darkness or in pelting rain, were tantalizing, and the lovely coastline with its bays and villages was quite invisible. Despite bitter rain and cold, despite having left my warm clothes in Istanbul, despite the startled, baffled and urgent warnings of the friendly American officers at my table, I clung to my original plan, descended on a pitch-black night at Hopa and was rowed ashore with a young Turk come from America to visit his father's grave at Rize.

Rize, the *çok güzel*, set among emerald hills, with coloured fishing-boats clustered at its feet, is famous for its warm and sunny climate. By the time I reached it the next day the weather had turned into a tornado, rain lashed down in sheets and waves beat on the shore. While my Turkish friend went off to find the cemetery, the kindly residents did all they could to ameliorate my miserable condition. Men in fur caps ran about looking for hotels, hot meals, taxis, anything I might need, and the *Gümrük* entertained me in their office, solicitously stopping up cracks in the door and holes in the windows to protect me from the bitter draughts, plying me with glass after glass of local Rize tea.

Wet to the skin, with nothing dry or warm to sleep in, I was soon in the depressed state when blood has ceased to circulate and petrification has begun in all extremities. Apathy was heavy on me when I finally found a *dolmuş* to take me along the coast to Trabzon, sharing it with my friend from the ship and several sad little men who wanted half-heartedly to get out of Rize.

All the lovely bays and villages between Rize and Trabzon, the terraced hills, rice fields and forests were shrouded in clouds of white rain. At one stage I waited in the car while the men plunged about in the mud with their heads inside the bonnet; at another I sat in a wayside café drinking tea while they mended the brakes, relieved that they had abandoned a proposal to continue on without them. Night fell and I dozed feverishly, disturbed by confused and fitful dreams. It was two o'clock in the morning when we arrived in Trabzon.

My friend led me to the Ülüsoy bus office, a little square box

lit by a naked electric light bulb, full of men standing about or
sitting rather hopelessly. They inspected me slowly, carefully,
as was their custom, while my friend spoke to the man behind
the desk. I must have looked tired or bedraggled for a wave
of sympathy went round the room and the gazing eyes took on
a kindly gleam. One of the men stood up and offered me his
chair, another handed me a cigarette, a cucumber, a third
called for tea. They gathered round me in a circle. Where did
I come from? Where was I going? What was the *Ak Deniz* like
. . . *Çok güzel?* What did I think of Turkey? What had I been
doing . . . where was my home . . . my family, my husband?
I answered all their questions in my halting Turkish; then the
man at the desk announced that though the town was full he
would find me a bed for what remained of the night. Saying
good-bye all round I followed him out into the storm.

We did not go far. He led me to the next-door building
where over the doorway a creaking sign flapped about saying
ÜLÜSOY PALAS OTELI. As we know, it is a Turkish custom
to call hotels *Palas*, no matter how humble, small or threadbare,
but I think in all my experience *Ulüsoy Palas* took the biscuit.
Led by a little man in a knitted cap, I crawled up a dark and
narrow stairway, past a noisome lavatory, through dull reverberating snores, until we were under the roof. Here, opening
from a landing so small that the proprietor and I had to cling
together, were two doors, side by side, both made of very thin
plywood. The one on the left shook with the snores of the occupant; the other was for me.

The *patron* switched on the light in the hall, pulled my door
open about twelve inches, gestured that I was to enter and slid
away down the black steps.

Teetering on the landing, I pushed my bag into the room,
then quickly slipped in after it before the door could push me
down the stairs; but when it shut I found myself in utter black-
ness. I was, in fact, in a cupboard. There was no room to move
and the only way to undress was to sit on the bed, for if I stood
on it – and there was nowhere else to stand – my head would
have gone through the roof, a tin roof supported by crumbling
beams, from which drooped cobwebs and fungoid growths.
The atmosphere was pregnant with a strong and powerful
smell, which, shut in and protected from any currents of outside
air that might have enfeebled its quality, was so subtle and

varied that it took all my skill and experience to analyse its components. Since the sheets were crushed and dirty and smeared with the blood of bedbugs, and the pillow carried the marks of many a drowsy head, I decided not to undress. I pulled a pair of pyjamas over my clothes, put on cotton gloves, and tying a scarf over my head to give maximum protection from the bed, I lay down with my camera, passport and *lire* huddled in my arms.

Sleep did not come; instead there was a violent metallic drumming just above my head as a fresh storm blew in from the *Kara Deniz*. Woven in and out of this background noise were the steady choking snores of my next-door neighbour and the scrabblings of rats which, emboldened by the darkness, took the planks between their jaws or frisked about the floor. Too petrified to move, I screwed myself up as small as I could, expecting each minute to feel the scamper of little claws across my face or sharp teeth gnawing my feet.

Disturbed by the rain or the rats or the waves of panic that emanated from my stiff form, the happy, earthy Turk in the next bed suddenly woke up and addressed himself to his female companion with such enthusiasm that not only the bedstead but the thin partition rattled and shook. So close were we all to each other that at times I had the feeling I was actually in bed with these unspoilt children of nature, for the walls, like those in South-Sea hotels, did not reach to the roof, and a wide gap at the top permitted all sorts of intimacies to enter. Throughout his performance the lover emitted characteristic noises, grunting, snorting and belching, from time to time falling into an exhausted sleep during which he gave strangled snores. His companion remained as silent as a corpse. I was just going off to sleep when there was a tremendous crash from behind the partition, followed by the prolonged sound of collapse usually associated with the falling of bombed buildings, and which proclaimed clearly that Hussein had kicked once too often against the foot of the bed. The mumble of voices that followed was suddenly supplemented by the frightened indignant bellow of a baby that has been rudely woken up. Sleep was impossible, for it would not be pacified, though its companions tried, between the three of them turning night into day. Finally the adults abandoned their attempt to fix the bed and carried on on the floor, while the baby yelled its head off in the corner. It was all so silly that I began to laugh and once started I could not stop. Giggling drunkenly to myself I lay watching the illuminated hand of my little clock until it was time to get up and join my bus.

'So this is Trebizond', I thought. 'The last stronghold of Byzantium against the Turks, the rich and fabled port to which the caravans from Persia came swaying with their priceless cargoes, across the mountains of Armenia; a city whose name is still an evocation of romance. The Towers of Trebizond; the *Ülüsoy Palas.*' My giggling became slightly hysterical when I remembered how, sitting in my suite aboard *Ak Deniz*, I smugly thought of seeking transport to take me into the mountains where Xenophon's Greeks came through and cried, 'The Sea! The Sea!' and wept on each other's necks. 'Very nice,' I thought. 'There's no doubt travel broadens the mind; and now for the rest of my life the name of Trebizond will evoke not Byzantine churches and narrow winding streets above the *Kara Deniz* but my night with Hussein and his love.'

At four o'clock I went down the stairs to the conveniences I had seen on the landing. One glimpse and I returned to my room to put away my sponge-bag and towel before setting out for the bus depot.

The rain was coming down in torrents and a cold wind was blowing out of the leaden sky. I shivered in my cotton dress. My neighbour in the bus, a fat woman muffled in shawls, with mountainous flesh distributed all over her, had opened the window as wide as she could, and when I asked her to shut it said firmly that she expected to be sick and must have it open all the time. She added that it was not cold.

It was five o'clock when we drove out of the bus yard at Trabzon and we expected to be in Samsun that evening. I had not brought any food with me, and had had no breakfast and no dinner the night before; but, I thought carelessly, Turkish buses always stop for meals, and food is easy enough to find along the road, apart from the snacks that your fellow-passengers press upon you. In this unsatisfactory state, cold, tired, with thunder rolling overhead, I started out along the Black Sea coast, in the wake of Xenophon and his Ten Thousand.

Occasionally, as the bus lurched down into some sylvan dell there were glimpses of hills and valleys of almost tropical richness, and dark beaches where women in striped shawls collected driftwood in deep U-shaped baskets strapped to their backs; but for the most part all was fog and nothingness. Nothingness, but not silence, for thunder crashed about outside, and within the bus, where the driver had managed to get two programmes on the wireless, the air was filled simultaneously with strong female singing and a lugubrious male voice reading lists. Back and forth across this confusion wove a thread of static, like the indirect colour in shot taffeta, and underlying all was the grating, grinding sound that means unsatisfactory tuning-in.

My neighbour, who had not been sick at all, still refused to shut the window, and I was soon so wet that a man across the aisle gave me his jacket. It was grubby and greasy but I accepted it gratefully.

Towards midday we stopped on the banks of a mauvish-brown torrent upon which heavy logs and blocks of timber were swirling. We had been there for some minutes before I realized that this was no ordinary halt and that a sense of permanency hung over the vehicles assembled round us. Suddenly the the air was full of voices. Shouting '*Köpru ... bozuk ... araba*' (bridge ... broken ... vehicle) the men jumped out, scrambling over each other in their excitement, and shambled off into the pelting rain. Penned in with the women and children I stared glumly at the remains of our bridge careering downstream and out to the open sea. An hour later the men came back, saying the water was too deep to cross and we must wait till the river went down.

We sat in the bus, alternately freezing with the windows open or grasping for air with everything shut. By the end of the third hour we were all hungry, and though the Turks had passed round what they had, there was very little to eat. Ironically, this was the first time in all my journeys that food was not thrust at us through the windows at every stop.

The men climbed down again and went scouring for food, returning with hands full of green unripe nuts from the hedges. We ate them thankfully. A friendly boy named Ayden showed me how to crack them, crushing two together in the palm of the hand. The flavour was pleasant but I suspected that they would not be too to easy digest.

For five hours we waited. Children fidgeted and cried, people slept and snored, arguments were held, windows opened and shut and the floor buried under a carpet of green nutshells;

then, with a great deal of trouble, the banked-up buses and trucks were turned round and we headed back to the nearest village.

The village buzzed with activity as people were drafted into all available hotels, inns and cottages. I was directed to the same hotel as Ayden and his family and arrived to find them battling with the management on my behalf. In a hall from which wet lavatories opened, a number of unshaved men were calling vociferously for attention and accommodation. The harassed little landlord was appalled at the appearance of a foreign female and his first impulse was to quarter me in one of the male dormitories; but Ayden made it clear that I was to have a room to myself, even if it meant throwing someone else out into the street. Grasping his hair with both hands the proprietor protested that he didn't have any single rooms, *yok, yok, yok,* but as Ayden insisted he flung down his pencil and led me to his own bedroom, snatching up his slippers from under the bed with a martyred, hostile glare.

Everything in the drenched village was bleak, cold and putting-off, but since I had not eaten for two days I went gloomily into the nearest *lokanta*. It had an earth floor and a tremendous draught blowing in through the open door and broken windows. One or two dispirited men sat about in outsized army uniforms and a dark indistinct figure hovered over a stove at the back.

It was all so depressing that I ordered a half-bottle of *raki* and the biggest possible meal, hoping to fall into a drunken stupor which would last till morning. By the time the bottle was finished I was drowsy, happy and relaxed. I floated back to the hotel, wrapped myself in the landlord's blanket and lay down on his bed.

The village was full of rumours next morning, mainly contradictory, all confusing. We were to go on; we were to stay; we were to go back to Trabzon; we could not get through; we should be here for three days; the river had gone down; it was in flood again. One of the passengers, weaker-spirited than the rest of us, had given up and died during the night. He was to be taken back to Trabzon for burial, but we were to continue on our way when the river was navigable.

At last all was settled. Word came that the river was subsiding; the corpse was packed up for its trip back to Trabzon,

the passengers aboard their buses and a yellow bulldozer arrived
to clear a path for us. Hopefully, cheerfully we set out, drawn
together by the sudden intimacy that grows between strangers
who have shared an unusual experience. In an excess of enthusiasm the driver turned the wireless full on and loud female
screams filled the air. Two little girls began to disgorge their
breakfasts into the aisle.

Back at the river-banks there was an hour of waiting and
fidgeting and eating green nuts; then a ford was cleared, the
men descended to lighten the load and the bus struggled across.
In a convoy of buses and trucks led by the yellow bulldozer,
we crawled along the narrow coast road towards Giresun. At
every river bridges had been washed away and men with tractors and bulldozers were clearing out the debris, reconstruc-
ting, trying to create temporary fords.

This landscape has all the brilliance of volcanic fertility,
and when the sun comes out, calling up warm steam from the
saturated soil, it is like Tahiti in the wet season. It is a land, as
Pliny says, numb with excessive moisture. The sand on the
beaches is black and on the bays and hills are fishing villages,
towns with crumbling walls and ruined castles. When we came
at last into Giresun, the ancient Cerasus, we had taken almost
as long as Xenophon and his Greeks, travelling on foot.

From Giresun's high cliffs is a view across Byzantine ruins
to the stormy sea. The water crashed in the bay below the town
and in the streets the people were well wrapped up, the men
with fur caps *à la russe*, the women in cotton shawls, striped red
and black and yellow. Round their waists were striped verandah-
blinds and on their backs deep *şalvar*-shaped baskets. They
were handsome friendly people, many with fair skins and light
eyes.

The Turks like to tell you that cherries were first brought to
Europe from Cerasus by Lucullus, who named them after the
town, but I was more interested to realize that on leaving Giresun
we were entering the land of the Mossynoici, a strange people
who kept boys specially fattened on wild chestnuts, such as we
had been living on. These boys were as broad as they were long
and their soft white flesh was tattooed all over with bright-
coloured flowers. They were given to talking and laughing to
themselves and stopping to dance in the middle of whatever
they happened to be doing; and like swine in the fields, would

lie down on the ground in promiscuous intercourse, not at all
disconcerted by the presence of others.

*   *   *

It was a day of flooded rivers, of waiting while washed-out roads
were repaired, of being towed from the mud, and when towards
evening we reached the banks of a great river and found ourselves once more in a line of stationary vehicles, incredulous
horror and despair descended.

The men got out and the women waited, and soon the news
came back. This time the bridge was so badly damaged that it
would take three days to repair. The tremulous foot-bridge that
had been rigged up was not strong enough for buses or cars and
we were too far from any village that might have sheltered us.

There was nothing to be done and it was growing dark.
Vehicles were collected on both sides of the river and in the
chilly dusk we talked things over. I wondered why we couldn't
all cross the footbridge and swap with the buses on the other
side, but the Turks looked grave at this suggestion. It was too
new, too bold; such a solution was far too simple; in any case
the buses were all owned by different companies and this, of
course, was an insuperable obstacle. *Yok!* We must just put up
with it. We must spend the night in the bus, said the men
gloomily and so must the occupants of all the other trucks and
buses banked up round us.

There came a little diversion. A corpse, travelling to Trabzon
for burial and already several days on the road, was carried
across the footbridge. A handful of relations followed, picking
their way like cats over the gaps in the planks. Arrived on our
side, the coffin was heaved up to the roof of a waiting bus and
lashed into place among the luggage and vegetables. We all
stood up respectfully as the bus set off back to Trabzon, the
coffin bouncing about on the roof with the other merchandise.

Most of us were now starving and I for one was suffering
from the green chestnuts I had been eating; but there was nothing to eat so we settled down together for a night on the road.

As soon as the sun sank the lovely green valley became icy,
and cold mists rose from the river and attacked the ankles,
stopping circulation. To keep out the creeping cold we shut all
the windows and in no time the inside of the bus was thick with
smoke. Gradually the air became full of strange smells, with

Q

the scent of hot, damp army socks predominating. In the darkness small children fidgeted and cried. People groaned and murmured. One or two fortunates snored.

I was terribly cold. My only extra garment was a cotton shawl I had bought at Giresun, and though I wrapped it round me, pulling it over my face and head like a peasant, it did not warm me. My seat was hard, with a rigid back. There was barely room for my legs and I soon had dreadful cramp in my knees. Behind me, drooling down my neck, was a crepitating Mongolian baby who heaved and blew and wheezed and wailed without ceasing. The young man across the aisle had removed his boots and put his feet upon the edge of my seat. His socks were, in a word, ripe.

In travelling, being small usually means that the person next to you – who is always fat – spreads out more and more, until they are occupying half your seat as well as their own. This was what happened now, for as my neighbour snored she spread, her folded arms digging into my side, her thighs gradually encroaching upon me until I was pushed off into the aisle.

Each time I dozed my head fell forward and woke me up, since there was nowhere to lean it, and I had just gone off into a fitful trance when a group of men, who had been cheering themselves up on the road with a bottle of *raki*, climbed into the bus and turned on the wireless. Loud caterwauling filled the air. Children stirred and cried, lights were put on and sleep was shattered. The men were arguing angrily about politics, and though the main theme was hostility towards Britain I was too tired to care and called out to them in English to shut up and let us sleep, for not a single Turkish woman dared complain. The men did not understand my words but recognized the tone of my voice and immediately became quiet. Though they knew I was British none of them took exception to my interference; in fact one offered me the *raki* bottle. I took a good swig at it and fell into an uneasy doze, hating Turkey and all the Turks.

When I woke again it was three o'clock, and the atmosphere was so intolerable that I crawled over the prone bodies and down into the road. The cold fresh air was stimulating and it was a night of incredible beauty. A new white moon hung in a purple sky. The valley might have been in the English countryside, so still and gentle and serene. All along the road the buses were parked with their passengers, and on the river banks were the little fires of workmen. I walked about trying to keep warm, reluctant to go back to the fetid bus, and at last the frosty moon paled into the morning sky. Then the sun came up and flooded the valley with light so that the thick dew sparkled on the cobwebs and among the leaves on the hedges.

Down the road some people huddling round a workman's fire called me to join them. A woman with two children was toasting the remains of a stale loaf over the glowing embers. She handed out a piece to each of us, and suddenly this simple gesture, so typically Turkish, cut right through my irritation, tiredness and coldness. There was only a mouthful for each of us by the time she had divided it but it never entered her head or those of her hungry children to do otherwise. What we had we shared; if we went hungry we did it together.

All my hostile feelings of the night vanished and I felt ashamed of myself. Sitting by the fire in my Black Sea shawl, with the dirt of four days travel on me, I suddenly smelt the fresh country scents, the smouldering logs of the fire, the beauty of a new day. I looked up at the hills with their cottages and summer villas, gardens and groves of trees, and glancing round me at the generous, kindly, unwashed, unshaved faces of my companions my spirits rose and I began to laugh. A little ruefully but with approval they smiled at me; then one after another, as the humour of our situation struck them, they laughed out loud, until we were all laughing together and our voices echoed through the valley and across the river to those on the other side.

CHAPTER TWENTY-SEVEN

AS FOR THE TURKS . . .

FOR some time people had been writing to me in an aggrieved way, wanting to know if I meant to stay in Turkey for ever. They could not understand what I was *doing* there, they said; surely by now I must have had time to take all the pictures I wanted . . . to see what the Turks were like? They felt it was time I moved on, since after all Turkey was not Greece or Spain or Italy or one of those countries people couldn't bear to leave.

Answering them, I wrote, 'I've taken more than seven hundred pictures; as for the Turks . . .'

I stopped. All travellers realize that the further they go and the more they see, the less they know and understand. How could I claim that my own impressions of the Turks were the complete picture, when others have seen different aspects under different circumstances?

'I've seen them as they showed themselves to me,' I wrote at last. 'You can't expect much more unless you stay for ever.'

*   *   *

I knew I could not stay for ever but I was doing nothing about leaving. Occasionally I looked up timetables and worked out routes between Jugo-Slav frescoes and Bulgarian villages, but more as a pleasant diversion than an actual prelude to departure. I was drifting along, grumbling with the locals about transport, the government, the inconveniences; I was used to Istanbul, which I hated and loved, philosophical about its disadvantages and possessive about its beauties. I was even used to Turkish music. I was feeling at home with the Turks in a way I had never expected possible, no longer questioning a country where women work as lawyers and engineers, and blue beads are still sewn into the backs of carpets as protection against the evil eye.

If you can't stay for ever, you should go before habit blinds you and familiarity ties your tongue. Because I was ceasing to question, I knew it was time to leave; so one day I ran down Galata Hill for the last time and over the bridge to the ferries. The mists were gathering round *Suleimaniye* and the *camis* were huddling down into their shawls, warming their backs against the setting sun. The crowds rushed, the traffic bore down on me, the noise of the demolitions crashed over my head, and at the bridge the ferries came and went, their silvery notes sounding high above the chaos of the town.

There was a typically Turkish departure at Sirkeci station, confused, noisy, affectionate, with last-minute presents of sugar-almonds, *lokum*, *raki*, and *baklava*, dangling ear-rings and embroidered slippers. My luggage, looking quite oriental, was stowed in by all hands – thirteen pieces, with *kilim* rugs in a sack, basketwork trays, even a string bag to hold the last-minute presents of food. There were loving farewells through the carriage window, embraces, moist eyes and urgent instructions from Beria about the Customs at the frontier. The conductor, bystanders and fellow-passengers were drawn in, so that when the train left there was the familiar feeling of being among old friends, and the Turks in my compartment sprang to help me stow away my parcels and presents.

I could not believe I was leaving, for departures from Istanbul, though not always so impressive, were familiar. It was not until the light had begun to deepen that, at a chance word from the conductor, I realized this journey would not end with a return to Çengelköyü. When I alighted from the train next day it would be in another country.

'But I don't want to go!' I thought, suddenly panic-stricken. 'It's all a mistake. I want to go back to Stamboul.'

The sun was going down over the plain, bringing with its light an instinct to turn back to the place just left, to hurry to reach it before nightfall, and I stared through the window feeling lost and confused, as though pitch-forked out into the world from a loving home and family. The express, screaming and swaying on its tortuous tracks, hurtled on towards the frontier, and slowly Thrace sank into the twilight; but even as it faded from my sight there began the strange distilling process by which one achieves the essence of a place, the final picture which cannot come till time and distance have brought perspective.

Countries are like people, sometimes inspiring love at first sight, an instinctive emotion, independent of reason, so strong that faults are accepted without question, and sometimes evoking the kind of love that grows almost unnoticed from respect and admiration and is discovered with surprise. Because it was not love at first sight I thought my regard for Turkey more cerebral than emotional; now I suddenly knew I was wrong. All through the months I was groaning about hotels and buses and lavatories I was falling in love; and though I was going away, I was leaving a part of my heart, as hostage against my return.

*   *   *

' *Teşekkur ederim, Anadolu. Allaha ismarladik.*' (Thank you Anatolia. Good-bye.)

Across the miles of ocean comes back the ghostly chorus, the kindly comic word:

' *Güle, güle . . . güle, güle.*'

EPILOGUE

At the Sydney Immigration Department I asked about sponsoring Mustafa and his Avanos friend, and Mehmet, the telegraphist from Kaş. The young man behind the counter, courteous, charming, dark as an Arab, quickly enlightened me.

'Turks are not accepted as migrants in Australia.'

I expressed astonishment and disbelief, but he assured me exceptions were made only for those sponsored by close blood-relations already living in the country.

'But I'm going to sponsor them,' I said. 'I'll take the place of relations.'

He said that was no good and repeated it must be a blood-relation.

'But it's ridiculous,' I said. 'These men are all educated; they all have a trade or profession. Two of them speak English and the third is learning it. One is a telegraphist, one a geologist and the other is an engineer specializing in the sinking of artesian bores. They would all be useful citizens; they are honest and prepared to work. They are not penniless and they come from a country where conditions are very much like our own.'

He shook his head. He was sorry but there it was. I could put in the application if I liked but it would be rejected.

'But why are they not accepted?' I asked. 'They would make excellent migrants. They are the most honest, decent, dependable people imaginable. They work very hard and can put up with the roughest conditions.'

'I'm sure you're right,' he said. 'But they're Asiatics.'

'Asiatics?' I said. 'Are you joking? The people of Anatolia live in Asia, but they're no more Asiatics than I am. And what about the people who live in Thrace . . . the people of Istanbul? They're not even geographically Asiatics; they're Europeans, like Jugoslavs and Hungarians and Czechs.'

He shrugged, slightly baffled.

'Well that's how it is,' he said. 'The White Australia Policy, you know.'

I was so stunned that I could not believe my ears.

'The White Australia Policy,' I said at last, 'is aimed at people whose skins are not the same colour as ours, isn't it? Brown people, yellow people, black people? Where do you think the Turks come into those categories.'

He looked a little sheepish.

'Oh well . . . they're pretty dark, you know.'

'Dark? Have you ever seen a Turk? Many of them are fairer than I am; and even the darkest are no darker than you.'

He laughed, slightly embarrassed.

'Well,' he said. 'I'm a Greek myself.'

FOR FURTHER READING

Apollonius of Rhodes, *The Voyage of Argo*, tr. by E. V. Rieu (Penguin Classics), Penguin Books, Harmondsworth, 1959.

Armstrong, H. C., *Grey Wolf* (Biography of Atatürk), Arthur Barker, London, 1932.

Arrian, *Life of Alexander the Great*, tr. by Aubrey de Selincourt (Penguin Classics), Penguin Books, Harmondsworth, 1958.

Arundell, Rev. F. V. J., *Visit to the seven churches of Asia*, John Rodwell, London, 1828.

Baynes, N. H., and Moss, H. St. L. B. (eds.), *Byzantium: an introduction to East Roman civilization*, Clarendon Press, Oxford, 1948.

Beaufort, Emily A., *Egyptian sepulchres and Syrian shrines, including some stay in the Lebanon, at Palmyra and in Western Turkey*, two vols., Longmans, London, 1861.

Bisbee, Eleanor, *The New Turks: pioneers of the Republic, 1920-50*, University of Pennsylvania Press, Philadelphia, 1951.

Blanche, Lesley, *The wilder shores of love* (chapter on Aimée Dubucq Rivery, the French Sultana), Murray, London, 1954.

Byron, Lord, *Letters* sel. and ed. by R. G. Howarth (Everyman's Library), includes letters from Smyrna, Hellespont, etc., Dent, London, 1936.

Casson, Lionel, *The Ancient Mariners* (chapter on the Pirates of Cilicia), Gollancz, London, 1959.

Ceram, C. W. (pseud.), *Narrow Pass, Black Mountain: the discovery of the Hittite Empire*, Gollancz, London, 1956.

Chandler, Rev. Richard, *History of Ilium or Troy*, James Rogson, London, 1802.

Choiseul-Gouffier, Comte de, *Voyage Pittoresque de la Grèce à Constantinople*, two vols. (in three parts), J. J. Blaise, Paris, 1822.

Dollot, Louis, *La Turquie Vivante*, Berger-Levrault, Paris, 1957.

Fellows, Charles, *An account of discoveries in Lycia: being a journal kept during a second excursion in Asia Minor, 1840*, Murray, London, 1841.

Frazer, J. G., *The Golden Bough* (St Martin's Library), Macmillan, London, 1957.

Gibbon, E., *Decline and fall of the Roman Empire*, The Modern Library, New York.

Gough, Mary, *The plain and the rough places* (Present-day Cilicia), Chatto & Windus, London, 1954.

Grabar, André, *Byzantine painting* (The Great Centuries of Painting), (includes colour-plates of Istanbul mosaics), Skira, Geneva, 1953.

Hahn-Hahn, Ida, countess, *Letters of a German countess, written during her travels in Turkey, Egypt, the Holy Land, Syria, Nubia, etc., in 1843-4*, three vols., Henry Colburn, London, 1845.

Herodotus, *The Histories*, tr. by Aubrey de Selincourt (Penguin Classics), Penguin Books, Harmondsworth, 1945.

Homer, *The Iliad*, tr. by E. V. Rieu (Penguin Classics), Penguin Books, Harmondsworth, 1950.

Howe, Robin, and Espir, Pauline, *Sultan's Pleasure, and other Turkish recipes*, Peter Garnett, London, 1952.

Kinglake, A. W., *Eōthen* (The Chiltern Library), includes descriptions of nineteenth-century Smyrna, John Lehmann, London, 1948.

Kinross, Lord, *Within the Taurus* (A journey in Asiatic Turkey), Murray, London, 1954.

——, *Europa Minor* (Travels in coastal Turkey), Murray, London, 1956.

Koran, The, tr. by N. J. Dawood (Penguin Classics), Penguin Books, Harmondsworth, 1956.

Kritovoulos, of Imbros, *History of Mehmed the Conqueror from 1451 to 1467*, tr. from the Greek by C. T. Riggs, Princeton University Press, Princeton, N.J., 1954.

Lear, Edward, *Journals of a landscape painter in Albania* (contains notes on Turkish customs etc.), Bentley, London, 1851.

Lewis, G. L., *Turkey* (Nations of the Modern World), Benn, London, 1955.

Lloyd, Seton H. F., *Early Anatolia: the archaeology of Asia Minor before the Greeks* (Pelican Books), Penguin Books, Harmondsworth, 1956.

Loti, Pierre, *Ayizadé: extrait des notes et lettres d'un lieutenant de la marine anglaise entré au service de la Turquie*, Paris, 1897.

——, *Les Désenchantées: roman des harems turcs contemporains*, Calmann-Lévy, Paris, 1923.

——, *Fantôme d'Orient* (a sequel to Ayizadé), Paris, 1893.

Luke, Sir Harry, *The city of dancing dervishes* (includes essay on Konya), Macmillan, London, 1914.

Mantran, Robert, *Turkey* (photographs with introductory text), (Hachette World Albums), Hachette, Paris, 1955.

Mayes, Stanley, *An organ for the Sultan* (Based on the diary of Thomas Dallam; includes descriptions of seventeenth-century Stamboul), Putnam, London, 1956.

Montagu, Lady Mary Wortley, *Letters from the Levant, during the embassy to Constantinople, 1716-18*, Rickerby, London, 1838.

Nerval, Gérard de (pseud.), *Voyage en Orient* (Les Nuits de Ramazan, etc.), Paris, 1851.

Orga, Irfan, *Portrait of a Turkish family*, Gollancz, London, 1950.

Ozbekhan, Hasan, *The Isle of Princes* (Novel about modern Istanbul), Gollancz, London, 1958.

Plinius Secundus, Caius, *Natural History* (Loeb Classical Library), Heinemann, London, 1938.

Rice, David Talbot, *Byzantine art* (Pelican Books), Penguin Books, Harmondsworth, 1954.

Sandwich, 4th Earl, *Voyage round the Mediterranean in the years 1738 and 1739* (Hellespont, Marmora, Constantinople, Bosphorus, Troy, Turkish life etc.), London, 1799.

Sandys, George, *Sandys Travels, containing a history of the original and present state of the Turkish Empire*, seventh edition (Descriptions of seventeenth-century Turkey), printed for John Williams Junior, London, 1673.

Schliemann, Heinrich, *Troy and its remains: a narration of researches and discoveries made on the site of Ilium and in the Trojan plain*, Murray, London, 1875.

Stark, Freya, *Ionia: a quest*, Murray, London, 1954.

——, *The Lycian Shore*, Murray, London, 1956.

Strabo, *The Geography of Strabo*, three vols. (Bohn's Classical Library), Bohn, London, 1854-7.

Tavernier, Jean Baptiste, *Les six voyages de J. B. Tavernier en Turquie, en Perse et aux Indes*, two vols., Paris, 1679.

Texier, C. F. M., *Description de l'Asie Mineure*, three vols. (nineteenth-century travel and discovery in Anatolia), Paris, 1839-49.

Ure, Percy Neville, *Justinian and his age* (Pelican Books), Penguin Books, Harmondsworth, 1951.

Xenophon, *The Persian Expedition*, tr. by Rex Warner (Penguin Classics), Penguin Books, Harmondsworth, 1952.

INDEX

241

Printed in Great Britain by
Richard Clay and Company Ltd.
Bungay, Suffolk.

BULGARIA

B L A C

THRACE

Edirne

ISTANBUL   Çengelköyü

Bolu

Bosphorus

Sea of
Marmara

Nicaea
Yalova
Bursa
× Mt Olympus

ANKARA

Gelibolu
(Gallipoli)

Çanakkale

Croy

T   U   R

A   N   A   T

Pergamum

Mytilini

Menemen

IZMIR (Smyrna)

R. Meander

KONYA
(Iconium)

Chios

Seljuk
(Ephesus)

Pammukkale (Hieropolis)
Denizli

Akseki

Çeşme

Aydın
Muğla

Antalya   Belkis

T   a

Bodrum
(Halicarnassus)

Marmaris   Elmalı ×
Fethiye
(Telmessus)

Side
Alanya

Cos

Mts Climax
& Solymna
Finike

Cyclades

Sonbeki Ada
(Symi)

Makri

Kaş

C. Chelidonia

Patara
Kalkan

Demre (Myra)
Andriake

Rodos Ada
(Rhodes)

Meis Ada
(Castelorizo)

M   E   D

T   E   R   R   A   N   E

CRETE